BESS OF HARDWICK

David N. Durant

BESS
OF
HARDWICK

PORTRAIT OF AN ELIZABETHAN DYNAST

Weidenfeld and Nicolson
London

To Christabel
and also to the memory of Sir 'Bunny' Pratt

CONTENTS

ILLUSTRATIONS

ACKNOWLEDGMENTS
FOR ILLUSTRATIONS

The author and the publisher are grateful to the following sources for their kind permission to reproduce the illustrations. The National Trust (Hardwick House) for illustrations 2, 4, 9, 10, 12, 13, 14, 20 (*photos: The Courtauld Institute of Art*); 6 (*photo: Edwin Smith*); 19 (*photo: Jill Langford*); 18. The Trustees of the Chatsworth Settlement and His Grace the Duke of Devonshire for illustrations 1, 7. The Bodleian Library, Oxford, for illustrations 5, 11. The Victoria and Albert Museum for illustrations 3, 8 (Crown copyright). The Controller of Her Majesty's Stationery Office for illustration 16. The R.I.B.A. for illustration 15, which is in the Smythson Collection. Angelo Hornak for his photograph for illustration 17. The Dean and Chapter of Derby for illustration 21 (*photo: Jill Langford*).

ACKNOWLEDGMENTS

This book could never have been written without the help of a great many people. I have been astonished that so many should have given to me more assistance than I had any right to expect. Over the five years of research which preceded the actual writing I made many good friends in unexpected places, friends who I can justly claim have been introduced to me by Bess herself. It is completely true to say that this book would never have been written had I not been provoked by my friend Mark Girouard into accepting the challenge and consequently Mark has felt responsible for the whole conception; my thanks are due to him for his stimulation and help.

My heartfelt thanks must also go to the Trustees of the Chatsworth Settlement and to the librarian at Chatsworth, Tom Wragg, and his assistant Peter Day, who gave me access to the Hardwick manuscripts there and permission to make the countless yards of micro-film from which I worked, and who never complained however many times I referred back to them. In this connection I must record that every page of the Hardwick manuscripts has been transcribed, typed and indexed. It has been a vast labour and together with all other manuscript sources has resulted in over ten thousand pages of typed transcripts; all this with the exception of Hardwick account No. 8, which I mention below, has been done single-handed and without any grant whatsoever. It seemed to me that if the biography of Bess was to be of any value then this programme of research, no matter how long it took, was the only way in which it could be done. The Folger Shakespeare Library in Washington, USA was good enough to supply me with micro-films of all their Talbot/ Cavendish manuscripts, and at the Sheffield City Library, the librarian and the archivist must have my sincere thanks for their assistance which went further than routine to my many enquiries connected with the Bacon/Franks and Arundel Castle manuscripts and their more recent purchases concerning the Talbot family.

Equal in importance has been the support given to me by the National Trust who own Hardwick Hall: I have spent many many hours in and around this fascinating and haunting house trying to disentangle the original purpose of the rooms and the symbolism of the decoration and hangings and so my thanks must go to Christopher Wall who is ultimately responsible for Hardwick and all it contains. I must thank Stephen Piret, the curator of Hardwick until 1973, and Clive Baker, the administrator since 1974, and his wife Kay, who became our firm friends. The staff of Hardwick, who have shown unfailing interest in my project and who may have thought that the book was never coming out, for my visits extended over many years, were always pleased to show me corners of the house I might have missed. I must thank too John Lane, the mason in charge of restoration of Hardwick, who has done his best to instruct me in some of the mysteries of stone masonry, and in this respect historians have a great deal to learn by asking questions of those who are experts in other fields. And not least my thanks are due to Francesca Barran, the Librarian of the National Trust photographic collection.

The help and support given to me by the University of Nottingham is particularly noteworthy. For the considerable assistance I have received I give thanks to the librarian, R. E. Smith, who has let me use the library facilities freely, and to his staff who have been unfailingly pleasant and helpful. But the greatest help has come from the Department of Manuscripts under the keeper, Mary Welch, and her assistant keeper, Alan Cameron, who never failed to spare time to answer my queries, and to Keith Harris of the photographic unit of that department who has developed so very many yards of film on my behalf. At the University of Sheffield I must thank in particular Vanessa Doe and her class, who during one winter untiringly transcribed and typed out the Hardwick account book No. 8 and so saved me many hours of time, thus speeding the completion of this biography; and also I thank the photographic unit of the library of the University of Sheffield who kindly arranged to put two Hardwick account books on to micro-film. Of

ACKNOWLEDGMENTS   *xi*

the University of London I thank Jennifer Montague and her staff
at the Warburg Institute, who spent time over my enquiries and
also my thanks to the librarian of the Witt Library at the Courtauld
Institute who during one memorable visit turned up a detail I would
have otherwise missed.

If I were to mention every County Record Office with whom I
have been in touch these acknowledgements would cover many
more pages, but I am nevertheless grateful to those anonymous
archivists who have replied to my letters in surprising detail. I must
mention my thanks to Adrian Henstock, the archivist of the Nottinghamshire Record Office, and his staff who have been such a great
help and encouragement to me, and I also thank Valerie Henstock
for her help over Elizabethan Latin translations. The staffs of the
British Library, of the Prints and Manuscripts Rooms, and the staff
of the Public Record Office must not be forgotten; and at the College
of Arms, Bluemantle Pursuivant found for me funeral regulations
which proved invaluable. At the RIBA I would like to thank John
Harris for his help over the Smythson drawings.

During the summer of 1973 Peter Thornton, Keeper of the
Department of Furniture and Woodwork at the Victoria and
Albert Museum, organised a symposium at Hardwick for those who
were interested in Hardwick Hall and its contents. On that occasion I
met John Hardy of the same department of the V. and A., Donald
King of the Department of Textiles, John Nevinson whose advice on
needlework has been unstinting and Gervase Jackson-Stops of the
National Trust whose kindness has been more than appreciated.
Whether or not anyone else got anything out of that symposium
I cannot say but from my point of view it was invaluable, for all
those I met subsequently gave their expert help whenever asked.
Leading on from this symposium I was in touch with Simon Jervis,
assistant keeper to Peter Thornton, who helped with advice on the
de Cerceau furniture at Hardwick Hall, and with Claud Blair, the
keeper of the Department of Metalwork at the V. and A., who found
for me the illustration of St Loe's armour. I must also thank Roy
Strong, director of the V. and A., who spent some hours of a very
busy day, discussing with me the problems posed by the portraits
at Hardwick and the symbolism of the frieze in the High Great
Chamber.

Most of the foregoing acknowledgments are due to individuals who work for their livelihood in organisations which are concerned with historical research in one way or another and this in no way detracts from my sincere appreciation of their help so freely given. But what has been impressive is the help I have received from many who have used their own valuable time. I shall always remember with appreciation a day spent at Althorp when the late Earl Spencer entertained me in his muniment room: entertainment is a just description for he knew all the contents of every drawer and cupboard and spoke of those long since dead as if they had been his personal friends. My old friend Norman Summers who made helpful comment on renaissance architecture, this contribution I gratefully acknowledge. Also I must thank another old friend, Keith Train, who read through the typescript and gave me useful advice. My thanks also to my friend Rosalys Coope for her help over the problems posed by the sources of Elizabethan architectural inspiration coming from the Continent. I must also mention with sincere appreciation George Potter who gave me so much encouragement in the early days of research, an encouragement which will be understood by those who had the luck to be his students when he was professor in the Department of Medieval and Modern History at the University of Sheffield. Alan Hardwicke, who is not a descendant of Bess but nevertheless is related to her through a co-lateral branch of the family, must be thanked for giving so much useful information on the early family history. Malcolm Airs who gave me help and welcome advice on Elizabethan masons is owed my thanks. Also Gordon Batho whose advice on the Talbot family is founded on his unrivalled knowledge of the Talbot papers in the College of Arms. Margaret Swain guided me skilfully round the pitfalls of the needlework of the Scots Queen. Hector Carter too must be thanked for his reliable and quick replies to my often frantic requests for details of manuscripts in the Public Record Office and the British Library. I thank too, the librarian at Hatfield House, R.H. Harcourt-Williams, for his assistance and comment on the Cecil manuscripts. And Patrick Strong, the librarian of Eton College, must have thanks for making available to me the account book of Henry and William Cavendish covering the time when they attended Eton College. I thank also Jennifer Worthington for tirelessly typing the manuscript of this book. And I am particularly grateful to Gila Curtis who by her masterly editing pulled so much into place and unfailingly saw to it that punctuation marks went where they were best disposed and was helpful too in countless minor dramas which inevitably attend the publication of any book. For some of the illustrations I am indebted to a dear friend Jill Langford, who with enormous enthusiasm marshalled her apparatus and lights so as to obtain the best possible results in bad conditions.

It is customary to thank one's wife and family for their support and help – the gesture has become almost automatic – but in my case, although following the custom, it is a genuine tribute, for they put up with a very great deal over the long period of gestation. My relief that 'Bess' has been reborn can be nothing to the relief felt by my wife Christabel and our three sons without whose full support nothing would have been possible.

1

YOUNG BESS
OF HARDWICK

Five miles north-east of Leicester are the ruins of Bradgate Manor. Here at the surprising hour of two in the morning of 20 August 1547, Elizabeth Barley, widow, born Elizabeth Hardwick and then aged about twenty was married to Sir William Cavendish, Kt, Treasurer of the King's Chamber. Whatever hopes and fears she might have had, she could never have seen how radically her life was to be changed by her marriage.

To remind himself of the event Sir William wrote carefully in a notebook. 'Memorandum. That I was married unto Elizabeth Hardwick my third Wiffe in Leestersheere at Bradgate House the 20th August in the first yeare of Kinge Edward the 6 at 2 of the Clock after midnight, the domynical letter B.'[1]

Bess's marriage to Sir William Cavendish, a successful civil servant and courtier close to the King, held in the home of Henry Grey, Marquis of Dorset, and his wife Frances, a grand-daughter of Henry VII, was an achievement for the daughter of a small landowner from Derbyshire, and would have satisfied many women. But Bess was no ordinary woman; like Sir William she was an opportunist and this, her second marriage, was the foundation stone of a remarkable and fantastic future.

A contemporary description of Bess gives her red hair and small eyes; the later evidence of portraits supports the colour of her hair, but suggests that her eyes were large and that she had a surprising resemblance to Queen Elizabeth I. If her funeral effigy in Derby Cathedral is accurate then her height was 5 feet $3\frac{3}{4}$ inches, an average height for a woman of that time. In her character she combined many traits which would bring success today: singleness of purpose, shrewd understanding and a managing ability, perhaps not feminine characteristics as we see them, but she was also said to have the charms of wit and beauty. A later description, after she had been dead for nearly two hundred years, stated that she was 'a woman of masculine understanding and conduct; proud, furious, selfish and unfeeling'.[2] But the writer was not one of her admirers. Bess was all of these and who is there who has never been proud, furious, selfish or unfeeling? Accounts of the early part of her life have been largely based on speculation pinned on to a few supposedly known facts. In many cases the facts have proved wrong and the speculation incorrect. In the period of her later fame there is so much documentary evidence that it becomes an embarrassment. When she was unknown and neither an object of interest nor a dispenser of patronage, she was seldom noted.

Even the year of her birth is uncertain. On her superbly ostentatious monument in Derby Cathedral is an epitaph put there by her grandson, the first Duke of Newcastle; and he, whilst detailed and glowing about his own material accomplishments, is cautious about giving her age when she died in 1608. About eighty-seven is as near as he allows. He was wrong. Bess had already become a legend and like all legends, it was becoming exaggerated.

It is likely that she was born no earlier than 1527. She could not have been born later, as her father died on 29 January 1528 and she had a younger sister Alice. It is also likely that she was born at Hardwick Hall in Derbyshire, the home of her father and his father before him.

Her ancestors had settled at Hardwick by the end of the fourteenth century when it was still early enough for them to call themselves 'de Hardwick' after the name of their manor. Documentary evidence shows that they settled at Hardwick before 1391[3] on what was part of the neighbouring manor of Stainsby; and they held Hardwick, not of the king but of the Savages of Stainsby, by tenure of one third of a knight's fee. This suggests that one of the Hardwicks originally married a Savage and the Savages gave the Hardwick estate out of their manor of Stainsby as marriage jointure. Hardwick Hall, a single large farmhouse away from any village, protected on one side by a sheer drop, suggests a date no earlier than about 1250 when Derbyshire had become peaceful enough to allow a settlement outside the protective shelter of a township. Whatever the date, by

1527 they had been established in the county for several centuries and must have seemed as permanent to the countryside as the hill which the house stood upon.

Derbyshire was a remote county. Communication with any part of the country was difficult in summer and impossible in winter. It was natural that the Hardwicks should marry into local families and theirs was a story repeated all over England. They held their lands neither prospering nor failing, generation after generation.

When Bess's grandfather, John Hardwick, died in 1507, the family owned over four hundred acres in and around Hardwick. Her father, another John, inherited the estate and married Elizabeth Leake who came of a local family at nearby Hasland. Three daughters besides Bess survived: Mary, Jane and Alice, the only one younger than Bess. James, the only son and next in age to Bess, was born in the period January to March 1526.

John Hardwick, Bess's father, was forty-one when he died, the average life expectation of the time, and he would have been considered an old man. To have left so young a family he had either married late or, more likely, had been a widower before he married Elizabeth Leake. In any case the combination of circumstances conspiring to leave his wife a widow with so young a family brought about a calamity of awful proportion.

Tudor landowners such as John Hardwick had the worry and fear that should they die before the heir was twenty-one, their land would be taken by the Crown – if it were held by knight service – and administered by the Office of Wards, which would hold the estate and use the income as the Crown wished, until the heir became of age. The apparatus of wardship was based on a medieval need to raise an army quickly and cheaply. The key to this apparatus was knight service, and the method was simple. In early feudal times, the Crown would award lands and manors in return for the provision of a mounted knight when needed – this was called knight service. The custom lapsed when knights in heavy armour became useless in war; nevertheless the fact that the service could be called for was never allowed to be forgotten by the Crown, ever jealous to keep its rights. Henry VII, in his pressing search for additional revenue, had revived the declining powers of the medieval Office of Wards. Henry VIII, in his greater need, had strengthened it. This

was no half-hearted revival and it was not concerned with the provision of knights, but solely with the revenue from the estates in
wardship and it was very profitable. The Master of Wards was
equipped with all the backing of substantial laws and a considerable
staff which enabled him to carry out his task far beyond the original
needs which had conceived the office centuries before. Obviously
when lands were inherited by a child under age, the knight service
could not be performed and with perfect logic the Crown took back
its lands in lieu of service until the heir would be old enough. The
result of this Tudor revival of an outdated medieval necessity was
a punitive inheritance tax, for the Master of Wards squeezed every
penny he could from an estate once it fell into his hands. It was
a tax far more severe than any modern capital transfer tax and its
direct consequences have been little appreciated.

Shortly before John Hardwick died, he made an attempt to avoid
his estate falling into wardship.[4] He gave, or said that he gave, all his
lands in Derbyshire and Lincolnshire, totalling over five hundred
acres and including the substantial Hardwick Hall, to seven feoffees
or trustees. Thus he supposed that when he died he would own
no lands at all; the trustees would have them. He was repeating
a legal artifice which his father had made years before. It had worked
then and its purpose was to keep the estate out of wardship. However, it is doubtful if any such legal document ever existed; had
it done so, all would have been well. Perhaps there was no time.

Exactly ten days before John died, when he was sick and knew he
was dying, he made his will. It is curious and complicated. Curious,
because he was attempting something which should never have been
attempted in a will – and it nearly came off. Wills were solely for
the disposal of worldly goods and chattels; land, which in principle
belonged to the Crown, could not be willed. And yet, indirectly,
this is what John Hardwick attempted to do. He mentioned the gift
of land to trustees; two were his wife's relatives, her father Thomas
Leake and her brother John, but he did not give the date of the
deed, and this makes its existence doubtful. He then specified that
the trustees were to hold the land for twenty years (until James
would be over twenty-one) for the use of his 'childur' and widow.
It was complicated because John mentioned five daughters, but only
four are known and perhaps of those Alice, the youngest, was then

unborn. Each daughter, he said, was to have a dowry at marriage of 40 marks. If Elizabeth was with child at the time of his death then that too would have 40 marks. As it is not known how many daughters there were, either born or unborn at the time John died, then it cannot be certain how much dowry Bess would have received, for the total sum was to be shared amongst the survivors. Bess could have had as much as 60 marks at marriage, the then equivalent of £40, or it could have been only 40 marks or £33·33. This would have to be found out of the estate as each married. It was not a great sum as dowry, but sufficient to get a husband of 'middling sort'. John was plainly worried about the future of his wife and 'childur'.

On 2 October in the year that John died, an enquiry was held, called an Inquisition Post Mortem. This had nothing to do with the manner of John's death, but was ordered by law to enquire how the lands were held; to seek out if possible, that fatal knight service; and to discover the age of the heir. All went exactly as John would have wished; the terms of his will were accepted and the fiction that the land had passed to trustees was respected. It looked as though the estate was safe. However, the watchdog of the Office of Wards, the Feodary, must have suspected something for another enquiry was called and held on 24 August, eighteen months after John's death. This time the calamity which John thought he had skilfully avoided, fell on his widow and young family. Notwithstanding all John's care, the Master of Wards took the estate, and Elizabeth was deprived of support at the very moment when she had most need of it. The findings of the previous enquiry were overthrown. The heir James was only 1¾ years old when his father had died and the fiction of trusteeship was not accepted. The whole purpose of the Office of Wards was brought to bear on the Hardwicks, and the family were left with no financial support.

For Elizabeth Hardwick to get her small son and lands out of the trammels of wardship there was one course open to her. If she was able to raise the money or to find a well-disposed relative or friend prepared to do so, then the wardship could be bought back into the family. But this she was unable to do.

The estate was surveyed on the same day of the last inquisition. The rents were valued at £20 annually, one quarter of which was

reserved for the jointure of one Amy Racheford (whoever she was
was not explained), but this money could not be touched by
the Office of Wards. A quarter of the interest in the land was sold
with the wardship to John Bugby and a more disinterested guardian
cannot be imagined. He was a Court official, an officer of the pantry.
By three instalments he paid a total of £20 and got in return lands
worth an annual £5 and the right to sell the marriage of his ward.

It is just possible that there may have been some compassion in
the administration of the Office of Wards, for just over half the estate
was kept in the King's possession and not sold with the wardship.
This was Hardwick Hall valued at £10 and the demesne land with
it, totalling in all £12, which may have been rented back to Widow
Hardwick, or she may have been evicted. But certainly the family
were at Hardwick in the period 1538–44, which was still within the
time of the wardship.

John Bugby made an undated complaint to the Star Chamber, that
John Leake esquire and Henry Marmyon (executors to John Hardwick's will) had led an attack on Hardwick Hall armed with arrows,
billhooks, staves and knives. They had forced an entry and broken
windows. They denied the charge and offered to defend themselves
in the Chancery Court. It is unlikely that this attack ever happened.
To bring a complaint of riot to the Star Chamber was one way to
get a speedy hearing in a legal wrangle – it was an attempt to sort
out some of the mess left by John Hardwick's will. In any case
Bugby should not have been concerned with Hardwick Hall at all
since it was not included in his purchase of the wardship. At the least
this complaint shows that the Hardwicks were having a difficult time
of it.

It is not easy to estimate their position at this point. At best they
may have been allowed to live on at Hardwick Hall, occupying just
over half the land; paying rent to the Master of Wards for the privilege and renting from Bugby the lands he was holding. Even this
would have been costly and would have drained and strained the
Hardwicks' resources. Their situation was financially perilous.

The Hardwicks were facing extinction and their neighbours the
Savages were in dire financial straits, but they were only a micro-
cosm of the whole, a story repeated all over England. Henry VIII
is credited with having altered the social structure of the country

and with having given opportunity to 'new men' of ability. The social turmoil was not Henry's direct intention but simply a by-product of his policies. In a nutshell the King was desperately short of money. After the ostentatious extravagance of 'the Field of Cloth of Gold' in 1520, Henry once again became entangled in war with France. To pay for this Henry was forced to turn to every means he could to screw the money he needed out of his subjects. The 'new men' of ability who rose to the top in situations of change were only too willing to devise all manner of ways for raising money: the Office of Wards was one; the commuting of prison sentences for fines another. Most profitable of all was the suppression of the monasteries.

To Elizabeth Hardwick and her young family these wider national events meant little. To the King's acute shortage of revenue they were indifferent and yet they and countless others were called upon to pay for it all.

With her income depleted, her estate removed from her care and her young son the ward of another, Widow Hardwick took the only course open to a woman – she remarried. The date is unknown but it cannot have been long after 1529. It would be interesting to know how a woman in her position came to find a husband. It was an age when marriage was very much a business transaction and property was a bargain between the two parties. Elizabeth Hardwick had nothing to offer but the small jointure from her marriage to John. Against her were stacked formidable disadvantages; the estate was in wardship and she had a family of five small children and yet Elizabeth remarried.

Her new husband was Ralph Leche, a younger son of the Leches of Chatsworth. He had no lands worth mentioning to bring to the marriage, only an annuity of £6 13s 4d (£6·66) out of Chatsworth, and some leases scattered over the midlands.[5] Neither could offer much to the other. Elizabeth gave Ralph the temporary shelter of the roof of Hardwick, and he brought to her a tenuous security. In some way they contrived to survive.

Elizabeth had three daughters by this marriage, Elizabeth, Jane and Margaret. It is a measure of her mother's success and that of Ralph the father and step-father, that all the girls made marriages into comparatively wealthy families. This could not have been done without provision of suitable dowries. They could have been found by making considerable sacrifice and a gauge of that sacrifice might be the fact that Ralph Leche was imprisoned for debt in the Fleet between 1538 and 1544.[6] He was only released when his creditors were satisfied from the sale of part of the leases and lands he had somehow acquired. The financial circumstances of Ralph Leche will always remain a mystery.

With this background of uncertainty and insolvency to Bess's early life, it is understandable that she developed an acute business instinct in money matters – a reaction to financial instability in her early childhood. But she also possessed the gift to recognise opportunity when it was presented, a gift not possessed by her brother James who, starting with greater advantages, contrived to lose a fortune he did not possess in stupid speculation and died bankrupt in the Fleet prison in 1581.

There is no certainty about any of this period of Bess's life, nor what became of her after the remarriage of her mother. It is likely that she was brought up with her half-sister Jane for she had a life-long fondness for this sister, the second daughter of her mother and Ralph Leche. Jane married Thomas Kniveton of Marcaston in Derbyshire and had eight children.

By any assessment these early years of Bess's life must have been tough nor could she look forward to a prosperous future. The women of the time, of whatever rank, were treated as inferior beings. Before marriage she was considered an infant and at marriage she became the property of her husband. Only when she became a widow was a woman in any way nearly the legal peer of a man. With this somewhat bleak future before her Bess entered the only career open to her: she married Robert Barley or Barlow (the two names are interchangable) of Barley in Derbyshire. Again little is known as to the date of this union of Bess's involuntary vocation. When Robert's father, Arthur Barley, died on 28 May 1543, it was stated that they had married 'in the life of his father'.[7] And Bess at the time of the marriage was under sixteen for she was said to be 'of tender years'. It looks as though these children were married over Arthur's death-bed when Bess would have been under fifteen and Robert thirteen years old and this seems the most likely probability. The two nearest contemporary accounts are agreed that both parties were very young. The Duchess of Newcastle in 1667, writing the life of her husband the First Duke, Bess's grandson, said that Robert Barlow 'died before they were bedded together, they both being very young'.

Nathaniel Johnson, the Yorkshire antiquarian, in an unpublished manuscript written in 1692, gives a longer and more romantic account. He claimed that he got the story from two old men whose memories must have been stretching very far back indeed. He wrote:

I have been informed by some ancient gentlemen that Bess's marriage was accomplished by her being at London Attending the Lady Zouch at such time as Mr Barlow lay sick of a Chronical Distemper. In which time this young gentlewoman making many visits upon account of them being neighborhood in the country and out of kindness to him being very sollicitous to afford him all the help she was able to do in his sickness, ordering his diet and attendance being then young and very handsome, he fell in love with her of whose great affection to her she took such advantage, that for lack of issue by her he settled a large inheritance in lands upon herself and her heires, which by his death a short time after she fully enjoyed.[8]

The main points in this account appear to be true, but there are some features which the old men must have added, perhaps to make a better story. Lady Zouch was a distant relative of the Hardwicks and she came from Derbyshire. It is no surprise to find Bess and Robert in the London household of this family. Robert could have been a page and Bess a companion for the Zouch children. Indeed it is likely that Bess's mother would have been glad to let her go; it would have been one less mouth to feed and it was the custom for children to be put into important households to learn something of the arts of music and the graces of court life. As the Barleys were near neighbours and kinsmen of the Hardwicks, Bess would have known of the family even if she had not already met them.

So far the account is consistent with other evidence, but on the matter of 'a large inheritance', the old men are quite wrong. Robert was a minor and his father was still alive when they married, therefore he did not have the disposal of the family lands. All Bess would have received from Robert was the customary marriage settlement of one-third of the total and for life only. In 1553 it amounted to no more than £8 15s (£8·75)[9] annually; very far indeed from making her an heiress.

Bess's young husband died, as the old men said, but not 'a short time' after the marriage. He died on 24 December 1544, which was at least one and a half years later. At his death when Bess was made a widow for the first time, her age was possibly sixteen and a half at the most, and although this was considered to be of age, her marriage jointure was firmly enmeshed in the legal jungle of the old Office of Wards now become the Court of Wards. For Robert had been a ward of that court. On his death the whole of his estate fell back into its machinery and Bess's marriage settlement became the subject of legal wrangling.

As the principles governing the operation of the Court of Wards were rooted in the medieval past, the revival of its powers posed many lucrative problems for lawyers. Its original purpose was no longer required and therefore many of its laws were either forgotten or misapplied. It is true to say that the legal profession was as much perplexed by its operation as were the courts themselves. All were agreed that if the heir to an estate was past the age of twenty-one then the estate was beyond the court's jurisdiction. But when it came to the marriage of a ward under age, then all fell into confusion; eventually some agreement was reached; indeed it had to be if the thing was to be worked properly. The age of consent in marriage for women was agreed to be twelve, and that of men fourteen, which meant that wards under these age limits could be married off by their guardians; over these ages the wards were considered old enough to make up their minds on the matter.

This point of age is crucial in the marriage of Robert to Bess, for had Arthur Barley died before the two children were married, then the guardian could have married Robert to whom he chose – to his own daughter perhaps – and so kept the Barley lands in his own family for a lifetime. But by the espousal (as these un-consummated child marriages were called) of Robert to Bess before his death Arthur could die in the knowledge that only two-thirds of his estate could concern the Master of Wards.

In the event, after the death of Arthur Barley, the wardship of Robert was bought by Godfrey Boswell, styled gentleman. He paid 100 marks for the guardianship, the equivalent of £66·33, but he would not have been able to buy control of the lands covering Bess's small marriage settlement which would have had to be kept separate. So that there was no possibility that Boswell should try to marry the young Robert off again; the official note of the transaction states that 'theyre is maryed in the lyf of his fader'. In any case Godfrey Boswell, gent., of Gunthwaite, Yorkshire, may not have been an ill-disposed guardian, for he either had married, or was about to marry, Bess's older sister Jane Hardwick.

Bess brought nothing to the marriage except her own small dowry – the Barleys were gaining no lands. Why then was the marriage permitted? As the two old men suggest, they might have married for love, but that would have been unusual. It is more likely that the marriage was a manœuvre to preserve the Barley estates and to keep them out of the Court of Wards.

The comment made by the Duchess of Newcastle, that Robert 'died before they were bedded together' is likely to be correct, since although fear of the Court of Wards was encouraging early espousals, it was also considered that early childbearing was not to be recommended; not out of concern for the young mother, but for the procreation of healthy male heirs, which is what it was all about.

On the death of Robert, his guardian Godfrey Boswell lost his investment of £66. The new heir was Robert's younger brother George, whose guardianship was bought by Peter Frecheville of Staveley in Derbyshire. The Barleys were left to pay out the widow's portion to Bess, which by 1589 had risen to £100.[10] The double wardship incurred by the Barleys must have contributed to their impoverishment by the end of the century.

Bess did not get her jointure without a fight, or perhaps the position was not clear in the confused state of the law concerning wardship. The settlement gave rise to three cases in the Chancery and was not finally settled until 1553. For those nine years she had to be content with something less than the full settlement.

So for those first impressionable years of her life, Bess and her family had faced setbacks which all but swamped them. She learnt that the world owed her nothing and that she would have to stand firmly on her own two feet. Later in her life, when she held enormous power through her wealth, she showed that she had never forgotten this early lesson. If Bess was forced to fight for a principle then she fought with no holds barred and used every means which her power gave her. Yet to those who depended on her for protection she gave generously. And never did she ever forget that the Crown had a greater power than she did.

From the date of her first widowhood at Christmas in 1544 until her marriage to Sir William Cavendish at Bradgate Manor in August 1547, one has to speculate what she was doing. It is likely that she went to Lady Dorset as a lady-in-waiting. This would have given her the opportunity to meet Sir William, for the Tudor world was a small one, particularly in the court circle.

At the time of his marriage to Bess, Sir William was about forty-two, some twenty-two years older than his bride. The Duchess of Newcastle, again in her biography of her husband, says that Sir William, 'being somewhat advanced in years, married her chiefly for her beauty'. He was a widower, already twice married, with three young daughters to bring up, so that it is understandable he should have married again. He had made his way in the world with success, and may have recognised the ambition and resolve in Bess's character as similar to his own. Of all Bess's marriages this undoubtedly was her most conjoint. She and Sir William thought along parallel lines, and their ambitions were united in a way which, had he lived longer, might have given him a greater place in history; a place ultimately reserved for their descendants.

'UTTERLY UNDONE'
1547-1557

The same year that Bess married Sir William Cavendish, Henry VIII died. His heir, Edward VI, was only ten, and not blessed with the stamina and good health to survive for long. After Edward, the line of succession was filled with uncertainty, brought about by Henry's understandable desire for male heirs, and his unforgivable methods of disposing of Queens who were able to supply only female or sickly babies. This uncertainty was the background to the marriage of Bess and Sir William; an uncertainty which was to influence their decisions over the coming decade.

William Cavendish was a man of considerable ability. He was born about 1505, the second son of Thomas Cavendish of Poslingford in Suffolk and his wife Alice. Younger sons had no inheritance but their own talents. William started with nothing and yet died seemingly a wealthy man. His father was Clerk of the Pipes, a legal position which would have given William access to Court circles. But the greatest help must have come from his older brother, George Cavendish, a gentleman usher of Cardinal Wolsey. George showed a devoted loyalty to Wolsey, and later wrote a biography after the great Cardinal's disgrace and death, not daring to put his name to the work.

It is likely that William started his career as a gentleman servant in the household of the cardinal. His ability helped him to survive Wolsey's fall and to be of value to his successor Thomas Cromwell; to survive his disgrace in turn and to become indispensable to the Crown. He weathered the uncertainties of the reign of Edward VI, and rode out the reversal of the Protestant cause under Queen Mary when he diplomatically became a Catholic. Any one of these turns of fortune could have been the undoing of a less able man, but with each change of power, William held on to his offices and survived.

His first big chance came when Cromwell engineered the dissolution of the monasteries. Although 1536 was the year in which the statute for the dissolution of the smaller monasteries was passed, Cromwell was taking and suppressing monasteries three years before that date. Whether the means were legal or not troubled neither him nor Henry. In 1530 William Cavendish was sent by Cromwell to enquire into a disputed lease at the monastery of Sheen near Richmond. That the matter was settled to Cromwell's satisfaction is not surprising, given the pressure which could be put on the unhappy prior facing an uncertain future. By 1534, William Cavendish was occupying, by leasehold, lands at Northaw in Hertfordshire which belonged to the Abbey of St Albans. The abbot in a letter to Cromwell was obviously steering a difficult course when he wrote that he had given to William Cavendish 'for Cromwell's sake a longer lease than ever granted before'.[1] The favour did the abbot little good for in March the following year William received an outright grant of the manor and lands of Northaw.

In April of 1536 he was appointed one of ten auditors to the Court of Augmentation, set up to deal with the sale of Church lands, and so called because the income augmented Henry's insufficient means. From then onwards William was involved completely in the work of dissolution. He covered the country with Dr Thomas Leigh, a commissioner appointed for the dissolution, taking the surrender of one religious house after another. The amount of work these two got through is astonishing. Their business with each monastery was put through in the briefest time, only long enough to enable them to take an inventory of the contents, transfer the property to the Crown and pay off the monks, before passing on to the next monastery with more long days in the saddle.

At some date early in the 1530s William Cavendish married Margaret Bostock, a daughter of Edward Bostock of Whatcross in Cheshire.[2] Their first child was born in January 1534. Altogether he and Margaret had four daughters and a son of which only three daughters survived: Catherine, Ann and Mary. His wife died in June 1540 and was buried at St Botolph's, Aldgate, where William's mother had been buried twenty-five years before.

Margaret's death occurred at a busy period of William's life. That year he was appointed one of three commissioners to survey Crown lands and twelve months later he went to Ireland to survey Church property newly seized by the Crown. He returned after a year and found time to remarry: a widow this time, Elizabeth Parris, at Blackfriars in November 1542. They had three children who all died: Susan, John and finally another girl who died a baby. Then Elizabeth died too and William was left a widower for the second time.

Another busy period followed. He was appointed Treasurer of the King's Chamber and to the Court of General Surveyors, all in 1546. These appointments, although a reflection of his merits and the appreciation of the Crown, would have been purchased by William as was the custom, and he would in turn expect to be paid for the favours and appointments which he handed to others. Finally he was made a Privy Councillor at Easter in 1546. The old King died in January of the next year and Sir William had leisure to marry again, this time to Bess Hardwick, a widow of little wealth.

Their first child, a girl, was born the year following their marriage at Bradgate. Sir William with his accountant's tidy mind, noted the details in his book with eccentric use of capitals: 'Frances my 9 Childe and the first by the said Woman was borne on Munday betweene the Howers of 3 and 4 at Afternone Viz the 18 of June Anno 2 R.E. 6. the domynical Letter then G. Memorandum At the Cristninge of the Childe my Ladie Frances Grace and my Ladie of Suffolks Grace weare Godmothers and my Lord of Suffolke Godfather at Bishoppinge.'

The godparents were all old friends from their Bradgate days with little political influence, but one of them was to be Bess's greatest friend and ally: Lady Frances, after whom the child was christened, was her old friend Frances Grey, daughter of Charles Brandon and his first wife Princess Mary Tudor. Lord Suffolk was Brandon's eldest son, then aged eleven and brother to Frances, and Lady Suffolk was Brandon's last wife. This was a family occasion and the association with the family of Frances and her husband Henry Grey, Marquis of Dorset (later confusingly made Duke of Suffolk) was not political. Grey had no ability or judgement; whatever influence he had derived from his marriage to Frances and that he happened to be the father of their daughter Jane Grey. Bess had not yet cast her net wider into Court circles.

But for the first time in her life, Bess had a home of her own, two in fact. Her life was divided between Northaw and a London house in Newgate Street, just north of St Paul's and rented from the Marquis of Northampton.[3] Reversing her previous role Bess had a gentlewoman, 'Cecily', and her sister, Jane Leche, also acting as gentlewoman, who was paid a wage of £3 per year. Altogether Bess ran an establishment of about fifteen servants some of whom were to stay with her for many years. Otewell Greves was still with her in the late 1560s; Francis Whitfield stayed until the late 1550s. But most trusted of all was James Cromp, who later supervised the building of Chatsworth, and in 1601 there was still a chamber named after him at Chatsworth, even though he had long since gone. None of these servants stayed with Bess till her death. By the end of her long life, she had outlasted them all.

The estate and administration of Northaw Manor had not kept pace with current methods of management and there would have been ample scope for improving rents and revenues by enclosing commons and waste. To the tenants this was no answer to their problems; in fact it added to them. They lost traditional free grazing and if they wanted grazing they had to pay for it in higher rents. At Northaw, Sir William was enclosing wasteland, when at Pentecost 1548, he faced something of a riot. The disgruntled villagers tried to pull down the enclosures and all his servants and the chaplain joined in the affray. Whatever the conclusion of this brawl, which must have been one of the first cases of peasant revolt Bess faced, it obviously never deterred her, for later she enclosed land time and again and even depopulated villages.[4]

However Bess's life was not all devoted to domestic matters. She and Sir William led quite a social life and were fond of gambling, particularly cards. Usually they lost a few shillings only, though on one occasion Sir William had gambling losses of £2. But a sum so large was not going to be ruinous to them. Their income from rents in 1549 was £250, on top of which there were Sir William's annuities of about another £400, and an unknown income from the sale of favours. Set against a total expenditure for the nearest known year of 1550 of £340,[5] it is obvious that Sir William could afford to play, no matter how badly. They lived well and by 1550 their income vastly exceeded their expenditure.

This interval of comfortable affluence must have been one of the happiest periods of Bess's life. An opportunist, like her husband, she would have realised that their prosperity depended on royal patronage and in recognising the transitory nature of political life she would have enjoyed what was offered. But her first priority was to have a family and after Frances, her children were born at almost yearly intervals, and their care became her primary concern. We know that Frances was only a year old when put into a waistcoat and red mantle, whilst underneath she had petticoats made of kersey, a partlett or collar worn under a bodice, hose caps and gowns, and that she was given a teething ring. Tudor children did not know the freedom of modern clothes and were dressed like little adults; it is a wonder that Frances did not die of constriction and frustration. Tudor babies had to be hardy to survive.

Sir William had brought with him a ready-made family, his two daughters by his first marriage: Catherine, aged thirteen in 1548, and Ann, then aged nine, were living with them. Bess referred to them as her daughters and treated them no differently from her own children; generous and expensive items of clothing were bought for them all. Mary Cavendish, Sir William's other surviving daughter by his first wife, would have been ten in 1548. No candies or rich silks were bought for her and unlike Catherine and Ann, she did not live with her father and Bess but boarded out, indicating perhaps a handicapped child. She was dead before 1556, and Bess used her name for her own seventh child.

Bess's second daughter, Temperance, was born at Northaw in 1549. Her aunt, Marcella Linaker, was staying with her and perhaps came up for the event. Temperence was born at two in the morning of 10 June. The midwife was paid the particularly large sum of 50s (£2.50) – perhaps it was a difficult birth – and in thanks 5s (25p) were given in alms. Bess's mother, out of it all in Derbyshire, sent nourishing food of brawn and capons, like many grandmothers before and since.

The christening of Temperance was held at Northaw and this time the choice of godparents was more far-reaching but still based on the friendship with Frances Grey. Lady Warwick, a godmother, stayed with them; she was the wife of John Dudley, Earl of Warwick, and her son Guilford was to marry Jane Grey, Frances's daughter. Jane Grey herself was also a godmother and for godfather they had the Earl of Shrewsbury who was a Privy Councillor. The christening over and Aunt Linaker in charge of the household, Bess and Sir William left for London.

By the choice of godparents and their association with Frances Grey, Bess and Sir William were committed to the Protestant cause. Their friends too were all without exception fervent Protestants. This could have been unwise. By the middle of 1550 the political future of England was not set fair. Religion, the over-riding problem of the whole century, was at the bottom of the concern. Edward VI, to whom his father Henry had passed the Protestant throne, was physically weak; after him in succession would come whoever proved the stronger; Jane Grey perhaps, or Mary the ardent Catholic, who was likely to hand back all the monastery lands. The great rebellions in the autumn of 1549 and the fall of Somerset, Edward's Protector, had frightened all those who wished for stable government. Bess and Sir William possessed the annexed Church lands at Northaw, and Northaw was on the main route from the north to London. This was an exposed position in every way, both from possible marching armies and Catholic monarchs set on reclaiming Church lands. Furthermore they had other Church lands in Cardigan which were too far away to administer properly, and they had a close association with Jane Grey. Clearly if Mary came to the throne and civil war followed they had a great deal to lose.

The problem was solved in a neat fashion. Bess's youngest sister Alice Hardwick had married Francis Leche of Chatsworth in Derbyshire. Leche had a considerable estate reaching from Bakewell on one side to as far away as Chesterfield on the other, but a lot of this was moorland and useless for anything more than poor grazing. It had been sold to Francis Agard in 1547–8[6] and by the following year, for an unexplained reason, Agard was trying to sell off half of what he had bought, including the old manor of Chatsworth. One of the problems of the age was the availability of ready money; the only security to put money into was land and if cash was needed quickly it was very difficult to find anyone with hundreds of pounds on hand to pay for a deal. This may have been the cause of Agard's problem. It was no problem to Bess and Sir William who had been selling off their Hertfordshire lands in small parcels.

To buy Chatsworth from Agard made a great deal of sense. Derbyshire had never been disturbed by the late civil war and it was not even troubled in that of the 1640s. It was Bess's home; she knew the land and its problems; her family were there and it was only four days' journey from London; not too remote and yet remote enough to escape trouble. On the last day of June 1549 they bought Chatsworth from Agard for £600. In the early part of the following year Sir William, with his spare cash, gave Bess a book set with gold and stones, with portraits of them both inside. It cost him exactly £14 6s (£14.30)[7] and perhaps this was in celebration of the successful outcome of their negotiations; certainly the gift was of great sentimental value to Bess for she kept it all her life and left it to her daughter Frances after she died.

The purchase of Chatsworth left the problem of finding a buyer for Northaw and the Cardigan lands. Through his position in the Augmentation Office Sir William was likely to know what properties the Crown held and their value; he was well placed to put through the deal which followed. On 15 June 1552 Sir William and Bess signed a profitable exchange of lands with the Crown – extremely profitable to Bess and Sir William. For the Hertfordshire and Cardigan estates, they exchanged lands in Doveridge, about thirty miles from Chatsworth; the manor of Meadowpleck near Chatsworth; and some oddments in Lincolnshire lately belonging to Tutbury Abbey, which they shortly sold. They gained a substantial amount on the deal. The lands in Doveridge alone must have amounted to more than the total value of the old properties, for it was and still is very good pasture land on the River Dove. The Crown Commissioners assessing the value of Northaw were sent a generous gift of game and fish by Sir William to make their job easier.

Bess must have had a considerable hand in these deals, although the negotiation and detail would have been carried out by Sir William. She knew Derbyshire and Sir William was relying on her local knowledge, and the trust between the two must have been absolute. Bess acquired her experience of accounting and estate management from Sir William; lessons she never forgot. In the first years of her marriage the accounts covering household and general expenditure were kept, as was the usual custom, by the clerk comp-troller. Every week the accounts were examined and passed by Sir William; with his accounting background it is not surprising that some of the entries are in his own hand, but it was unusual for the time. What is more unusual is that Bess made occasional entries, mainly concerned with her own purchases of items of dress, entries which became more and more frequent as time passed and she took over from Sir William who was becoming a sick man. Later she kept the accounts entirely herself.

The tragedies and triumphs of domestic life do not wait on mat-ters of land exchange and purchase, nor on the uncertainties of the political future. Temperance, their second child, died whilst still a baby. The last reference to her was in October 1549, when a nurse was paid 5s (25p) 'Given when Temperance was sick'.[8] She must have been very sick for so large a payment. Temperance, although only Bess's second child, was Sir William's tenth, and of those ten only four had survived beyond childhood.

Their first son, Henry, was born in mid-December 1550, and was no doubt welcomed as an heir. Much later the emotion turned sour for Bess; she was to call him 'my bad son Henry'. This time ambi-tious, they chose as godmother the Princess Elizabeth, the future Queen. Considering the uncertainty of the succession, it was a sur-prising choice; once more they were committing themselves com-pletely to the Protestant party. The two godfathers were the Earl of Warwick, future father-in-law to Jane Grey and a Privy Coun-cillor; and finally Henry Grey the husband of their old friend Frances – all of them firm Protestants.

It seems surprising that Bess did not entertain the Greys at their London house during this period of their close friendship, although we know they had supper at the Greys' home on at least one occasion. Neither did Bess and Sir William entertain any other of their powerful friends and the explanation must be that their house was not big enough to accommodate the large number of servants these high potentates found it necessary to take with them. But about the time that Northaw was sold they moved to another Lon-don house, perhaps larger than the Newgate Street house and even if they were unable to entertain their patrons they made up for this lack by inviting the less exalted; there were usually three or more to every meal. Sir John Berends, the family priest, was present through most of 1552–3; Bess's mother was with them during four days in November 1552; in April the following year her brother James, who had repossessed Hardwick in 1547, had dinner with them bringing a Derbyshire friend, Sir James Foljambe. One frequent visitor was Lady Port who was probably a childhood friend, for she came from a local Derbyshire family, the Fitzherberts. She was the second wife of Sir John Port then recently knighted at the coronation of Edward VI and later a knight of the shire in Mary's parliament. Usefully he was sheriff of Derbyshire in 1553, and perhaps more usefully one of his daughters by his first marriage was married to George Hastings Latur, Fourth Earl of Huntingdon, and therefore it is not surprising that the good earl sent a venison pasty to the Cavendishes.

In common with the custom, the hall of the London house was given over to the servants and those of visiting guests, whilst Bess, Sir William and their guests supped or dined in the parlour off the hall. Bess invariably decorated her parlour with flowers and boughs. Breakfast was a meal seldom mentioned; dinner was served at eleven in the morning and supper at six in the evening. With these meals they offered considerable refinement: a harpist and two minstrels were part of the permanent establishment, they had silver and the finest linens and napkins, whilst their servants wore a blue livery. As far as diet was concerned London provided everything from far and near though some of their dishes were perhaps spoiled in the cooking, at least according to modern taste: fresh salmon was boiled in ale, for example, though apples frittered in ale might just be acceptable. Stewing and boiling over the fire was a constant stock pot which had yeast and herbs thrown into it from time to time and no doubt the scraps from the leftovers. Saltwater and freshwater fish were plentiful; crabs and oysters, and even 'red herrings' which were kippers; eel soused in ale, and cods' heads which were a favourite dish; all these were generally eaten on Fridays although towards the end of Mary's reign the habit tended to drop away. Lamb, mutton, veal, beef, bacon and ox's feet, rabbits and neats' tongues comprised the meats, and for poultry chicken, pheasant, blackbirds, and what must have been a messy dish of '12 great birds and 12 dozen small birds'. Quantities of herbs were used for salads and cooking, as well as pepper, cloves, vinegar and mustard, cinnamon and ginger; whilst for fruit Bess had dates, raisins of the sun, currants, figs, oranges, lemons and pippins; and on one occasion custard was served. Poor Frances, who may have been suffering with her health, was the only member of the family who had regular amounts of milk to drink either on its own or with saffron, and once – what must have been the vilest of all potions – with garlic.

Enormous amounts of ale were drunk; and wines, claret, Rhenish, malmsey and sack were sent out for by the quart and gallon, suggesting that there was no cellar large enough to store what was needed. Sir William himself would drink two pints of wine with dinner and the same again at supper while his habitual purgatives were helped down with sweetmeats. Often, in the evening, a posset was taken made of sack – a white wine – mixed with milk and herbs. For Sir William and Bess there was nothing in London, or for that matter in the known world, they could not buy: dates, prunes, raisins dried in the sun, almonds from Jordan and salt from the Bay of Biscay.

Wine, ale and provisions could be bought at any hour of the day or night; occasionally their oven was used to bake cakes, but never bread, which was bought expensively from a baker. Theirs was a busy London household living in considerable comfort and luxury; their life centred on the Court such as it was, surrounded by a bustling city which never slept, a city of narrow lanes and complicated streets which made the use of the river, when possible, a comfortable and safer alternative for travelling about.

The expense of such a life-style was enormous; from early November in 1551 through a period of eleven weeks, Sir William spent £352[9] and on top of this would have been the household expenditure and wages. A grocer's bill from this period has survived: Robert Harrison submitted his account for 'all thynges from the begynynge of the world to thys day. £6 11s 10d' [£6.59] and the day was 2 December 1552.[10] The average weekly expenditure in 1551–3 could have been as high as £40 or £2000 a year, without taking into account the expenditure at Chatsworth, nor Sir William's marriage settlement on his daughter Catherine when she married Thomas Brooke. This expenditure was conspicuous extravagance of the order expected of very rich noblemen, and even with

their estates, annuities and bribes of office they did not have this
sort of income; later evidence suggests that they fell far short of
living within their means. It may have been a calculated gamble
based on the estimate that a nation troubled with civil war would
not have time or energy to check its servants' accounts. Bess and
Sir William certainly knew what they were up to and whatever Sir
William was doing Bess was party to it.

This conspicuous extravagance was only part of the story. After
buying Chatsworth and exchanging Northaw and Cardigan, they
embarked on a policy of buying lands in Derbyshire on a considerable scale.[11] The Manor of Ashford, close to Chatsworth, together
with eight thousand acres, was bought in 1550 from the Earl of
Westmorland. This acquisition was followed by purchases which
by comparison were smaller but nevertheless, taken together,
amounted to a large acreage. In 1553 they bought two hundred and
fifty acres in Chatsworth and Baslow; in 1554 another seventy acres
around Chatsworth and at the same time part of Edensor, the neighbouring village to Chatsworth. This was a policy of consolidation
in and around Chatsworth; there were no additions to the
Doveridge lands. All would have to be paid for somehow and it
could never have been done from Sir William's profits and rewards
of office.

The manner in which these properties were conveyed and recon-
veyed to trustees and then back again to Sir William and Bess jointly
shows an adroit awareness of the problems of establishing a good
and indisputable title to their lands. By holding the estates jointly
in both their names for their lives, whichever lived the longer,
assured that on Sir William's death there could be no question of
wardship for the heir Henry, for the land would all be held by the
surviving Bess. This was a lesson she had learnt from her childhood
and furthermore, unlike many of her contemporaries, Bess never
dabbled in the profitable but detestable buying and trading in wardships. Always acute to recognise a profit, Bess had her limits and
from her personal experience the purchase of wardships was an
insupportable practice.

Whilst Bess was running their London home, no doubt smoothly
and efficiently, their family was continuing to grow. William, their
second son, was born at the new London house on Sunday morn-

ing between two and three o'clock on 27 December 1551. There
must have been some concern at his birth for a Dr Bartlett gave
advice and although it was usual for the christening to follow closely
on the birth, Sir William only wrote to William Paulet, the
powerful Lord Treasurer, on 4 January asking him to be godfather
and the ceremony must have taken place many days after that. The
sole godmother was Elizabeth Brooke, wife of William Parr, Marquess of Northampton. This gesture was not completely political;
admittedly he was a Privy Councillor but there was to be a marriage
connection indicating that Parr was a member of the Protestant
circle to which Bess and Sir William belonged. William Parr had
been married before, but had at length, and almost uniquely,
obtained a divorce. It had been a tangled and unhappy case but
now Parr had married Elizabeth Brooke whose brother, Thomas
Brooke, son of Lord Cobham, married Catherine Cavendish the
eldest daughter of Sir William from his first marriage. William Parr
and Catherine Cavendish therefore had both married into the same
Brooke family; they became part of the web of friendship and marriages centred on Protestantism, which built up round Bess and Sir
William. Young William's other godfather was William Herbert,
Earl of Pembroke; a Privy Councillor tinged with Protestantism and
a brother-in-law to the same Elizabeth Brooke. To count these con-
sequential officers of State amongst their friends and marriage connections shows how far Bess and Sir William had moved since
Frances was born two years earlier.

These births in quick succession which were the inevitable lot
of any married woman were no trouble to Bess, who throughout
her long life enjoyed what can only be called robust health. This
was as well for the medical knowledge of the time was, if not ineffective, downright dangerous. It was based on the absurd concept that
the health of the body was governed by the balance of humours
in the blood, wet and dry, hot and cold; too much of one caused
illness. An illness could be cured by taking blood – to drain off the
humour – and possibly any life the patient might have left in him.
Bess was sick in February 1553: it may have been a miscarriage
for no child was born until late November that year, but whatever
the cause, she was given a pint of malmsey wine, a pleasant and
harmless remedy. Sir William may have suffered from varicose veins

for his legs were washed with herbs. By keeping to purgatives, malmsey wine and herbs, Sir William and Bess were showing a great deal of common sense.

This was the only period of Bess's life when she lived more or less continuously in London. Later she would make extended visits but never again was her life centred on London. Although the precise position of their half-timbered house is never mentioned, it was evidently close to the river; provisions were brought to the house by river and, Ann Cavendish, when she visited the Greys at Suffolk Place, went by boat; Sir William on his frequent Court visits took his own boat. And on one occasion the river overflowed into their inadequate cellar and it had to be baled out. Sometimes Bess and Sir William visited their friends on horseback when the river was not a practical means and sometimes, more comfortably, went in their litter lined with green quilted silk.

The prosperous existence which the Cavendishes were enjoying was abruptly called into doubt when, not unexpectedly, the young King died in July 1553, and the prospect of civil strife became a strong possibility. In the spring of 1552, Edward had an attack of smallpox which developed into tuberculosis and by the summer of 1553 it was obvious that he was dying. The Earl of Warwick, created Duke of Northumberland, had succeeded Somerset as the King's Protector and with the prospect of his power slipping away with Edward's death he had made a determined and desperate attempt to preserve his position. In May 1553 he married his son, Guilford Dudley, to Jane Grey and persuaded the dying King to make a will having Jane as his successor. This had no legal basis as Jane's mother, Frances, was still living and above all it set aside Henry VIII's will that Mary and then Elizabeth should succeed after Edward's death. It also overlooked the Act of 1544 which laid down that it was high treason to tamper with the succession.

On Edward's death, Northumberland proclaimed Jane Grey Queen of England. Mary Tudor, in Norfolk, rallied her supporters at Framlingham Castle and Northumberland marched out of London for Cambridge at the head of his troops, passing within a few miles of Northaw, confirming that Sir William and Bess had been right to fear being in the path of warring armies. Mary's support was overwhelming and the Privy Council arrested Northumberland

at Cambridge; the succession of Mary was proclaimed and an uneasy transition had been achieved with no bloodshed. Northumberland was executed and Jane Grey, her husband Guilford Dudley
and her father Henry Grey would all have followed the same way
had it not been for the intercession of Frances Grey with Mary.
Frances's influence must have been considerable for though her
husband Henry detested Catholicism and all Mary stood for, he was
let off with a heavy fine; their daughter and son-in-law remained
alive but in the Tower. Bess and her husband had tied their cause
to both parties for Sir William later claimed that when Northumberland marched with his army, he raised a number of men in support
of Mary at his own very dear cost of nearly £700.[12] Sir William
survived for the moment and retained all his offices, but little Henry
Cavendish lost one of his godfathers when Northumberland was
beheaded.

In November following these events, Bess's third son Charles was
born and Sir William celebrated his arrival by asking the Queen
to be godmother; this surely was the height of diplomacy. But the
choice of Henry Grey, Duke of Suffolk, as godfather was a bizarre
and loyal act of friendship and one that associated Mary with a man
who had lately tried to engineer her downfall. The association can
only have been held together by Frances Grey's influence with her
cousin the Queen, and it must have been Frances who extricated
Bess and Sir William from a very difficult situation. The other godfather was Stephen Gardner, Bishop of Winchester, 'Wiley Winchester', as he was called; his portrait still hangs at Hardwick and
the description is a fitting one.

For the next few years Bess and Sir William divided their time
between Chatsworth and London. In Bess's absence from Chatsworth, she left her sister Jane in charge of the household with Francis
Whitfield, her bailiff, responsible for running the estate. Some
attempt was made to repair what was decayed in the old house, but
almost as soon as they had taken over the property they started
rebuilding. At the end of 1551, Roger Word, a mason who was to
work for Sir William Cecil at Burghley, supplied a plan for 20s (£1),
and ironwork for two gates was sent up from London. The work
continued fitfully, suggesting that funds were not always available.
Not only funds, but skilled workmen were scarce. In 1555 Sir William

wrote to Sir John Thynne from Brentford (a house Thynne had built in 1549) who was then starting his interminable building and rebuilding of Longleat, asking for the loan of his 'connynge plais-terer at Longlete which hath in yor hall made dyverse pendants & other pretty things', adding that his hall at Chatsworth was 'yet onmade'. Sir William's hall was to stay unfinished until 1570. But this did not prevent Bess and Sir William furnishing Chatsworth in splendid magnificence which must have been unequalled in Derby-shire and neighbouring counties. A steady stream of furnishings, hangings, plate and wines went up to Chatsworth. By an inventory of 1553[13] there were 2124 ounces of silver and gold plate, which if valued at the then current 6s (30p) per ounce was worth £640. There were fifty-eight pieces of tapestry; thirteen bedchambers were each furnished 'en suite', the earliest reference in England to bedchamber furniture with matching coverings throughout. Their bed was described as being gilt carved work with the arms of Sir William and Bess, and a single valance of 'red cloth inlaid with red silk and silver'. Other beds, even more costly, had valances of cloth of gold embroidered with pearls; reds, purples, blues and yellows were mixed with colours which must have clashed alarmingly and presented a sumptuous spectacle of jangled disharmony, which never troubled the Elizabethans. In addition there were quantities of bedding and other household equipment; then finally the livestock, forty drawing oxen, five hundred ewes and six hundred wethers. Chatsworth, with this furnished splendour, was fit to receive the monarch, and Bess and Sir William obviously had their sights set high. Again, all this magnificence had to be paid for somehow and it could never have come from Sir William's ordinary rewards.

Another daughter, Elizabeth, was born in March of 1555. For godparents she had to share one with her brother William, Elizabeth Brooke after whom the child was named; the other godmother was an astonishing choice; Jane Grey's sister Catherine. Her father, Henry Grey, had failed to learn his lesson and now involved himself in the popular rising known as Wyatt's Rebellion, a serious protest against Mary's rule and one in which France had a hand. Inevitably Grey was re-arrested, tried and found guilty. It was obvious to Mary that as long as the Greys remained alive they would be a source of trouble to her. Notwithstanding her friendship with Frances

Grey, Mary had Jane Grey and her husband and father brought from their prisons. Jane, being of royal blood, had the privilege of being executed privately within the Tower, so avoiding the public spectacle afforded by the execution of her father and husband on Tower Hill. The gleaming axe rose and fell and three more victims were added to Mary's growing list of judicial murders.

Catherine Grey had been married to Lord Herbert, the son of the Earl of Pembroke, on the same day that her sister had married Guilford Dudley. Pembroke annulled the marriage after the trial of Jane Grey and the disgrace of the family; Catherine was left an outcast. To choose her as godmother was therefore astonishing and showed no hint of the old ambition. It was a loyal and devoted act of friendship on the part of Bess and Sir William to their old friend Frances Grey, Duchess of Suffolk, the mother of Catherine, and from whose house Bess had been married only eight years before.

Two more children followed after Elizabeth in 1555. Mary was born eleven months later and finally Lucretia, who died young, was born in March 1557. Apart from having Elizabeth Brooke's husband, William Parr, Marquis of Northampton, as godfather to Elizabeth, Bess and Sir William this time played safe by calling on members of her own family and Derbyshire friends for the remaining godparents. Lucretia may have been born at Chatsworth as the godparents were entirely and safely local gentry. And in the choice of a name for his last child Bess was picking a classical heroine whose virtues of chastity and liberality she worked into a hanging for Chatsworth much later, and which still exists today at Hardwick.

In the August following Lucretia's birth, Bess left Chatsworth for London,[14] taking with her Elizabeth, then aged two and a half. There was nothing to suggest that the journey was hurried; they took four days and three nights and it could have been done in less. Sir William, then in London, was in trouble and he was also sick. But there was no suggestion of great urgency in Bess's arrangements – after all they had been in trouble before and come out of it.

Sir William had been called upon by the Lord Treasurer, William Paulet, to explain a huge discrepancy of £5237 5s 0¾d (£5237.26) in his accounts.[15] Sir William had purchased his office, he had been appointed at a very low salary, and could take the profits. He was expected to make up for the low pay, which was all the Crown could afford, by the sales of favours which in effect amounted to an indirect tax; this was one of the facts of Tudor Court life and Sir William had been doing no more than similarly placed officials were doing. No doubt some of the accounting between his private and official business life got mixed up but this again would have been normal. Sir William said that he had 'two books all ready engrossed [made up] and nine other rough journal books not yet sorted together nor engrossed'; plainly his accounts were in a bit of a mess. It looked as though someone in the Lord Treasurer's office had gone to immense trouble and ferreted out payments and receipts concerning Sir William going back thirteen years and had discovered the discrepancies. But that was not what had happened for it was plainly an impossible task. The reason was political. England was at war with France; Mary's husband Philip had deserted her for Spain and her policies at home were desperately unpopular; she felt herself surrounded by malevolent Protestant advisors and was determined to get rid of them. It is very likely that Sir William had been syphoning off royal revenues; in fact the money to build Chatsworth and to buy all the splendours had very likely come from that source. But Sir William and Bess may also have been associating with Mary's rival, her sister Elizabeth; and there was certainly a great bond between Bess and Elizabeth after she became Queen. Sir William had become a liability to Mary and he had to be got rid of.

He must have known the blow was coming long before it fell; this sort of thing could not have been kept secret in that small Court circle and whispers and hints must have been dropped into his ear. Furthermore he knew that once the charge was made there would be no denying it and his only hope was to ask for leniency in the light of his past loyalty. He tried to defend himself by explaining that a servant in his office, Thomas Knott, whom he had taken on from the previous Treasurer of the Chamber, had run away with £1231 during the 'tyme of my sickness'; but even this was far short of the total sum lacking. He pointed out that he had often been out of pocket under the two previous monarchs who had promised sums which had never been paid; he displayed his loyalty to Mary by telling of the expense he had been put to by paying for the men he had raised in her defence when she was threatened by Northumberland. Finally he asked for mercy, painting a harrowing picture of his 'poor wife my miserable and innocent children and formerly now kneeling and standing before me (not without the number of sorrowful tears) presenting our misery'. Pathetically he pleaded that if forced to repay the full sum he would find himself 'and mine Innocent Children utterly undone, like to end our latter days in no small penury'. A theatrical exaggeration and it got him nowhere.

That was the situation when Bess returned to London at the end of August 1557. Sir William had been accused and was making up his defence, possibly the worry of it all was making him ill. Sir William may also have had a drink problem for the total of ale and wine he drank over these weeks could have done him no good at all. Meanwhile the life of the London household went on as usual; there were guests to many meals and Bess went to supper with Frances Grey. But the crisis had gone too far for Frances's help and she may have been as far out of favour as Bess and Sir William, for her Protestant devotion was well known. Perhaps an omen, on Thursday 7 October a priest said mass in the house. On 12 October, Sir William sent his secretary, Robert Bestnay, to the Privy Council with his statement of defence, saying that he was too ill to go himself. Thirteen days later Sir William died and was buried on the last day of October at St Botolph's church, Aldgate, where his first wife had been buried seventeen years before and his mother twenty-five years before that.

Bess completed her husband's notebook, finally writing in it:

Memorandum. That Sir William Cavendyshe Knight my most deare and well beloved Husband departed this present Life of Mundaie being the 25th daie of October betwixt the Howers of 8 and 9 of the same daie at Night in the yeare of our Lord God 1557. the domunicall Letter then C. On whose Soule I most humbly beseeche the Lord to have Mercy and Ridd mee and his poore Children out of our greate Misserie. Elizabeth Cavendysshe.

It can be certain that she meant every word.

LADY
ST LOE
1557-1565

Sir William left Bess with considerable problems. By then thirty, and widowed for the second time, she had six children of her own and two step-daughters (although by then one may have married). It was an intimidating prospect. Above all, the outstanding matter of the missing £5000, which Sir William had been unable to account for, was now Bess's responsibility. A bill against her was passing through parliament.

By the next decade, Bess admitted to debts. Although the sum of these is never revealed, it is likely that they were not inconsiderable and had been raised to cover the purchase of Ashford Manor from the Earl of Westmorland, and other small parcels of land bought before 1555. The total of the debts is never revealed because usury was illegal, although widely practised. Loans require the payment of interest and this would have been added to Bess's financial burden. To keep what she already had and to bring up her young family in the face of these difficulties, required financial acumen beyond the ability of many. Once more Bess showed that she was no ordinary woman.

At this point Bess could have chosen the easy way and sold land to pay off what was owing, married a local squire and lived in comfortable obscurity. It is doubtful if she ever considered this as a solution. Bess's obvious later ambition must date from this time. She made up her mind to build on what her late husband Sir William had begun, a great dynasty of Cavendishes founded on such wealth that it could be swept away only with difficulty; it was to be a dynasty which would be involved in all the future glories of the English nation. Men are mortal, material possessions decay, but a dynasty might last for a thousand years. It was a very Elizabethan vision – a

vision motivated in Bess by her early childhood fears from the near extinction of the Hardwicks by the State through the Court of Wards.

The London account book for the period immediately before Sir
William died stopped at 13 October 1557,[1] exactly twelve days
before his death. It began again the following year eight months
later on 13 June 1558. By then Bess had given up the London house
and had sent to Chatsworth for the children to come to her at Brentford where she was probably renting the same house from Sir John
Thynne as her husband had two years before. By that June it was
plain to all that Queen Mary was seriously and incurably ill. Bess
was well placed at Brentford, a village far enough away from London
for her to be unobtrusive and yet near enough for her to miss nothing
when Mary died.

In early November messengers were sent to Hatfield Palace telling Princess Elizabeth that Mary had named her as successor to
the throne and from that moment Elizabeth began selecting her
councillors and Court.

Through that tense autumn Mary's health continued to
deteriorate and as the Queen became weaker, Bess became involved
in mysterious comings and goings. She was at Brentford until the
end of September, then she vanished but turned up in London on
13 November; it is quite possible that she had been to Hatfield in
the meantime. On the day that Mary died, 17 November, Bess
apparently was absent again, and the best surmise is that she was
again with Elizabeth and would have heard her first public speech
made on 20 November in the hall at Hatfield Old Palace which is
still very much as she left it. Bess was definitely back in London
by 25 November and had started furnishing and provisioning the
new house. Hangings were put up, half a thousand billets of wood
were sent for to air the place, and one of her sisters came to stay.
Elizabeth was crowned on 14 January; Bess's daughter Frances,
then aged ten, and perhaps Elizabeth aged nearly four, under the
charge of her step-daughters Ann and Catherine, watched the procession as the Queen passed in a horse litter on her way to Westminster Abbey. Her sons Henry, William and Charles, in London
for the excitement of the royal occasion and with their hair cut only
two days earlier, were probably in the Abbey to watch a scene to
remember for the rest of their lives.

Bess's friendship and support of Elizabeth now paid off; she was appointed lady-in-waiting to the Queen and could have asked for nothing better. The reign of one of history's most brilliant women was just beginning. Her Court naturally attracted men of all kinds, the clever, the wealthy and the loyal, as well as the adventurers, the shifty and the perfidious. Bess's Court appointment would have let her meet them all.

The Court was the centre of power and the fountain of patronage; it could also be a well of despair. The backbiting and intrigues as well as the gaiety and grandeur were as familiar to Bess as anyone and she also knew that the sixteenth-century pursuit of royal patronage could provide the shortest cut to prosperity and, by displays of material wealth, a shorter cut to bankruptcy for the unwary. But Bess would not be taken in by the pitfalls of Court life; immensely practical in all things she never allowed her head to rule her heart; she would know when to spend money to bring a good return.

Marriage was a matter of wealth and the wealthy tended to display theirs in their dress at Court; a betrothal was a bargain in which one bid was set against another; those with wealth could expect to be matched with equal riches. Bess's income in 1558 from her rents was approximately £300 a year and in that year, which involved some expensive living at Brentford, she spent £200.[2] On these estimates Bess was living within her means but they do not include any payment of interest on her debts. They do show that she would have been unable to pay back anything of the £5000 owing to the Crown. Bess had a twofold reason for attending Elizabeth's Court; the urgent hope that she might abate the ruinous payment of that £5000; and the opportunity to find a third influential husband. To fail in either meant insolvency and an uncertain future.

That year of her coronation, Elizabeth rewarded her supporters. Among them Sir William St Loe, her Captain of the Guard, was appointed Chief Butler of England with an annuity of 50 marks or £33, on 9 December 1559, and the following day he was given another annuity of 100 marks. This was a Court appointment carrying with it a responsibility of almost constant attendance on the Queen and a performance in the complicated ritual which was an essential part of the daily life revolving round the monarch, a ritual designed and evolved to impress all beholders with the might of majesty and with the additional benefit of keeping idle courtiers fully occupied. Sir William was moderately wealthy and immensely loyal to Elizabeth. Within a few weeks after 15 August 1559, Bess and William St Loe were married.

Sir William, Bess's third husband, came from a Somerset family who were ancient and landed.[3] They had settled near Bath by the time of Richard I and had remained in a state of suspended nonentity until Sir William, who was born about 1520, entered upon a career of service to the Crown by way of the army. He was sent to Ireland and by 1548 was Lieutenant of the King's Forts in Leinster. Then, as now, Ireland was a perplexity and a distress to the English. Primitive and wild, it was not a comfortable country to serve in. The next year, whilst in Ireland, William St Loe was knighted, and in December granted an annuity of £40. By February 1553 he had left Ireland, no doubt with relief, and was appointed Keeper of the Horse to Edward VI, a Court appointment. Following Edward's death he became a gentleman attendant to the Lady Elizabeth, the future Queen. Here he displayed his loyalty by being committed to the Tower on 28 February 1554, charged with being an accomplice in Wyatt's rebellion. He was imprisoned with many distinguished Protestants; some were pardoned and some executed, but Sir William was fined £200 and released in January 1555. With this career of honourable service to the Protestant cause it is understandable that Elizabeth should reward his loyalty. This would have commended him to Bess. A further recommendation was his possession of lands at Tormarton in Gloucestershire, Chew Magna, the evocatively named Owlspring Manor and others in Somerset. Thirty years later the income from these lands was £700 annually; in 1560 they would have brought in something like £350 which, added to his annuities, would have made a total income of around £500.

Obviously St Loe was comfortably off. Why then did he marry Bess who was encumbered with debt, who had £5000 to repay to the Crown and who had daughters and step-daughters to marry, requiring dowries? No doubt at Court Bess gave the impression of wealth, and her estates in Derbyshire would have lent support to that impression, but the world must have known of that missing £5000 and speculated as to how it was to be repaid. The background to Bess's financial problems must have been known to St Loe and he must also have known that when he married her he was taking not only a bride but some considerable future expenditure. The only conclusion must be that St Loe was fascinated by Bess and loved her. A portrait in the Long Gallery at Hardwick, after the style of Hans Eworth and wrongly marked 'Maria Regina', is of Bess and gives some indication of her personality. By the dress it was painted in the early 1560s – about the time she and St Loe were married. Her hands, wearing four rings are clasped demurely before her, holding a pair of gloves. She wears an expensive black gown lightly trimmed with fur round the edge and collar; the puffed sleeves, ending just above the elbow, reveal undersleeves heavily embroidered and although they exactly match the collar, would have been separate and held by laces. On her light-reddish hair Bess wears a bone grace 'of the new fashion'. She looks down from her frame, almost but not quite smiling; her dark eyes look past us to the right; she seems lost in contemplation. By this portrait we can see why St Loe married his expensive bride; she has an attractive face, a pleasant expression and above all it shows one who was competent and not likely to suffer fools gladly. It shows the charm which Bess had in abundance when she cared to use it; the concealed smile is perhaps hiding the wit which she was said to have. Unfortunately the letters which survive from Bess do not do her justice for they show no wit and little charm: obviously Bess found it difficult to express herself but the evidence of these gifts is there in the portrait.

Three letters only survive from Sir William St Loe to Bess and they are all touching in their affection.[4] Poor Sir William had to spend so long at Court, he missed her and signed himself 'farewell my own sweet Bess'. He tried to get leave from his Queen to visit Bess but often failed; and when he was with Bess the Queen complained and called him back again. He was serving two mistresses at the cost of his love for Bess. It has been said with truth that in affairs of the heart there is one who loves and the other who lets themself be loved, a giver and a receiver. With Sir William and Bess, undoubtedly he was the giver; but Bess as the receiver must not be thought any the less sincere in her affection.

Inevitably, Sir William St Loe's attendance at Court meant long absences from Bess, but his frequent visits to London with the

Court gave him the chance to deal with urgent matters which otherwise would have required Bess to make the long trek herself. The
Cavendish boys were growing up and Sir William was deputed to
visit Eton College to arrange their schooling.[5] On one of his rare visits
to Chatsworth in August 1560, he returned to Court after his leave
was up, by way of London. Four days were spent buying spices,
medicines and other items to send back by carrier to Chatsworth
– items unobtainable in Derbyshire. He also bought books for the
Cavendish boys, three French grammars and two copies of *Cosmo-
grafie de Levant*. Sir William joined the Court at Winchester but
was no sooner there than the Queen moved back to Windsor. On
4 September Sir William wrote to Bess, directing the cover 'To my
owne dear wyff Chatsworth delyver thys'. He addressed Bess 'My
owne, more dearer than I am to myself'. The Queen, he explained,
had admired his horse on the road to Windsor and he had given it to
her; he sent messages of affection from Bess's Court friends and
in reference to the building of Chatsworth called her his chief over-
seer of his works. Adding a postscript to his letter, he commended
himself to Bess's mother, her sister Jane and her brother James
Hardwick, 'not forgetting Francke wyth the rest of my chyldren and
thyne'. This referred to Bess's daughter Frances and her other children: he did not mean his own children for he had none. The 'thyne'
was a commendation to Bess herself. With the Court at Windsor,
Sir William was able to visit Eton College where he paid a term's
tuition fees, 19s (95p), for Henry and William Cavendish then aged
ten and nine respectively. The almoner of the college told him 'no
gentleman's children in England shall be better welcome nor better
looked unto'.

During this period at Windsor, the news of the death of Amy
Robsart, the wife of the Earl of Leicester, was published on 11 September. Her mysterious fall downstairs at Cumnor Place has never
been solved. Was she pushed? Certainly her death was convenient
if Leicester were to marry the Queen as was commonly believed.
On that same day Sir William St Loe was having a basket made
up of artichokes, cucumbers, Spanish silks (for embroidery), red
frisado and a pound of wire for stringing a virginal, to go to Bess
at Chatsworth along with a firkin of olives and a barrel of sturgeon.
But it all went up to Derbyshire by Sir William's manservant,

Greves, and was not taken by himself, as he had hoped in a letter. It was two weeks later that Sir William finally got leave from Court. On 10 October he bought paper 'to wryte home' and his letter was dated the 12th. It was brief and told Bess that he was returning to Chatsworth with his brother Clement and 'towe or thre good felloes'. But the party which eventually arrived at Chatsworth on 21 October was more than two or three: it totalled ten in all, with thirteen horses.

On the same day that Sir William and his brother arrived at Chatsworth, Bess's sons Henry and William Cavendish, entered Eton College; they must have passed on the road. The two boys arrived in the care of a manservant, who in addition to looking after his charges kept an account of expenditure, heading his accounts with an appropriate thought: 'He that ordainyth a wand for a other man often tymes doth chanse unto the same himself' – Bess would have approved. Within the next twelve months purchases were unremarkable, a few books, ten pairs of shoes, and clothes, and they paid 3d 'to see bayre bayting and a camell in the colledge as other schollers dyd'. Late in November 'serten chambre stuff' arrived by barge, sent by one of Sir William's servants the day before from Westminster Bridge. Now that their hangings and furniture had arrived they could move into college from their lodgings outside. The total cost for the two boys for the year came to £25.

Sir William's visit to Chatsworth was a short one. By 3 November he was once more on his way with his brother Clement, this time to visit their mother Lady Margaret St Loe, in Somerset, taking with them as gifts for the old lady jewellery and cloth to make a pair of sleeves. It was more than just a visit of two dutiful sons to their mother; there was serious trouble with their brother Edward St Loe, who resented Sir William's marriage to Bess.

What happened between Sir William and his brother Edward when he went down to Somerset that November can only be guessed, but the trouble certainly went back to when their father Sir John had died in 1559.[6] The lands in Somerset and Gloucestershire were left to his heir Sir William. As Sir William was not married at the time and had no children there was no entailment; he could dispose of these lands as he wished. In the normal course of events it would have been usual for the estate to have gone to Edward on

Sir William's death, since Edward was the next heir. But there was an impediment. Edward was jealous of his brother and had tried to make trouble between Sir William and their father. It is a certain guess that Sir William's visit to Somerset was to break the news to Edward that it was his intention to leave all his lands to Bess; and this would have provoked a row of combustible proportions. It was considerate of Clement to have gone along with Sir William; his support would have been needed.

Edward St Loe was a thoroughly bad lot. Even his mother Lady Margaret had no good to say of him. Edward had married a Mrs Scutt who was 'by nature a verye lustye yonge woman'. She had been married to old Mr Scutt, who was ninety, when he suddenly died and it was suspected that Edward had poisoned him. Almost immediately and with indecent haste he married the widow Scutt who was pregnant. But within two months she too was dead.

One more example of Edward's perfidy should suffice. Whilst Edward was briefly married to Widow Scutt, old Sir John, his father, found a suitable bride for Sir William. This of course did not suit Edward who could see that once his brother was married he would have children and the estate would pass out of his reach. So Edward persuaded Sir William that the bride his father had chosen was not suitable by making disparaging remarks and then, having killed off his own wife, Edward married her himself!

Early in 1561 Edward and his mother went to London to visit Sir William and Bess. The occasion was not a success. There was no animosity on Bess's side towards her brother-in-law and she went out of her way to please him. Nevertheless Edward reverted to his old habits and Bess and Sir William were given poison during this visit. Old Lady St Loe, writing to Bess later that year, said, 'I was suer yow wher powsonyd when I was at London and yff yow had not had a present remedy ye had dyed'. Neither Bess's mother-in-law nor her husband were under any illusions as to who could be behind this attempt.

It is likely that this drama took place at John Mann's house in Red Cross Street, where Sir William often stayed in London, and Mann, who felt some responsibility towards his guests, brought an accusation against Hugh Draper who kept a tavern in Bristol and was a near neighbour of Edward St Loe. On 21 March 1561 Draper was charged with having a 'conjurer or sorcerer practise matter against Sir William Saint Loe and my Ladie'. Draper denied the charge saying that he had given up astrology and burnt all his books a long time before; all the same he was found guilty and committed to the Tower. Mann also accused Francis Cox who was likewise found guilty and sent to the Tower. Sir William St Loe gave information which resulted in Ralph Davis ending up in the Tower as well. With this trio safely put away, it was an odd justice which allowed the author of the attempted murder, Edward St Loe, to remain free. But Sir William never accused his brother and so he was never charged. Cox was committed to the Tower on 25 March 1561 and was released thirty-eight weeks later on 19 December. Davis had forty-six weeks inside from 1 April to 11 February 1562, when he was brought before the King's bench and released on sureties. What became of Draper is not known. He was probably eventually released like the others, but on the wall of the Salt Tower is scratched into the stone a drawing of a sphere for casting horoscopes along the top of which is written 'Hew Draper of Bristowe made thys spheer the 30 daye of Maye anno 1561'.

In view of the uncertainty of life, it was a sound policy for Sir William to make an indenture whereby he and Bess held his lands jointly. This removed any incentive for Edward to kill off his brother since Bess would keep the land. Also Sir William knew the extent of Bess's debts and the security his estates gave her.

Bess has often been accused of influencing Sir William to make over his lands to her and so making herself wealthy at the expense of his family. Sir William answered this himself, by saying that before the sensation of the poisoning Bess bore his brother very good will both before and after their marriage:

She prswaded the same Sr Willm Stlowe to entaile the Remaynder of all his Lande for faulte of issue of theyre Bodyes to the sayd Edwarde Stlowe & ever refused the joynt feesimple thereof wt the said Sr Willm untill prceyving his Brothere to moche unaturalnes & unseamely speaches of hym and his wyfe did of verye good will towarde her convey the same unto her.[7]

That comment by Sir William exonerates Bess of any suggestion of influence; quite the contrary. If Edward had not been a fool as well as a villain, he would have kept his interest in the St Loe lands with Bess's blessings.

It is tempting to see Bess's influence in the purchase of a wardship by Sir William on 28 March 1560. 'Grant to William Seyntlowe, knight, of the wardship and marriage of Anthony Scute, son and heir of John Scute and Bridget Seyntlowe, late his wife; with an annuity of £9 10s [£9.50], from 4 Dec 4 & 5 Ph & Mary,'[8] (1557 – the year Bridget died). Anthony Scute was the son of old Mr Scutt, and Bridget was 'the verye lustye yonge woman' Edward St Loe married and shortly poisoned. But this was two years before Bess and Sir William were married, although in the small Court circle they must have already met.

The unfortunate dramas with Edward St Loe were hardly over when, in the late summer of 1561, Bess unwittingly got into serious trouble. It was not of her making and one of the few times in her life when it can be said with certainty that she was innocent of any intriguing. There may, of course, have been evidence suggesting her involvement but if there was then that evidence has been lost; and it would have been completely out of character for Bess to be involved in serious matters of State outside her family interest.

Catherine Grey, born to misfortune and tragedy, was pregnant. It was a sad story of young and romantic love.[9] Some two and a half years earlier, in the time of Queen Mary, Catherine had fallen in love with Edward Seymour, Earl of Hertford. She met Edward for the first time when she was lady-in-waiting in the household of his mother, the Duchess of Somerset. Edward recalled that it was when his sister, Jane Seymour, was brought home ill from Court on a horse litter. Although Catherine was wasting her time on this indifferent little man, that was not the way she saw the situation and her love, apparently, was returned. The affair had progressed and Edward had asked her to marry him; when the Court was at Westminster, he proposed to her in a closet or small private room which his sister Jane had off the 'maidens' chamber of honour'. Jane was there at the time and a witness. They kissed, embraced and held hands; romance had come into the life of the unhappy Catherine.

The marriage had been discussed with Catherine's mother, the Duchess of Suffolk, who had not disapproved. However, by an Act of 1535, all those of royal blood required the monarch's permission to marry and Catherine of course was a great-grandchild of Henry VII. Her mother, Frances, after the beheading of her previous husband, had caused some comment by marrying her master of horse, Adrian Stokes, who remembered that a letter to the Queen had been drafted but unfortunately Frances had died before it could be sent. This was only one of a long chain of misfortunes which dogged the life of the unlucky Catherine. Then Queen Mary became seriously ill and eventually died. It hardly seemed the time for Catherine to bother anyone with the question of her marriage, particularly if the answer was likely to be a definite no. But Edward Seymour was in no hurry; in fact he had not troubled to tell his own mother. Poor Catherine had a fit of jealousy when she believed Edward was courting another. To settle her suspicions he told her that he would marry her 'owt of hand' when a convenient moment could be found. In throwing her jealous fit, this may have been the end Catherine had in mind.

In November 1560, within a few days of this final proposal, the Queen left Westminster for Greenwich, but Catherine, who had a swollen face, stayed behind with Jane Seymour and several others of the ladies-in-waiting. The swelling was not bad enough, however, to keep her away from Edward Seymour. They met and it was arranged that Catherine, with Jane, should go the following day to Edward's home, Hertford House in Cannon Row down by the river. He would have a priest there and they would be married with his sister as witness. Accordingly the next morning the two girls left Westminster Palace by the water stairs. It was low tide and they walked along the sand by the river's edge to the watergate at Hertford House, arriving about 11.00 am.

They went straight up to Edward's bedchamber but there was no priest. Jane slipped out, returning fifteen minutes later with a priest, who was presumably in the area by chance. The marriage was conveniently performed in the bedchamber and Edward gave Catherine a gold ring of four links with a verse engraved on it. Sadly, she later admitted that she did not know if he had got it specially for her. The ceremony over, Jane gave the priest £10; Edward gave him nothing. Shortly Jane left the room and the young couple undressed and went to bed. After about an hour-and-a-half they had

had enough of each other, dressed again and left the bedchamber. Edward saw Catherine off by boat at the watergate with a kiss. She and Jane were rowed back to Westminster Palace in time for the mid-day dinner at the comptroller's table where – not surprisingly – Catherine ate nothing.

The marriage was mentioned to no one. Secretly the newly-weds met several more times at the Cannon Row house and had a few hours together. This was the extent of Catherine's romantic loving. It was all the consequence of her royal blood: Queen Mary had said that the Grey sisters should remain spinsters, but had gone back on this; Elizabeth saw no reason to alter the original policy. Edward Seymour soon found that he had business in France, to look for 'a kinsman of his that was fledd ... with certaine money'. It seems an unlikely story and this was almost certainly a diplomatic absence.

Catherine cannot be accused of not knowing what she was doing. She had been warned by many, including Sir William Cecil, the Secretary of State, not to let Edward Seymour run away with her affections. Perhaps at twenty-one she had given up all hope of ever being allowed to marry with the Queen's blessing. This marriage to a man she loved, the unsatisfactory Edward Seymour, who had been called 'our little man and a great bladder', was all she could hope for. If Catherine imagined that she could ride out the storm of inevitable discovery she underestimated Elizabeth and the situation. Elizabeth, who never tolerated a rival, particularly a woman, would not have considered the marriage as at all suitable. Not only was Catherine openly canvassed as her successor, but Edward was the son of the late Protector Somerset. Politically it was totally unacceptable.

Almost inevitably Catherine became pregnant. It is easy to imagine her anxiety. She kept the matter a secret from all, except that she wrote to tell Edward, who showed no hurry to return from France. But pregnancies, however unwelcome, cannot be forgotten. About six weeks before the baby was due Catherine, unable to keep her torment to herself, unloaded her anguish into the unwilling ears of Bess, her mother's old friend. Bess 'fell into great weeping and saying that shee was very sorrie that shee had so done without the consent and knowledge of the Queen'. That, seemingly, was the extent of her involvement and her contribution to Catherine's marriage. Bess offered no advice or consolation and was no help at all to the agitated Catherine.

Receiving no comfort from Bess, Catherine then went to Lord Robert Dudley. Creeping into his room late one evening, the unhappy girl poured out her whole anguished story. But this time the effect was electric. Dudley went straight to the Queen who received the news of this unwelcome conception with predictable fury. Catherine was immediately put under arrest and bundled into the Tower and it was there, six weeks later on 24 September, that her baby, Edward Seymour, was born. Her husband, the dilatory Edward was sent for out of France; he was arrested at Dover whilst having his breakfast and also taken to the Tower. Cecil, obviously suspecting some deep plot in all this innocence, sent instructions to Sir Edward Warner, the Lieutenant of the Tower, to question Catherine very closely and added,

Ye shall send to Alderman lodge for sentloe and shall put hir in aw of dyvers matters confessed by ye lady Catheryne and so also deal with hir that she confess to yow all hir knoledg in the same matters, it is certayne that there hath bene great practises and purposes and sence ye death of ye lady Jane, she hath bene most privy and as ye shall see occasion so ye may kepe sentlow II or III nights more or less.[10]

Bess was arrested on 20 August, ten days after Catherine, and she too went to the Tower. But for more that two or three nights.

There was no trial. Catherine and Edward were subjected to interrogatories, or questions, by a number of eminent statesmen and churchmen, including the Bishop of London. These questions, with the answers, were sent to the Privy Council for their judgement. The evidence of the two does not agree. For a matter so vital, Catherine was surprisingly vague and Edward even more so. He said that there had been a written assurance of £1000 per year for Catherine; she could recall none. They were both agreed that the priest was of medium height and wore an Abraham beard; they were also agreed that neither would recognise him again. Understandably the priest never came forward and as Jane Seymour was by then dead, the two principal witnesses to the marriage were lacking. It is not surprising that the council, interpreting the Queen's wishes, found the marriage not legal. To make matters worse Catherine, with the connivance of the Lieutenant of the Tower, Sir Edward Warner, continued to see Edward. She was so far successful that she had another baby by him, still in the Tower. Edward, in due course, was found guilty of seducing a virgin of the royal blood and fined the huge sum of £15,000 which was later commuted to £10,000 of which finally he paid only £4000.[11] Both were kept in the Tower until an attack of plague struck London and he was moved to his mother's house, whilst Catherine, whose spirits, hopes and health were crushed, was sent first as a house prisoner to her uncle Lord John Grey, and when he died to Sir Owen Hopton, until she in turn died in January 1568.

Just why Bess should have been sent to the Tower at all is perplexing. The evidence of her interrogation, which might have revealed more of Bess's involvement, is missing, and we are left guessing. Bess was detained for thirty-one weeks which was more an inconvenience and anxiety than anything else. She was comfortably accommodated; she had a servant and was allowed £1 6s 8d (£1.34) per week for food, when ordinary prisoners had to manage on 10s (50p); the total bill for food, fuel and candles came to £56 16s 8d (£56.83), which was far from hard living. But it must have been galling to Bess to have to share the Tower with the three who so lately had tried to poison her. The punishment may have been meant as a sharp reminder that her loyalty was with the Queen, for the priest was said to have been Catholic; and in the recent reign of Mary, Bess had diplomatically become Catholic. Certainly some were concerned about the Queen's serious flirtation with Robert Dudley and feared their eventual marriage might cause a rebellion.

Before these unfortunate events overtook Bess, she had been arranging the marriage of her eldest daughter Frances, then aged thirteen years. She had been to see Sir George Pierrepont at Holme Pierrepont, a few miles south-east of Nottingham. With Sir George, she discussed the possibility of a marriage between Frances and his son and heir Henry, then aged fifteen and a half. The Pierreponts had lived at Holme Pierrepont for many generations and they were impressively wealthy. When Sir George died in 1564 his personal chattels including silver were valued for probate at £400, and his funeral cost £127.[12] From Bess's point of view this was a very suitable alliance.

In the bargaining which went on during this visit, it is likely that Bess had the upper hand, for Sir George was far from well and in a great deal of pain from what was possibly rheumatism. The silent pressure of the menace of the Master of Wards would have been working on Sir George's mind. Skilfully Bess used her influence to help Sir George over some trouble he was having with a Mr Whalley, whose family came from Rufford in North Nottinghamshire. No doubt Bess used her bargaining power to the limit. Her daughter was of the right age and it was simply a question of arranging the amount of Frances's dower. In the circumstances it is likely that she got away with the lowest possible figure against the usual one third of the Pierrepont estate, which would be settled on Frances for life.

The agreement was made; Sir George wrote to Bess at London in November 1561 confirming all they had discussed, it only remaining, he said, to see if 'the gentillwoman your doughtr lyke or boye uppon syght as well as I and my wife lyke the yong gentillwoman'. He also added that he would 'not shrinck one worde from yt I said or promised'.[13] Frances went as a gentlewoman attendant to Lady Pierrepont, to see if she 'lyked'.

Bess was released from the Tower on 25 March 1562 and shortly afterwards Henry Pierrepont visited the St Loes in London. Obviously all went well and Frances 'lyked', for on 18 May Sir George wrote thanking Bess for entertaining Henry in London and urging that the marriage contract be drawn up. He was still in considerable pain and discomfort and refused an invitation to Chatsworth on that account. He was in a hurry to get the marriage fixed and the two children were married some time during 1562.

In the autumn of 1561, during Bess's time in the Tower, she used the services of the Lieutenant of the Tower, Sir Edward Warner, as one of the parties to an indenture covering the dowry of Ann Cavendish, her only remaining step-daughter still unmarried.[14] Sir William St Loe agreed to give Ann 1000 marks, which was £666, if she married within one year a husband selected by Bess and one other trustee. If no husband was offered within this time, then she could keep the 1000 marks, but if she refused a selected husband then she would only get 600 marks. With this pressure it would be hard for Ann to resist. Considering that Sir William was in no way related to or connected with Ann, it seems a generous gesture; it also indicates the sort of price that was put on a girl to buy a husband. At twenty-one Ann was comparatively long in the tooth and because Bess had been unable to put up the money before, she had remained undowered and unmarried. Now with her price tag of 1000 marks, the marriage market worked for Ann: within the year she married Sir Henry Bainton.

Sir William St Loe's money was used by Bess not only for marrying off her step-daughter but for more building at Chatsworth. The work had been suspended over the crisis period of her second husband's illness and death, and for two and a half years afterwards Chatsworth and its building remained in suspension. Parts of the old house were still standing and parts of the new were unfloored and unroofed, with Bess and her family living in what was inhabitable of the old and what could be used of the new. By this time Bess's mother, Elizabeth Leche, had been widowed and was also living at Chatsworth. James Hardwick had taken over the Hardwick estate in 1546 and the Leches moved out sometime during the late forties or early fifties.

The wages at Chatsworth for the autumn of 1559 cover payments for hewing wood, threshing, winnowing and other agrarian activities.[15] Nothing is shown as being spent on rebuilding although a roof of the old house is repaired. Typically, Bess is enclosing land: the twenty-four-acre Lark Meadow at Ashford is taken in, ditched, hedged and improved. The year ends and the new begins with ploughing; the mill at Chatsworth is repaired. It is a picture of the passing of timeless rural seasons, of sun and rain, frost and snow. Bess was keeping her estates ticking over and improving them as opportunity presented.

This eternal rural scene changes cautiously on 13 April 1560. The weekly wage bill until this date had been an average 10s (50p). Significantly there is a payment that week to one man for four days' getting limestone. Two days later coal is got from the shallow pits near Chatsworth. These two items of payment, perhaps on their own meaningless, together show that Bess was restarting her building. The limestone was for making plaster, the coal for firing the lime kiln and this is confirmed the same week that the coal was dug. A page proudly headed 'payde to workemens that hathe wrought on the worke aboute the newe byledng' shows plasterers and glaziers at work with a slater mending the old house. Immediately the weekly average payments jump to over 30s (£1.50). Bess is building again. Payments to joiners, sawyers, plasterers and glaziers consume the bulk of the expenditure, whilst three masons only are employed occasionally, showing that the work was not that of erecting new walls but of roofing, plastering, flooring and completing the work which had stopped two and a half years before. Doors are made, windows glazed, the carpenter is kept almost continually busy cutting great timbers for floors and roof.

On 25 April that year Bess wrote to Sir John Thynne, who was then trying to complete his first rebuilding of Longleat. She comes straight to the point and asks outright for the speedy loan of the plasterer who had flowered his hall. She signs herself Elizabeth Cavendish, then crosses it through and puts Seyntlo. It is doubtful if she got Thynne's plasterer, who had more than enough work at Longleat. This sudden high expenditure on building at Chatsworth was the direct result of her marriage to St Loe, when she was able to use the money which he had inherited on his father's death only twelve months before.

Through the early half of the 1560s the building continued, and became more than just the completion of what had been started earlier, new but unspecified work being undertaken. Bess was constructing a house of magnificence, suitable to the dynasty she was founding. In Bess's absences from Chatsworth, James Cromp, Bess's servant from the time she had married Sir William Cavendish, was left in charge. She sent frequent instructions to Cromp on how the work was to be done and where the masons were to be found. When Cromp was away on other business, Francis Whitfield, another old Cavendish servant, was directed: the porch was to be finished before the battlements were started, the crest was to be of the same stone as the porch. All this in letters interrupted by messages to the children and to her Aunt Marcella Linaker who was living at Chatsworth and who was instructed to make a little garden beside the new house ('I care not whether she bestow grate cost thereof') and was sent bundles of garden seed. In December

1560 a grill and a knocker for 'the great gate at Chattesworth' costing 12s (60p) was sent up from London.

By the end of October 1564, the phase of the building was over. William St Loe, a relative of Bess's husband, writing from London where he had been doing some business for her, wrote that he was glad that she was in good health and that the sight of *her newly finished building* would continue it, and then added that Sir William St Loe must stay there. Sir William, who seldom got to Chatsworth, might have wondered at so much expenditure on a house he hardly used.

By their attendance at Court both Sir William and Bess would have been in a position to press the Queen for the abatement or cancellation of the £5000 owing to the Crown. They were unsuccessful in their efforts until the summer of 1563. In August that year Sir William St Loe paid a fine of £1000 on behalf of Bess and her son, Henry Cavendish, the heir, and all three were made to ask the Queen's pardon.[16] Bess's session in the Tower for the very small offence of listening to Catherine Grey may have been part of the bargain made between Bess and Queen Elizabeth and Bess may have suffered her months of imprisonment in return for being let off the full repayment of the £5000. This seems the most likely explanation. It was hard on Sir William for he paid out £1000 and gained nothing while Bess kept her lands. Elizabeth was certain henceforth of Bess's absolute loyalty, and the future would show that Elizabeth got the best of the bargain.

Seemingly, St Loe had no regrets about the expenditure he was called upon to pay out on Bess's behalf. What few letters survive show only his patient adoration and longing to see her. It is impossible to do more than conjecture on Bess's feelings, for none of her letters to Sir William have survived, but no doubt she accepted his support and admiration willingly and then got on with her rebuilding at Chatsworth, using his money to pay for her schemes and settle her debts. There must have been more to their affection than this cynical surmise and her portrait at Hardwick belies it; Bess undoubtedly made Sir William a happy man. Sadly, their life together was short, for with the problem of Bess's debt to the Crown safely settled, fate seemingly had finished with St Loe and he died. The exact date of his death is a matter of guesswork. He was definitely alive on 22 October 1564 for he was mentioned in a letter to Bess of that date. By 25 March the following year Bess asked in a letter for more time to consider the settlement of her lands and Sir William was dead by then. The likely time of his death is early 1565. He was buried in the church of Great St Helen in Bishopsgate beside his father, Sir John St Loe,[17] and Bess was left a widow for the third time.

MY LADY SHREWSBURY
1565-1570

Bess was in her late thirties when she was widowed for the third time. Her children were growing up; the eldest Frances was then married and Mary the youngest was ten. For the past six years, since she had married St Loe, Bess had been more or less continuously at Chatsworth, but remaining at Chatsworth as a widow was a different matter. After St Loe died Bess returned to Court for the serious matter of selecting a fourth husband. Bess knew her market value as a bride and the Court gave her access to the highest bidders.

She probably returned as one of the Ladies of the Privy Chamber. She was a close friend of Lady Stafford and Blanche Parry, both in attendance on the Queen, and their friendship may have come from sharing a similar appointment. Blanche was senior lady-in-waiting, widow of Sir Thomas, and introduced her Cousin John Dee to the Queen, starting him on his career as Court mathematician and royal seer. By the end of 1567, Elizabeth had only four women of the Privy Chamber: Blanche Parry, Lady Stafford, Elizabeth Knollys and Dorothy Bradbelt; by then Bess had remarried and left the Privy Chamber.

Bess was not the only woman at Court looking for a suitor. At this time the Queen was debating the merits of marrying the Archduke Charles of Austria, the son of Emperor Ferdinand of Germany, a marriage of political convenience which would have made an Anglo-Spanish alliance and a balance against French ambitions of conquest, or of marrying her favourite the Earl of Leicester for love. That she married neither does not matter; it was part of Elizabeth's diplomacy which she played with skill almost single-handed through her long reign. In simple terms the overriding problem was one of religion. England was a small Protestant island off the coast of a mainly Catholic Europe devoted to bringing the 'true faith' to England. Elizabeth in her wisdom knew instinctively how far her people would go in their toleration of Catholics, but this was a knowledge denied to her antagonists, Pope Pius V and Philip of Spain, who were dedicated to converting England by any means, marriage, or war and invasion. Both believed that the English people would leap at any chance to overthrow their heretic Queen and her tyrannies. From the start Elizabeth had been tolerant towards Catholics and permitted them to practise their beliefs. However in 1570 Pius, acting on divine instructions, was so misguided as to excommunicate Elizabeth. This had the effect of uniting Protestants to her support and branding Catholics as agents of treason. Pius, who was not blessed with the material benefit of an army, encouraged Philip who had both an army and a navy, to invade England. These were the external consequences dictating Elizabeth's home and foreign policies which were inextricably bound up in her courtships. The Queen tended to leave the detail of her diplomacy to William Cecil, her principal secretary, and let Leicester act as her social secretary.

This was the background to Bess's Court life. Her main financial worries had been left behind but she was not completely free of cares. A letter from the faithful James Cromp[1] at Chatsworth, dated only 20 November but most likely 1566, explained that her two sons Harry and William would join her in London as soon as he could send them off. The delay was caused by the old complaint of footwear; William 'hath no boots that will keep out water'. Cromp then quoted William as saying 'all this learning he now hath shall do him small pleasure'. The learning came from their late tutor, Henry Jackson; there had been trouble and Jackson had gone. The ex-tutor had been spreading slander against Bess; the matter was serious enough and Bess important enough for the Queen to intervene personally. In a letter to the Ecclesiastical Commission, dated 29 September and no year given, the Queen instructed that Jackson be punished severely, 'by corporal or otherwise, openly or privately, for spreading slander against Lady St Loe, who has long served with credit in our Court'. Tantalisingly no one mentioned what the slander was.

After the failure of Henry Jackson, William Cavendish entered
Clare Hall, Cambridge, at Michaelmas 1567. He was fifteen, below
the average age for undergraduates. Cambridge then, as now, was
insufferably cold in winter; the bitter blasts of Arctic wind blew
from the fens piercing every chink of clothing. But winter was the
healthy time of year; summer saw the almost certain return of the
plague, when students and pedagogues stopped exams and lectures,
leaving the town for the healthier countryside. William probably
stayed at Cambridge until 1571; the bachelor and master's degree
took four years and the curriculum had barely changed since the
Middle Ages – geometry, astronomy (such as it was), theology,
arithmetic, mathematics, medicine according to Hippocrates or
Galen, dialectic, rhetoric, Greek and Hebrew, but above all else the
study of Plato and Aristotle. As an education it was pretty useless
in preparing William for earning a living, but that was not the point
of Cambridge; it turned out useful lawyers and useless gentlemen.
Bess in her wisdom knew that William would need a grounding in
law and from Cambridge he was admitted to Gray's Inn in 1572.

With her sons away at school and university, her daughters would
have remained at Chatsworth. And whilst Bess was in London or
at Court her family was looked after by her mother and her aunt
Marcella Linaker; the running of the estate was left in the hands
of her half-sister Jane Kniveton, this arrangement leaving Bess free
to attend to the serious matter of making a worthwhile and profitable
marriage. Whatever estimate is made of Bess's wealth after the death
of St Loe – and this of course was the key to her remarriage – there
was no denying that she gave the impression of considerable
affluence. Chatsworth for the moment was completed and it was
furnished in a sumptuous manner. Forty-two tapestries covered the
walls of the ten principal chambers; Bess's own bedchamber still
had the old bed which she had shared with Sir William Cavendish.
The bedstead of gilt with their arms carved on it, had '5 curtains
of mokado red' and 'one quilt of red sarsenet'. The furniture in the
room included 'one great chair green checked silk'; on four tables
were pictures of her two late husbands, Cavendish and St Loe,
another of herself and 'an other of my Lady Jane', presumably Jane
Grey, who had been beheaded by Queen Mary (now that Elizabeth
was on the throne all this was in the past and the portrait could

be displayed). Like the earlier decorations and furnishings, all was a splendid disharmony of rich colour and richer luxury, but it was first and foremost a mansion for the Cavendish dynasty.[2]

Bess's ambitions were founded on her Cavendish family; she was the archetypal ambitious mother; with the exception of her sincere loyalty to the Queen, nothing was too great a sacrifice for her to make, or to force others to make. St Loe had realised this and had willingly placed his love in second position to Bess's priorities. After St Loe died Bess might have stayed on, living in obscurity and widowhood, at Chatsworth; this she chose not to do, either because her debts were so serious that she had to find a wealthy husband or because her dynastic ambitions drove her beyond being satisfied with what she had already won. In fact there was no single reason behind Bess's decision to attend Court and choose a fourth husband; her debts and her ambitions and her feminine instinct may have told her that if she did not take this chance in her late thirties, by her forties she would regret it, and all combined to bring the widow, Lady St Loe, to Court and a-courting.

Financially, Bess was better off than at any time in her life. She now had her late husband's Western Lands, as they came to be called; she had the Cavendish estates in Derbyshire and the debt to the Crown had been paid off. She still had her other debts, though these were not generally known, but her gross income would have been about £1600 per year in 1566. Bess gave the appearance of being a wealthy widow of considerable ability and great charm. Therefore in the way of things she could expect to marry into greater wealth.

Through the whole of 1565–6 Bess dallied at Court. The gossips had their day but not their way; a letter possibly addressed to Sir William Cecil, the Queen's Principal Secretary, in January 1566 told him 'either Lord Darcy or Sir John Thynne shall marry Lady St Loe and not Harry Cobham'. (Sir John Thynne was her old friend at Longleat and Harry Cobham alias Sir Henry Brooke was a family connection whose brother had married Bess's step-daughter Catherine Cavendish.) But Bess was not to marry any of these. All three would have been perfectly suitable for Bess as far as wealth went, but obviously she was not going to throw herself away on the first comers. In fact it is unlikely that she knew then who she was to marry, for her fourth husband was not a widower until the end of 1566.

Of all the courtiers surrounding the Queen, one of the wealthiest, the most powerful and most loyal was George Talbot, Sixth Earl of Shrewsbury. Elizabeth, with her girlish fondness for nicknames, called him her 'old man'; in fact he was only four years older than the Queen and the same age as Bess; his tall figure, 5 feet 11 inches by his funeral effigy, his rather slow manner and sombre expression may have been the cause of the nickname. His appearance, from the few likenesses left to us, was lugubrious; his long face made longer by a pointed beard, receding hair and large melancholy eyes, gives little clue to his character which was uncomplicated. His greatest asset was an immense loyalty to his Queen and having said as much there would be little more to add except that he was not overblessed with intellect. However, George Talbot was said to be immensely rich and was regarded as one of the richest noblemen in England at that time. He had been married to Gertrude Manners, sister to the Earl of Rutland, who had died in late 1566, leaving him with four sons and three daughters. He was possessed of vast areas of land in Yorkshire, Derbyshire, Nottinghamshire, Shropshire and Staffordshire. He enjoyed eight principal houses: Sheffield Manor, Sheffield Castle, South Wingfield Manor, Rufford Abbey, Welbeck Abbey, Worksop Manor, Buxton Hall and Tutbury Castle leased from the Crown. In addition he had two houses in London and another outside the city in the village of Chelsea on the riverside, as well as other minor manors such as Shifnal in Shropshire. He was Lord Lieutenant of Yorkshire, of Derbyshire and of Nottinghamshire, he was Chief Justice in Eyre north of the Trent and Constable of Radnor and Wigmore Castles, Chamberlain of the Receipt of the Exchequer and a KG. George Talbot was a Prince whose princedom was north of the Trent.

Some time during the autumn of 1567, Bess and the Earl of Shrewsbury were married. Their marriage must not be looked on as anything other than an amalgamation of assets from which both sides would benefit. In Bess's case the marriage made a lot of sense, for her Derbyshire lands touched his in many places. And for the Earl it can be said that he could expect on marriage that Bess's income would become his and likewise any unsettled lands in her possession. In the way of the market for prosperous widows in 1567, it is doubtful if the Earl could have done better and Bess certainly could not have found anyone more suitable.

It is surprising that this wedding, which would have provoked considerable comment and amazement, should have passed by unnoted; but if it was mentioned in contemporary correspondence then the gossip has been lost. As far as the Court was concerned all eyes would have been on Bess when they were not on the Queen and Leicester; her future was the curious concern of many and yet no word of this ceremony has survived. Its date and place are uncertain. It is likely that it took place at All Hallows, Sheffield, away from the Court, but the date can only be conjectured from two pieces of evidence.

Two lists of Bess's jewellery, dated 27 August 1567, show twenty-seven pieces of astonishingly rich *bijouterie*: 'one book of gold with 10 rubies, 3 sasers & one diamond with 2 pictures in the same' is the book which Sir William Cavendish had bought for her in 1552 with their two portraits inside; 'one agate given to me by my Lady Marquess' was from Frances Grey, dead for eighteen years but not forgotten; a ring with a seal in it and 'one wedding ring'. At the bottom of the second list are five items in Bess's distinctive writing headed 'given to me by my Lord' – George Talbot, Sixth Earl of Shrewsbury. This seems to indicate they were married by 27 August 1567 but too much reliance should not be placed on the two lists of jewellery. Bess had a habit of adding items after lists were completed – it saved the trouble of making another. Nevertheless they could have been married slightly before 27 August 1567, the date of the two lists, and they were certainly married before 7 January the next year. There is a second piece of tenuous evidence in a letter addressed to Bess as Countess of Shrewsbury from her half-sister, Elizabeth Wingfield, which carries only the date 21 October and no year. Mistress Wingfield quotes the Queen as saying to her husband, Anthony, 'I have been glad to see my Lady Saintlo, but now more desirous to see my Lady Shrewsbury,' and then talking for an hour about Bess and the Earl. The year could be 1567 or 1568, but if the latter then Bess had been married for at least nine months and it would hardly have been novelty enough worth discussing for an hour. The probability is that Bess was married not many weeks before the letter was written and the year was 1567. It is certainly safe to say that Bess and the Earl were married in the autumn of 1567 and probably best to leave it at that.[3]

Unfortunately their marriage settlement, which would have revealed so much, particularly about the bargaining which went into the arrangement, has vanished. Perhaps, after the later disputes, it was left in some attorney's office, or handled so much that it fell to pieces. Certainly Bess got the usual third of the Earl's unsettled estate at his death. But like most Elizabethan marriages based on the amalgamation of properties – and this one was no exception the lands settled on the wife were held for her lifetime only. If there were children then the lands would be passed on in succession. By this time Bess was forty years old and past child bearing, and a straightforward partnership in marriage was rather less than her ambition would have been content with. If Bess herself could have no more children, then she had sons and daughters who could. Part of the bargain was that two of Bess's children should marry two of the Earl's. So the advantage of marrying into the Earl's lands would not end at Bess's death.

The indenture for this marriage of their children has survived[4] and a more revealing document on the Elizabethan attitude to marriage is hard to imagine. It is a straightforward, cold assignment of lands and assets. The date is 7 January 1568: Bess and the Earl were already married. Two trustees were named, Anthony Wingfield, who had married Bess's half-sister Elizabeth Leche; and John Byron of Newstead. Gilbert Talbot, the Earl's second son, then aged fourteen and later Seventh Earl of Shrewsbury, was to marry before Easter Bess's second daughter Mary, who was twelve years old. If Mary died before the marriage or 'before carnal knowledge betwixt them', then Gilbert was to marry Bess's next youngest daughter Elizabeth. So the eventuality of an untimely death spoiling the arrangement was avoided. But it went further than that, for if Mary was bereft of Gilbert by some disaster, then she was to marry one other of the Earl's sons – Edward, or if he failed then Henry Talbot. Such was the determination to bring about a union that every permutation was covered. The indenture just manages to say that the marriage was only if 'Mary agrees', although it would have been difficult for a dutiful twelve-year-old to have disagreed in the circumstances. As if the one marriage was not sufficient seal on the bargain of land, a further marriage was proposed between Bess's eldest son Henry Cavendish, then eighteen, and the Earl's youngest daughter Grace, who could not have been older than eight at that time. Again all mischance was covered by offering alternative brothers and sisters in descending and ascending order of ages.

In the event all the partners originally chosen lived and did as they were told. Gilbert Talbot married Mary Cavendish and Henry Cavendish married Grace Talbot. The double wedding with the two child brides took place one month and four days after the date of the indenture at Sheffield in the Church of Saints Peter and Paul on 9 February 1568.

The lands involved in these marriages were to be enjoyed by the Earl and Bess for their lives, then by the two married couples and their heirs – this was the point of the whole complicated arrangement. Furthermore the gift of lands to the children could be revoked by Bess and the Earl by payment of 10s (50p) to the parties, but of course the couples would stay married. However calculated and cold-blooded this double wedding might appear, and the children's feelings in the matter were hardly of any account, it was no more calculated than the marriage of Bess to the Earl. Once married, the couples were expected to get on with the business of having children as soon as the wife was old enough, and to cohabit in appearance if not in harmony. Elizabethans did not acknowledge that temperament existed at all in marriage; land was all. And of course to inherit the land, heirs had to follow.

Although the majority of marriages in Elizabethan landed classes were made on this basis they were not any the less successful for it. Marriage was final until death ended it and when that is understood more tolerance and acceptance comes in. Having married therefore, Bess and the Earl could be expected to accept each other as they were. That is, so long as the financial side remained as they supposed it to be.

The Earl's letters to Bess in the early years of their marriage were affectionate. He invariably addressed her as 'My dere none', and psychologists can make what they like of that.[5] When he visited London in the autumn of 1568, he wrote to Bess, 'If I should judge of time, methinks time longer since my coming hither without you, my only joy, than I did since I married you: such is faithfull affection, which I have never tasted so deeply of before.' Clearly Bess was keeping to her part of the bargain – he was a happy man.

The London visit that autumn of 1568 by the Earl was possibly made in response to a summons by the Queen for she had something to tell him. He had some business to attend to; his Bolsover tenants had been causing trouble and had made a petition, perhaps to the Queen. Shrewsbury was petitioning the Master of the Rolls for a lease of land at Abbot Stoke in Lincolnshire. He thought the asking price of £500 too much and, undecided, wrote to Bess asking if she thought his offer of £400 too little. Whatevever the price, he got the lease. The Court had moved from London to be away from the plague and Shrewsbury had the interview with his Queen in the gardens of Hampton Court. He wrote to Bess on 13 December, 'I should well perceive she did so trust me as she did few. She would not tell me wherein, but doubt it was about the custody of the Scots Queen.' In another letter written a little later, 'Things fall out very evil against the Scots Queen. What she shall do yet is not resolved of.' He ended his letter 'Your Blak man [himself] is in helthe. Your fathfull husbande till my ende', then added a postscript, 'Now it is sarten the Scotes Quene cumes to Tutbury to my charge.'

The Queen's decision would not have taken Shrewsbury and Bess by surprise. The eventual fate of the Scots Queen had been openly discussed almost since the day she had landed in England in the spring of 1568 and the general opinion was that the honour of lodging the fugitive during her sojourn in England should go to the Shrewsburys. Indeed the Earl looked on his selection as the Scots Queen's jailor as an honour bestowed by his Queen; from his point of view she had selected him above all others and that was sufficient. Mary's stay, perhaps, would not be too long and Shrewsbury's reward would be his service to Elizabeth. Her stay with the Shrewsburys was in fact sixteen very difficult years, but this was a misfortune which could never have been foreseen at the beginning, and it is to the credit of the Earl and Bess that, notwithstanding the problems and disaster their prisoner brought them, had Elizabeth asked them they would probably have done the same again.

On 16 May 1568 Mary Stuart, Queen of Scotland and Dowager Queen of France, fled by boat from Scotland. Her policies in ruins and her marriages tragic disasters, Mary had been forced to abdicate her throne whilst a prisoner at Lochleven and pass the crown to her infant son James VI. Pursued by Scottish rebels, she chose England as her asylum, and asked her cousin Queen Elizabeth for help. The Scots Queen landed at Workington in Cumberland with only the clothes she was wearing and attended by a small Court. Her tall figure and strikingly beautiful appearance, as she stepped ashore at this small border port, understandably caused consternation. She was received with puzzled caution by the Deputy Governor, Richard Lowther; in London the news was received with perturbed agitation. Acting on her usual policy, Elizabeth felt her way cautiously before making any irrevocable decisions.

Until the end of July, Mary was accommodated at Carlisle, whilst Elizabeth and her Privy Council struggled towards a decision. Mary was not a prisoner and enjoyed a limited freedom; she had appealed to Elizabeth to help her return to Scotland and regain her throne. She had no reason to regard herself as anything other than a temporary guest of Elizabeth. However, rumours about her future were circulating. As early as 19 July the French ambassador, de la Fôret, reported that Tutbury Castle was being made ready for Mary – 'a very beautiful place, as they say, especially for hunting, in which the Earl of Shrewsbury, who has a portion of his estate in the neighbourhood, is ordered to give her his company'. This was inspired speculation. On 26 July Mary was removed from the dangerous proximity of the border southwards to Bolton Castle in Yorkshire, in the care of Sir Francis Knollys. The move, although with Mary's reluctant agreement, was not made without tears and rage on her part. Tears and rage were Mary's refuge when she found that she was no longer mistress of her destiny.

To hold her cousin a prisoner was distasteful to Elizabeth; Mary was of royal bood like herself, and to deprive a Queen of her freedom was almost unthinkable. Yet to leave Mary free to come and go as she wished posed danger to Elizabeth; Catholic Mary was a focal point for the northern Catholics. The Scots Queen was not averse to using her influence to assemble the army which Elizabeth would not provide, and returning to her country, so involving England in yet another war with her neighbour. Mary's sudden, unexpected arrival had caused the needle of diplomacy to swing in unforeseen directions and time had to be given for the position to settle down. The circumstance was as complicated as it was difficult; slowly Elizabeth and her Privy Council reached a decision.

Mary's power had been usurped by her half-brother, James Stuart, Earl of Moray. It suited Moray to have his sister a prisoner in England. From Elizabeth's point of view, if it was unthinkable to lend an army to reinstate Mary, it was less unthinkable to have her a prisoner; but the decision should not appear to be Elizabeth's. There was the unresolved question as to whether or not Mary was responsible for the murder of her husband Darnley. For Mary to be put on trial in England for matters which had taken place in Scotland was inconceivable; yet here was the Scots Queen in England. With Mary's agreement a compromise was found to this seemingly intractable problem. A conference was held at York in October 1568; the result was inconclusive. Moray revealed the famous Casket letters and the whole matter was referred to a commission at Westminster. As it was all a device to make Mary's eventual imprisonment appear to be a judicial decision and not Elizabeth's, it is not surprising that both conference and commission were stage-managed to bring about the eventual desired result. The commission at Westminster was still sitting when the Earl of Shrewsbury was writing to Bess that 'the Scotes Quene cumes to Tutbury to my charge'.

In choosing Shrewsbury as Mary's keeper, Elizabeth was considering a number of essential points, most of which fitted the Earl's qualifications. He was an apparently wealthy nobleman and therefore Mary would not feel affronted; he was as passionately devoted to Elizabeth as he was to the Protestant cause, therefore there was no likelihood of the Earl falling under Mary's spell or charm; his estates were in the Midlands and conveniently far from Scotland and France from where rescue attempts might be launched; he had a number of large houses to accommodate the Queen and, apart from Sheffield Castle, they were all sufficiently far from any town to avoid unnecessary contact with strangers. The Earl was flattered to have been chosen for this duty by his Queen. As it turned out Elizabeth could not have picked a more devoted or suitable servant for her cause. On the Earl's part it was to cost him his wife, a slice of his fortune and possibly his health. Could Elizabeth have asked for more?

From the beginning nothing went smoothly. A letter to Leicester from Shrewsbury dated 7 January 1569, plaintively asks for news and instructions.[6] He has been told to stay put until he hears from the Queen; he has heard nothing. It will soon make him greyheaded, he complains; and he would like to know what day the Scots Queen is arriving. Poor Shrewsbury was made to wait for another four weeks.

Tutbury Castle was not a residence in a fit state to receive a Queen. The Shrewsburys used it occasionally as a hunting lodge and the furniture was scanty, the roof leaky and its walls cracked in many places. But it certainly answered all the requirements of remoteness and easy fortification against possible rebellions. Standing on a ridge over the valley of the Dove on the borders of Staffordshire and Derbyshire, it was surrounded by a high wall, and the only access was by a single gateway. Later Mary described it:

I am in a walled enclosure, on top of a hill, exposed to all the winds and inclemencies of heaven. Within the said enclosure, resembling that of the wood of Vincennes, there is a very old hunting lodge, built of timber and plaster, cracked in all parts, the plaster adhering nowhere to the woodwork, and broken in numberless places; the said lodge distant three fathoms or thereabouts from the wall, and situated so low, that the rampart of earth which is behind the wall is on a level with the highest point of the building, so that the sun can never shine upon it on that side, nor any fresh air come to it; for which reason it is so damp, that you cannot put any piece of furniture in that part of the building without its being in four days completely covered with mould .... The only apartments I have for my own person consist – and for the truth of this I can appeal to all those who have been here – of two little miserable rooms, so excessively cold, especially at night, that but for the ramparts and entrenchments of curtains and tapestry which I have had made, it would not be possible for me to stay in them in the day time .... This house having no drains to the privies is subject to a continual stench; and every Saturday they are obliged to empty them, and the one beneath my windows, from which I receive a perfume not the most agreeable.[7]

To furnish the lodgings of the Castle, nineteen tapestries were sent from store in the Tower along with bedding, chairs and Turkey carpets; gold plate was provided from the Queen's storerooms.[8] It was left to Bess to supply the rest. The fitting out of Tutbury was done in a rush; Bess was told only two weeks before Mary's arrival. In a letter to the Earl of Leicester of 21 January, she acknowledged the receipt of his letter of instructions, which had arrived only the night before at six o'clock. She was grieved, she said, not to have had the letter sooner,

> The house being unready in many respects for the receiving of the Scottish Queen coming at sudden. I have caused workmen to make forthwith in readiness all such things as is most needful to be done before her coming and God willing I shall cause forthwith three or four lodgings to be furnished with hangings and other necessaries and rather than I should not with true and faithful heart answer the trust reposed by the Queen's Majesty I will lack furniture of lodging for myself.

Sir William Cecil writing to Shrewsbury on 26 January 1569 to give orders for the safekeeping of his charge admitted that the castle was not as fit as was thought, and that he might use any of his other houses. Further instructions were that no one was to visit Mary without permission and that Bess should see her only 'should she be sick or wish to speak with his wife the Countess', and that 'very rarely'; no other gentlewoman was to be admitted. Above all Mary was to be treated as a Queen.

On 26 January, Mary left Bolton Castle with her small Court numbering just over sixty people, carefully guarded by an escort and still in the charge of Knollys, whose wife had just died. It cannot have been anything but an unpleasant journey, made in mid-winter over all but impassable roads. Mary's lady-in-waiting, Agnes Livingston, the wife of Lord Livingston, became ill on the way and had to be left at Rotherham. Mary herself had to stop the following day with a violent pain in her side. Knollys would have liked to rest her at Sheffield Castle, but as he wrote to Cecil, the place was bare because 'my Lady Shrewsbury had conveyed all the hangings to furnish Tutbury'. The cavalcade arrived at Tutbury on 4 February where Mary was received by Bess and the Earl, not as a guest but as a state prisoner, and taken to her dank and gloomy apartments. The Earl, reporting the safe arrival of his prisoner to Cecil, stated brightly, 'The Queen of Scots arrived yesterday afternoon in good health, though some of her women were sick by the way' – one way to describe a frightful journey in which he had taken no part. The Earl politely asked Mary to reduce her attendants from sixty to thirty and then, as he was expected to make up the difference in cost for feeding and warming so large a number of people, he asked Cecil for £500 at least, as he had not sufficient. This was to be a recurring request.

Soon after Mary's arrival, Nicholas White, one of Cecil's subordinate colleagues, found reason to visit the Scots Queen on his way to Ireland; curiosity can have been his only motive. Mary received him, sitting in her murky chamber beneath the little canopy of her cloth of estate with the embroidered motto '*En ma fin est mon commencement*'. White noted this and confessed it was a riddle to him. This is odd for the Elizabethans loved such riddles. The words were borrowed and adapted from her mother's *impresa* and referred to the phoenix rising from the ashes. White reported his visit to Cecil,

I asked her Grace, since the weather did cut off all exercise abroad, how she passed the time within; she said, that all day she wrought with her needle, and the diversity of colours making the work seem less tedious, she continued so long at it till the very pain made her to give over; and with that laid her hand upon her left side, and complained of an old grief increased there.

By 13 March Shrewsbury wrote to Cecil, 'Mary daily resorts to my wife's chamber, where with Lady Leviston and Mistress Seton, she sits devising works.' So that Cecil should not think that Bess was too much influenced by Mary, he said 'her talk [was] altogether of indifferent trifling matters, without any secret dealing or practice I assure you. Of which resort though I think there can be not danger, but rather more surety.' Apparently Bess and Mary had built up a friendship, which if the Earl is correct was based on a shared appreciation for embroidery. It would have been extraordinary if Bess and Mary had not become friendly, for in that remote prison, apart from her ladies-in-waiting, Mary had no one to talk to and for the moment her mind was not occupied with schemes for escape. She had all the time and disposition to pass the day with Bess.

The Scots Queen was twenty-seven. If Bess's life had been eventful, those events were insignificant by comparison with Mary's past.

When only six years old, she had left Scotland to live in France for thirteen years, the homeland of her mother Marie de Guise. At fifteen she was married to the Dauphin of France later François 11; Mary had been brought up in the Court of Catherine de Medici. She must have watched Fontainebleau being built. When she became Queen of France in 1558, Chambord was still building. Mary was widowed for the first time in December 1560 when François died. She returned as a Catholic Queen to Scotland in 1561 where the parliament had recently established the reformed Protestant religion. In 1565 Mary married Lord Darnley, the son of the Earl and Countess of Lennox, and when pregnant had watched in terror the savage murder of her secretary David Rizzio. Darnley in his turn was found murdered in 1567, immediately after an attempt to blow him up in Kirk 'o Field, and Mary was suspected by some to have been responsible. Within months she remarried, this time the Earl of Bothwell who was universally detested. Within weeks Mary, still in her twenties, had lost her throne and left Scotland for ever.

On Bess, who never left England, the younger woman's experience and intellect must have made an impression; although it is impossible to disentangle what exactly, if anything, Bess gained from her association with Mary. Bess was no provincial bumpkin, she was used to the ways of Elizabeth's Court and would have been no stranger to tales of foreign lands. In architecture Mary gave Bess nothing: the Chatsworth Bess built before she knew Mary was a typical large Tudor court-yard house; the Hardwick which she was to rebuild in the 1580s, after she had known Mary, shows no understanding of European renaissance architecture which Mary might have introduced to Bess. The reason for this lack of instruction by Mary is not hard to find. She had no books with her illustrating French buildings or the palaces with which she was familiar; it was a subject of no interest to Mary. However, she did have books showing woodcuts suitable for embroidery designs and in this respect her influence on Bess was not insignificant. These were Mary's books rather than Bess's who never showed a taste for reading.

During the 1550s Bess had sent to London for silks, metal thread, pins and needles for embroidery. But it was only when Mary was Bess's unwilling guest that Bess herself shows up as a needlewoman.

In that letter written by Shrewsbury, Bess with Mary and the ladies-in-waiting, Agnes Livingston and Mary Seaton, are together busy embroidering. The four women are caught at their needlework, sitting working in the light from a window, their heads and hands concentrating on their work, occasionally stopping to discuss some point or a design to be selected from an open copy of Gesner's *Icones Animalium* and Mattioli's *Herbal*.⁹ Usually Bess employed a male embroiderer who was part of the household; he would draw out the designs and work the embroideries on Bess's clothes, and when not doing that he would have been employed on cushion covers and larger pieces. At this time Mary had a 'tapissier' Florens Broshere, another male employee, who although really an upholsterer sometimes served to fill in the background embroideries. By leaving the larger pieces to these servants, Bess and Mary were left free to work on smaller pieces which could be held in the hand, picked up and put down as they felt inclined. Many pieces from this period of Mary's association with Bess have survived and form a set of hangings now at Oxburgh Hall, comprising three bed curtains and a valance.

The Oxburgh embroideries were not made as bed hangings; they are in fact random pieces which have been put together by a later 'tapissier' and mounted on green velvet curtains. Each of the curtains has a square central panel, originally a cushion cover, which is surrounded by 'slips' or small panels showing motifs of flowers and herbs taken from Mattioli; and birds, animals and 'fantastic' creatures so loved by the Elizabethans, taken from Gesner's book. These 'slips' were convenient, for they could be applied to dresses, upholstery, or hangings, or to whatever took the fancy. In the case of the Oxburgh hangings the 'slips' are octagonal with the Mattioli designs and anagrams, and cruciform with the Gesner designs. There are other similar cruciform 'slips' elsewhere – three at Holyrood Palace and two recently found at Hardwick Hall. Of the octagons there are no less than thirty used in a screen at Hardwick and these are curious for each emblem is surrounded with a Latin tag taken from *Adages* by Erasmus which was likely to have been one of Bess's books. It is doubtful if Bess understood Latin for the inscriptions have little to do with the emblems they surround. For a stinking iris to be bound by 'Pluck not the Crown' might have been a warning to Mary perhaps, but it had nothing to do with an iris.

The boredom and frustration of Mary's imprisonment were lightened by these sessions with Bess. Through her embroideries Mary could express something of her feelings. A design headed 'A Catte', now at Holyrood, was more than Gesner intended: the cat, personifying Elizabeth, sits watching a mouse significant of Mary herself, and a later embroiderer has given the cat red hair and a crown to underline the inference. This was harmless enough and amusing to both Bess and Mary. Less harmless was the meaning behind the central piece of the Oxburgh curtain known as the Marian hanging – the so-called Norfolk panel – made as a cushion cover by Mary and sent to the Duke of Norfolk as a present. The design shows a hand with a pruning-hook cutting back unfruiting vines, across which is embroidered '*Virescit Vulnere Virtus*' ('Virtue flourishes by wounding'), a motto associated with Mary, also found on a small silver bell and used on gaming counters in Scotland in 1579. Norfolk would easily read into this the cutting back of Elizabeth the barren vine and the substitution of Mary as Queen of England. When sent to him this embroidery became treasonable.

Some thirty of these embroideries carry Mary's cypher, either a simple anagram of M.A., or M.A. with the Greek letter ϕ signifying her first husband François II. One such 'slip' shows a small black and white dog called 'Jupiter' – not from Gesner – which surely must be one of Mary's 'pretty little dogs' of which she was so fond.

It is not so easy to assign embroideries to Bess for she used no personal signature. The central panel of the Cavendish hanging – another cushion cover – may be from Bess's hand. It is a mourning panel dated 1570, using the silks drawn from the same sources as the Norfolk panel. The central motif, tears falling on quicklime, has embroidered across it '*Extinctam Lachrimae Testur Vicere Flammam*' ('Tears witness that the quenched flame lives'), the *impresa* of the widowed Catherine de Medici and suggested to Bess by Mary; around the border are symbols of Bess's three widowhoods. Two of the 'slips' on this same hanging are associated with Bess and could be her work: one 'A Buke' or Stag, signifying the Cavendish stag; the other knotted serpents, which became the

Cavendish badge and was used by Bess in embroidery for the first time, borrowed from Mary's book by Gesner.

Curiously, each of the three hangings has an octagon 'slip' with the names 'George Elizabeth Shrewsbury' surrounding an anagram which makes up the names 'George, Marie, Elizabeth, Shrewsbury'. If this indicates anything at all, it shows the friendly relationship then existing between captive and captors.

The most extraordinary hangings of all to have survived are a set of goddesses and their virtues – there were five but are now only four – made up in applied work using the plain parts of religious copes, perhaps left from Sir William Cavendish or bought by St Loe. This was a set which Bess was very proud of for she put them in the state withdrawing chamber in her new Hardwick. Penelope, Cleopatra, Zenobia, Artemisia and Lucretia, each woman had a history which could apply to Bess's life and must have been suggested by Mary with her knowledge of the classics; the forbearance and patience of Penelope and the constancy of Artemisia were virtues Bess tried to emulate; but other virtues such as justice, liberality, charity and wisdom were compliments to Queen Elizabeth.

Mary had arrived at Tutbury with no furniture of her own and what had not been provided by Elizabeth's bounty had to be found by Bess. At the end of 1570 Mary was importing her own and sent[10] Ange Marie, her *valet de chambre*, to France for furniture. It is likely that the four pieces of French furniture, including the well-known sea-dog table based on designs published in 1560 by Jacques Du Cerceau, a French Huguenot architect and decorative designer, all of which are best described as royal, were given to Bess by Mary and were some of the pieces imported in 1570. Early in 1577 Mary wrote to France asking for a rich bed to be sent to the Shrewsburys with six '*Grand chandeliers de salle qui se font à Croutelles*' (crystal chandeliers), but it is doubtful if they ever received these two gifts. However, an undated list of Bess's jewellery has six items headed 'Given by the Scots Queen to my Lord and me'. Mary was not beyond offering gifts to Bess nor Bess too proud to accept.

For the moment the duty of keeping Mary was not particularly arduous for Bess and the Earl. For the present Mary had no need to make plots for escape. She was planning to marry the Duke of Norfolk; she was sure that this would eventually have Elizabeth's

approval and that she could return to Scotland as Queen married
to an English nobleman. There were of course several drawbacks
to the scheme; Elizabeth knew nothing about it and Mary was still
married to her third husband, Bothwell.

Even though these were the halcyon days of Mary's stay with
Shrewsbury, the responsibility of accommodating the Scots
Queen's miniature Court had considerable problems. By the beginning of March it was apparent to the Earl that the sudden arrival
of something like two hundred people at Tutbury in the middle
of winter was putting a severe strain on the local peasants. Wood,
coal, corn and hay were short or, as the Earl put it, the good people
of Tutbury 'are marvellously molested', and he asked permission
to move Mary to his house at South Wingfield. It was no easy matter
to trundle this royal prisoner from place to place. In a letter to Cecil
written on 17 April, Shrewsbury told him, 'I am presently moving
to Wingfield where my wife has been this senight preparing it.' The
local justices were called upon to provide assistance on the journey
and the Earl paid the full cost himself; for this was an expense Elizabeth did not finance.

Wingfield Manor had very much better accommodation than
Tutbury. It was a larger house for one thing, and for another it
was used as a residence rather than an occasional hunting lodge.
The drawback was that it was not so easily defended. The buildings
of the manor formed two courts, an inner and an outer one. The
entrance to the outer or service court was by an arched gate on the
east side, to the left of which was the now restored castle barn; the
other buildings round the court provided quarters for guards and
servants, with stables and outbuildings. Access to the second court
was by way of another gateway leading from the service court. Here
were the great hall and the state apartments where Mary was lodged.
It was a house very much better able to accommodate the large
number of people seemingly necessary to guard and attend the Scots
Queen; the state apartments alone had two garderobe towers, each
providing four garderobes.

Mary as usual was involved in one of her incessant intrigues, and
was expecting with some impatience the arrival of a messenger from
Scotland. The message when it came brought bad news. Her plans,
whatever they were, had misfired. Mary took her usual refuge in

illness. Elizabeth tended to over-react to Mary's attacks of ill health; she could not afford at this point, to let her royal cousin die in her charge. Two doctors were summoned from London and Shrewsbury reported their arrival to Cecil: 'As since their coming, there is within these two days grown in the next chamber to her a very unpleasant and fulsome savour, hurtful to her health, by continual pestering and uncleanly order of her own folks.'[11] The Earl went on to say that he was moving Mary to Chatsworth for two or three days whilst Wingfield was cleaned out.

Mary recovered her health but her doctors were still at Wingfield when the Earl himself went down with a sickness. He had been to Chatsworth about some matter when he was taken ill. So that Mary should not remain outside his care, he had himself carried back to Wingfield on a litter. Three days later he was more or less recovered but wrote to Cecil telling him that 'my sickness was so extreme that I cannot forget it'. Two days later Bess wrote to Cecil on 19 June, confirming that Shrewsbury had recovered and that Mary was as well guarded as before. Elizabeth and Cecil reading between the lines guessed that the Earl was in a worse state than Bess was confessing. To ensure Mary's safety, the Earl of Huntingdon, a near neighbour of the Shrewsburys at Ashby-de-la-Zouch, was ordered to attend at Wingfield if needed, and Sir Ralph Sadler was sent to reinforce Bess's able but temporary lone guardianship of Mary.

The two doctors who had been sent to attend Mary were ordered to give their help to the sick Shrewsbury. A report to Cecil by Dr Francis makes quaint reading; the Earl on his return from Chatsworth in an open litter had drunk a quart of metheglin, 'so inflaming his body full of humours ... so that many hot and choleric vapours went from his stomach to his head'. As far as Shrewsbury was concerned it had been a bad attack of gout and he had felt dreadful. However he was not clear of his troubles, for just as all were congratulating themselves on his recovery, he fell ill again; so ill, in fact, that he and all around him thought he was dying. Sir John Zouch, a neighbour, was sent to take over the responsibility of Mary's keeping. Once more Shrewsbury recovered and on 3 July wrote to Cecil that in future he would be more precise in obeying the physicians.

So far the duty of keeping watch on Mary was not as arduous

to the Shrewsburys as it later became. But the period of peace was coming to an end. Mary's hopes of returning to Scotland were shattered at the end of July when the Perth convention voted by forty to nine against her return and ruled that her marriage to Bothwell was valid. Although this was a convention of Scottish nobles there is no doubt that they reflected the popular opinion. Scotland did not want Mary back. By mid-July Elizabeth knew everything about the proposed marriage to Norfolk, who, when he presented himself at Court, met with a characteristic storm of abuse. The Earl of Huntingdon and Viscount Hereford were sent to Wingfield to assist Shrewsbury, and Mary was bundled back to the safety of the hated Tutbury where she was allowed neither to send letters nor to receive them; her coffers and chambers were searched with such unnecessary violence that she complained to Elizabeth; her retinue was reduced once more and Mary became sick. Poor Shrewsbury, in trying to be on good terms with both parties, ended by being distrusted by all.

Shortly after his disastrous visit to Court, Norfolk was arrested. This provoked a Catholic rising in the north under the Earls of Northumberland and Westmorland whose rebel armies were determined to free Mary and moved towards Tutbury. Three days after his departure Huntingdon was back again to help in the hurried removal of the captive Queen to Coventry, another of those uncomfortable journeys accomplished under difficulties with protest and complaint by Mary.

The lodging of the prisoner at Coventry was another problem. Queen Elizabeth, who always felt uneasy when Mary was mingling with crowds and could pass messages unseen, raised objections about the choice of accommodation and Mary was moved within days of arriving. The upheavals and journeyings were far from easy for Bess and the Earl: the keeping of their prisoner had become a full-time occupation for both and cut them off from their friends and all outside activities. At Coventry, Shrewsbury was receiving letters almost every day from Cecil; instructions and directions followed orders, all of which had to be answered. There was disagreement with Huntingdon; accommodation to be found for four hundred attendants and guards; in addition to the usual baggage accompanying Mary, there were the valued chattels which Bess and the Earl took with them for safety – gold and silver plate. At some point in all this turmoil Shrewsbury found time to give Bess a gold cup weighing fifty pounds which had been his father's. He still remembered this fifteen years later.[12]

By 3 January the danger had receded and Mary was back at Tutbury Castle again. But life within the castle was henceforth to be constantly disturbed by the intrigues of the captive Queen and the suspicions of the reigning one. The honeymoon was over and the long years of mistrust of Mary by the Earl had begun. It was a period which brought a burdensome strain into the domestic life of Bess and her husband.

THE SCOTS
QUEEN
1570-1575

Within eight weeks of Bess's return to Tutbury with Mary, Shrewsbury wrote to Cecil telling him that Mary was down again with fever, that the water 'waxes so evil and scant' that his servants were falling sick daily and he suggested a move to Chatsworth.[1] Twelve weeks later on 24 May the Shrewsburys, Mary and her attendants, with all their accompanying baggage, were on the move.

Chatsworth, although Bess considered it to be hers, was, now that she had married the Earl, as much his. It was another house which he had at his disposal and only a short distance from Wingfield and Tutbury. It was as well that the three were so conveniently close, for the problem of accommodating about two hundred people had two acute sides to it; one was the difficulty of finding sufficient food and fuel in the area, and the other, equally critical, concerned sanitation. The medieval garderobe systems, which were all these houses were equipped with, could not be in continuous use by so large a number of people and remain effective; also they tainted the water. The constant peregrinations of the Earl and Bess with Mary and her attendants were in part due to Mary's complaints about the state of the garderobes, the Earl's concern for her health, and the local population's pleas that they could not find sufficient supplies for the Earl's requirements and their own needs. The move from Tutbury was to be Mary's last sight of that detested castle until she left the care of the Earl for good in 1584; Tutbury was found at last to be quite unsuitable for accommodating so large a number of people. For the remaining fourteen years of Mary's time with the Shrewsburys she was kept mainly at Sheffield at the castle, the manor, or the lodge which the Earl built in 1574 specially to accommodate her. Over the full period of nearly sixteen years in the Earl's charge, Mary was moved a total of forty-six times; so much human baggage bundled from one prison to another. Complaints were made of the 'expense caused by the transport of her books and other weighty trumpery, on which she placed much importance'. And the moving of the prisoner and her trumpery was paid for out of the Earl's pocket.

From the start Mary was a costly captive. Elizabeth allowed the Earl and Bess £52 a week for the lodging and keeping of the Scots Queen and all her attendants but this was inadequate. In February 1570 the Earl noted that Mary had been with him for fifty-four weeks and therefore he should have been paid £2,808; in fact he had received only £2500 and was £300 out of pocket. He also received an allowance of 'cote money' and wages for the soldiers needed to guard the Queen, but this again was inadequate. Part of the trouble was that Mary was a magnet for exiled Scots who would attach themselves to her Court. The numbers crept up to over sixty and more many times before an order would be sent by Cecil to reduce the number to thirty. The extra hangers-on were not budgeted for by Elizabeth and the cost of keeping them had to be found by the Earl. Later Elizabeth deliberately delayed and withheld payments to the Earl, provoking him to squeaks of poverty, but this may have been part of a deliberate policy to force Mary to spend her own money to pay for her keep, rather than using it to finance her eternal intrigues throughout Europe. As the widow of François II, Mary had a dowager's pension of £12,000 annually, paid irregularly. But notwithstanding Elizabeth's guile, Mary continued to use this to finance her plots and plans for escape and the Earl was left to make up the cost of keeping his expensive prisoner.

The move to Chatsworth made Mary's life more comfortable, because for the moment Bess's building was finished. Indeed Elizabeth would never have let Mary go to Chatsworth if this had not been so. Her apartments faced inwards on to the court-yard and were high up over the great hall in the east wing of the house. They comprised a withdrawing chamber, a bed chamber and a servant's chamber. In 1601 when Mary had been dead for thirteen years and the apartments dismantled, they still had a bedstead with a canopy of velvet and cloth of gold, with sarcenet curtains which could very well have been hers.

One of the many attempts to free Mary was made at Chatsworth that summer of 1570. Cyphered messages were passed; Mary was to be spirited out of one of the windows and away by boat to the Isle of Man. The plot was betrayed but it showed Bess and the Earl how far Mary's admirers were prepared to go on her behalf. One of the plotters, John Hall, was a disaffected gentleman servant to the Earl; in his examination, dated 13 May 1571, he confessed that he had been in the Earl's service for six years but had left four years previously because he 'did mislike my lord's marriage with his wife as divers of his friends did' – though he failed to say on what grounds he disapproved.[2]

In September 1570 Cecil, with Sir Walter Mildmay and John Lesley who was Bishop of Ross and Mary's ambassador in London, made a three-week visit to Chatsworth. Their purpose was to persuade Mary to give up her claim to the English throne; to return to Scotland as Queen and to leave her infant son James as hostage in London against her good behaviour. There were other items in a long list of articles, some of which were unacceptable to Mary but in the main she was prepared to fall in with the plans. However, these negotiations came to nothing because the Scots refused to accept anything invalidating Mary's abdication which she had signed under duress at Loch Leven in 1567. The entertainment of the three statesmen would have let Bess catch up on national and international news, and Court gossip. Cut off by her preoccupation with Mary's captivity, Bess had been keeping herself informed by means of long newsletters sent to her by professional newswriters in London. Although shut away in Derbyshire, Mary was still a piece on the chessboard of European politics, even though her influence was slipping away. Often it must have seemed that Mary, by her secret letters, knew more of what was going on than did Bess. Elizabeth and Cecil were apt to intrigue as much as Mary, telling the Shrewsburys nothing of what they were doing. Unless Bess and the Earl could keep in touch with the mainstream of events, the intrigues of their prisoner would have been bewildering.

For the first half of 1570, Mary continued her ploys with comparatively little interruption. Indeed her letters and answers in secret went and came with surprising freedom. Sometimes her letters were written completely in code and others had the vital and revealing names substituted by seemingly innocent alternatives. At Sheffield, where Mary was taken in December, the Earl's servants found secret letters hidden under stones and once a message was found inside the hollow staff of a visitor; there was no end to the ingenuity employed by Mary and her friends and it required all the wits the Earl possessed and the absolute loyalty of his servants to forestall Mary in her plottings. But as long as Norfolk was alive Mary was content to bide her time, making no plans for escape.

Norfolk was released from the Tower in August 1570. Mary continued her efforts with the Pope to get an annulment of her marriage to Bothwell, which was the impediment to her marriage with anyone else. Her diplomacy was hindered by the fact that her ambassador, the Bishop of Ross, was in the Tower for a period of six weeks. Nevertheless, Mary considered herself affianced to Norfolk; there had been an exchange of gifts, and on his part he had given supplies of money to Mary. In fact it was partly over this money that Norfolk was rearrested in September 1571. He had unwisely become involved in an attempt to send Mary's money to Scotland by one of his own servants. But this was a less serious charge, for he was also discovered to be implicated in the Ridolfi plot, by which Philip of Spain was to invade England from the Spanish Netherlands, depose and behead Elizabeth and put Mary on the throne. Norfolk's servants were racked and tortured in the Tower and more was revealed. The cypher which Mary had used in secret letters to Norfolk was found, also her letters and copies of his replies. It was all very damning for them both. Reprisals followed immediately; Mary's attendants were reduced to sixteen and she was more closely confined.

For some time Elizabeth had been toying with the idea of marrying the Duke of Anjou. From the start it was a hopeless diplomatic gambit. Anjou was a dedicated Catholic and insisted on freedom of worship for English Catholics which was quite unacceptable to Elizabeth and the vast majority of her subjects. The matter was dropped with some embarrassment. With the obvious threat of invasion by Spain it was clear that England must have an alliance with France, if not by marriage then by other means. In April 1571, by the treaty of Blois, an Anglo-French defensive alliance was signed.

France withdrew from her unofficial support of Scotland and abandoned the cause of the Queen of Scots. Mary was more isolated
than ever.

The Earl of Shrewsbury was summoned to London to preside
as Lord High Steward at Norfolk's trial. Sir Ralph Sadler arrived
at Sheffield Castle on 28 December to take charge of Mary in the
Earl's absence. Mary's distress during the time of the trial was described by her temporary jailor who noted, 'And my presence is
such a trouble to her, that unless she come out of her chamber I
come but little to her; but my Lady Shrewsbury is seldom from
her.'[3] In the face of all the conclusive evidence, Norfolk could only
be found guilty of high treason and sentenced to death. The news
was sent to Sadler as soon as the verdict was declared on 16 January
1572 and he immediately told Bess, asking her to inform Mary. Unfortunately bad news travels fast and had already reached Mary,
who was in the first agonies of grief when Bess, entering her
chamber, 'found her all be-wept and mourning'. Tactlessly Bess
asked what ailed her, although the cause must have been obvious.
Patiently and with sadness Mary replied 'that she knew her ladyship
could not be ignorant of the cause, and how deeply she must be
grieved for the trouble of her friends, who fared the worse for her
sake ... she feared the Duke of Norfolk fared the worse for what
she had lately written to Queen Elizabeth.' Bess replied 'that she
might be sure that whatsoever she had written to the Queen's
majesty could do the Duke neither good nor harm touching his con-
demnation; so if all his offences and reasons had not been great,
and plainly proved against him, those noblemen who sat on his trial
would for all the good on earth, have condemned him'. This, being
true, may have brought Mary no comfort at all. The Scots Queen,
said Sadler, 'thereupon with mourning, became silent, and had no
will to talk more in the matter, and so like a true lover she remaineth
still mourning for her lover.'

There is some tactlessness in Bess's reported comment to Mary,
but there is also an element of double-talk. Sadler was at her elbow
and Bess knew that her words would be reported back to the Privy
Council and the Queen. Mary, in fact, was living in a world of intrigue and knew that nothing said to her in public could be taken
at its face value. If Bess and Mary were allowed any privacy at all,

perhaps Bess was able to say then what may have been in her heart.

Understandably, with all this harrowing news, Mary became ill again. With her indifferent health, which was made worse by the conditions of her captivity and the number of confounding setbacks she received, the wonder is that she lived on at all. Hope of release or escape can only have kept her going. Mary must have been an extraordinarily tough and resilient woman. Shrewsbury returned from London to take charge of his unhappy prisoner once more. Sadler left and life at Sheffield returned to what must have passed for normal.

On 22 April 1572[4] Shrewsbury signed a remarkable deed of gift, which was to cause him so much frenzy later. By this deed he gave to William and Charles Cavendish all the lands Bess had brought to him at their marriage, Bess keeping a life interest. In return, Shrewsbury was let off paying 'great Somes of money whych he the said Earle Standeth Chargeable to pay as well to the yonger chyldren of the said Countesse as also for the debts of the said Coun-tyesse and for dyvers other weighty Consyderations'. Later he claimed that he was ill at the time and did not know what he was doing. This can be dismissed as untrue; he wrote that same day to Lord Burghley, as Cecil had now become; it was a perfectly straightforward letter, obviously written in full command of himself and he made no mention of being sick. He also later claimed that the deed was a forgery; but the signature is genuine and this claim can likewise be dismissed. He stated quite correctly that it had not been legally enrolled which was a legal quibble. It is certain that Shrewsbury knew what he was doing when he signed this deed, notwithstanding his later regrets.

As the details of the Shrewsburys' marriage settlement are lack-ing, one does not know what the terms were, nor what the 'dyvers other weighty Consyderations' were, and one cannot be certain what the debts were, for which Shrewsbury was no longer responsible. In the early years of their marriage Bess had no opportunity to run up debts, she was buying no lands and had no extravagances and she was too much occupied with the problems of guarding Mary. The debts may have been those she had incurred long ago before her marriage, and the paying of them by the Earl must have been written into the settlement. By this deed Bess was giving up some of the rights granted to her and they must have been considerable. In return she was getting back her own lands valued at £1050 per year, which by this deed were settled on William and Charles under Bess's life control. A peculiarity about the deed is that there were no witnesses to it and it was signed only by the Earl. Later when the heated disputes between them came to the boil and the Queen intervened, this deed of gift was taken taken to be genuine: the Queen must be believed. If on the evidence Bess appears to have got away with a lot, in order to do so she had to give up a lot.

One does not have to look very far for the reason for this deed of gift which later became so important. William Cavendish, older than Charles by one year, was twenty-one at the end of the year of the deed, 1572, when Shrewsbury would have become liable to pay out a cash settlement 'to the yonger chyldren of the said Countesse'. In this case the cash would go only to William; Charles would have to wait two years for his. The Earl signed the deed willingly and was pleased to do so for he did not have the thousands of pounds in ready money, which he would have had to pay to William, and to Charles in his turn. Later Shrewsbury said, 'My riches they talk of are in other men's purses,' and he had indeed been called upon to pay out very large sums of money in recent years. Francis Talbot, his heir, had married Anne Herbert the daughter of the Earl of Pembroke in 1563 requiring an enormous marriage settlement; the marriage of Gilbert to Mary Cavendish in 1568 again required another settlement; Grace Talbot's marriage to Henry Cavendish had brought the settlement of more lands; all these had been a great drain on Shrewsbury's wealth quite apart from the expense of keeping the Scots Queen. By 1580 Shrewsbury had serious debts and said so; in 1572 when he signed the deed he was happy to do so; it got him out of paying 'greate Somes of money' which he did not possess. When Shrewsbury later tried by all means fair and foul to repudiate the deed, he was acting disreputably.

At her marriage to Shrewsbury, Bess's gross annual income was £1600; this went to her husband. However, he only enjoyed the full sum for five years, because Henry Cavendish became twenty-one in late 1571 and the income from the lands settled on him by his father which had been coming to Bess, whose ward Henry was, then went to Henry. These lands were worth about £550 per year in 1572 when Henry took possession, and that income was lost to Shrewsbury. All the Earl was giving up by his deed of gift was the remaining income of £1050 per year.

Henry and Grace had been married for five years and there were still no children. For Henry, as Bess's heir, to have no children was a serious matter; this would not make the dynasty Bess was determined to create. But one must be fair: Grace was eight years old at the most when she married in 1568 and well below the age considered safe for child bearing, and Henry had been sent abroad almost immediately after their marriage. Henry's education had been suitable as a background for the heir to the Cavendish lands; after Eton he had returned to Chatsworth and been tutored by the disgraceful Henry Jackson. Instead of going to university, Henry had eventually married Grace and afterwards been sent on a tour of Europe with his new brother-in-law Gilbert Talbot. It was the custom in such child marriages for the groom to be sent away until the bride reached child-bearing age. And although Gilbert's wife Mary was twelve and of that age, Gilbert was nevertheless packed off as a companion for Henry. By the end of June, Henry, already on the Continent, was arranging to meet Gilbert shortly at Hamburg; in November they were both at Padua for study and a year later staying at Venice.[5] This interlude meant that Henry was away for possibly two years of his married life. Nevertheless it may have been in Bess's mind that Henry might have no legitimate children and that William, her second son, would have to be provided with suitable estates to support the honour of her heirs which the Earl's deed of gift gave her freedom to do.

In addition to his financial problems, the Earl was not having an easy time with his prisoner. The massacre of the Huguenots in France on 24 September, St Bartholomew's Day, 1572 had brought a frisson of horror to all Protestants in England and a reaction against Catholics. There had been plans to move Mary from Sheffield Castle across the way to the manor for a change of air; all this was cancelled. Elizabeth wrote to Shrewsbury on 5 September ordering that Mary 'be kept very straightly from all conference'.[6] Her attendants were reduced in number once more to sixteen. Elizabeth felt that the problems the Earl was facing deserved some reward; he was made Earl Marshal, a post made vacant when Norfolk was beheaded. Shrewsbury was grateful to his monarch for the honour, and it cost the Queen nothing.

Mary's existence had by now become more than an embarrassment to Elizabeth. Her constant intrigues, and the fact that she had a claim to the throne and could become a Catholic successor to her cousin, made her a constant danger.

It seemed that the only answer to this political problem was that Mary should die and yet Elizabeth could not consider this as a way out of the dilemma. It was Elizabeth who stopped the bill of attainder which was passing through Parliament. Now that there was no possibility of Mary's return to Scotland, the future of the Scots Queen could only become more and more bleak. Shrewsbury tried to make his charge as comfortable as he was allowed to; he must have had in mind that if through mischance Elizabeth died, then Mary could take her place on the throne of England. Her liberty was only curtailed in times of national tension, and her household cut down when London heard of mounting numbers.

For some time, Mary had been asking Elizabeth for permission to visit 'La fontagne de Bogsby' as she quaintly termed Buxton. Perversely Elizabeth put her off with the excuse that the house Shrewsbury was building there was not ready, but on 10 August 1573 Burghley wrote to Shrewsbury giving the Queen's consent for Mary to visit Buxton. Accordingly Shrewsbury accompanied Mary on that first visit, which lasted for five weeks from 22 August. Both Bess and the Earl owned property in the town, but it was the Earl who had been responsible for building the Hall which was where Mary was accommodated. Built before 1572, it was adjoining the springs and comprised a square block four storeys high, with thirty lodgings and a great chamber.[7] A Dr Jones, writing at the time of this first visit, recommended the benefits of using what he called the 'Ancient Bathe of Buckstones'. Certainly by the 1570s and '80s Buxton had become a very popular health resort. Although Bess has been credited with the development and popularising of Buxton at this time, there is nothing whatsoever to suggest that she had anything to do with its success. It is far more likely that the six visits which Mary made during her time with the Shrewsburys, combined with the visits which Leicester and other statesmen made when staying at nearby Chatsworth, provided the publicity which caused its development as a health centre in the late sixteenth century.

The preoccupation of Bess and the Earl with their charge may have caused Bess to relax some of her authority over her own children. Henry, now returned from the continent to his wife Grace, had his own establishment at Tutbury Abbey. In an undated letter of the early 1570s he sent an urgent note to his mother.[8] There had been a brawl between two of his servants, who had fought a duel with two swords apiece and one had been killed. The survivor, whose name was Swinnerton, had wisely run off and Henry's men were even then searching for him; Henry supposing the two to have been friends, expressed his surprise. Swinnerton was obviously known to Bess for she sent Henry's letter on to the Earl with her own comment written in the margin.

My Juwell, thys saterday at nyght I resavyed thys leter meche to my greffe for the myshape [this letter much to my grief for the mishap] yett was ever lyke that swenertone shulde cometo some great fayte, he was a vane lewd felow. Fare well my deare harte. your faythfoul wyffe. E Shrouesbury.

In 1574 Henry himself was involved in another affray in Staffordshire, in which a man was killed. This was serious enough to occupy the attention of the Privy Council which ordered an enquiry. These were serious cases for Henry to be involved in; his brother Charles, who was an engaging youth, was also always involved in some escapade or other. He was the cause of a letter from the Earl to Bess in June 1573 from Sheffield Castle. 'Charles your son', he wrote, 'he is easily led to folly for within two nights after you went from me his man Morton enticed his master, Blyth and my armourer to go stealing in to Staly Park in the night and I would wish you to advise him from these doings.' But this was a harmless prank and the Earl may have been more worried about the effect these midnight larks with his armourer and the like might have on discipline amongst his servants guarding Mary.

By the summer of 1574 Bess still had one daughter unmarried, Elizabeth Cavendish, aged nineteen. Shrewsbury, writing later to Burghley said 'there is few noblemens' sons in England that she hath not prayed me to deal for at one time or other'. There had certainly been at least one attempt to arrange a marriage for the girl. A letter addressed to Bess from a relative, Hugh Fitzwilliam, written from London on 3 February 1574, outlines secret negotiations.[9] The husband of Bess's half-sister Elizabeth Leche, Anthony Wingfield, had been having conversations with Mr Bertie and 'her grace' about a possible marriage between an unnamed young lady and a young gentleman at Gray's Inn. The matter was so secret that Fitzwilliam did not mention names; but Mr Bertie was married to Catherine, the widow and fourth wife of Charles Brandon, Duke of Suffolk, who continued to call herself the Duchess of Suffolk and their son Peregrine Bertie, later Lord Willoughby de Eresby, was at Gray's Inn. The negotiations concerned a possible marriage between young Bertie, then aged nineteen and Elizabeth Cavendish. Fitzwilliam was trying to arrange a meeting between Bess and the Berties, but Bess had done nothing in the matter. It looks as though the initiative had come from the Berties and Bess was biding her time with other plans for her daughter.

That summer Margaret, Countess of Lennox, petitioned the Queen to be allowed to go north to her estates at Temple Newsam.[10] The Countess was the daughter of Henry VIII's eldest sister, and mother of Darnley, Mary's second husband. Her petition was granted but Elizabeth, suspecting something, made the condition that she was not to visit Mary either at Chatsworth or Sheffield. The old Countess replied that she could never forget the murder of her son Darnley and had no intention of seeing Mary. Margaret Lennox had not had a happy life, which may have contributed to her peculiarities: she had spent parts of her life imprisoned, her son Darnley had been murdered, and out of her eight children only one had survived. Charles Stuart was then eighteen and little is known about him; the Privy Council had arranged for a Protestant tutor for the boy to counteract his mother's Catholic beliefs, and Margaret admitted that he was her 'greatest dolour'. If the later word of the Scots Queen is to be believed then Margaret Lennox had deliberately lied to Elizabeth about her relationship with her daughter-in-law; but she was in a precarious financial position and the means might have justified the end.

That summer, Mary made her second visit to Buxton. Quite when is uncertain but it may have been at Whitsun, 19 May 1574. She was back at Sheffield by 9 July. During that time Mrs Bertie, as the Duchess of Suffolk, made a visit to Chatsworth which was frowned on by Elizabeth, though the Duchess was a fervent Protestant and detested all Mary's beliefs and it is unlikely that Elizabeth had anything to worry about. Just what Bess and the Duchess had to talk about is undetermined; it may have been further marriage negotiations between Elizabeth Cavendish and young Bertie. If so then they came to nothing for Shrewsbury later said that Elizabeth had been 'disappointed of young Bartie'. The Duchess may have been taking letters to Mary from Margaret Lennox or she may have been acting on Margaret's behalf with Bess over quite another matter.

La Mothe Fénélon, the French Ambassador in London, had his ear close to the ground and sent a despatch to Paris as early as 24 September reporting that the Countess of Lennox was proposing to journey north.[11] Clearly he did not believe the trip was all it appeared, for he said that she was going on to Scotland to visit '*le jeune Prince, son petit filz*'. On 3 October the Privy Council authorised the provision of two teams of horses or oxen for the 'removing of the Lady Lennox's stuff from Hackney into her manor of Temple Newsam in Yorkshire'. Fénélon, in a later despatch dated 15 October, reported that the Countess was planning to leave London in five or six days. He was suspicious about the whole trip, adding that she was going to Stirling to visit her grandson and, astonishingly, to kidnap him to England.

Fénélon was partly right; the trip was not all it appeared. At Northampton the party stayed with the Berties and Mrs Bertie, the Duchess of Suffolk, accompanied them as far as Grantham. On reaching Newark they received a message from Bess, who by chance was at Rufford Abbey, another of the Shrewsbury houses, inviting them to the Abbey, a little way further off the road. The Countess in her later excuses claimed that the 'place [was] not one myle dystante owte of my weayea and a muche farer way as well to be perceved'. Bess went out to meet old Margaret Lennox and her party on the road, to escort her to Rufford. Was it chance that Bess's daughter Elizabeth Cavendish should have been with her mother at Rufford? Was it chance again that the old Countess was too sick or tired with the journey to move from her chamber for four or five days leaving her son Charles and Elizabeth Cavendish to their own devices? The whole business has the aspect of being cleverly managed by Bess and Margaret Lennox as the result of the plotting at Chatsworth. The only thing left to chance was the affections of the two young people and in this Elizabeth did not let her mother down. According to Shrewsbury's account, 'The young man, her son, fell into liking with my wife's daughter ... and such liking was between them as my wife tells me she makes no doubt of a match .... The young man is so far in love, that belike he is sick without her.' The marriage was not delayed, indeed the whole thing had to be tied up before the Queen could stop it. Fénélon in another report on 17 November said that the marriage had taken place and went on to say that the Queen had ordered the Countess and her son to return to London. He concluded that they would be put in the Tower. Fénélon was a perceptive observer for he expressed relief that the trip to Scotland had been interrupted and pointed out that Bess's friendship with Margaret Lennox would make her the enemy of Mary Queen of Scots.

From Bess's point of view the marriage was a triumph. Her daughter Elizabeth was now married into kinship with the Queen of England, and her grandson, should there be one, could rule over England and Scotland. For a Derbyshire squire's daughter she had come a very long way indeed. On the Lennox side, by marrying into the Cavendish family they had allied themselves to the Shrewsbury wealth, which was what they were most short of.

In her defiance of the Queen, Bess must have calculated that the influence of her husband the Earl would deflect some of Elizabeth's notorious fury. That she might be sent to the Tower was possible but for how long could the wife of the keeper of the Scots Queen be decently kept prisoner? Obviously she could not be shut away as she had been over poor Catherine Grey's marriage to Edward Seymour.

Excuses poured into the Court to Burghley, to Leicester and to the Queen.[12] The Earl's letter of 5 November was the first the Queen heard of the marriage. Shrewsbury himself must have been a worried man, for the scales of diplomacy had received a jolt and it was not clear how matters would settle down, nor how his position would be affected. In a letter of excuses to Elizabeth, written on

4 December, Shrewsbury explained that the marriage had been 'dealt in suddenly and without my knowledge'. No doubt this was correct, for Bess, had she asked her husband's opinion, would have had all the opposition of which he was capable. He hoped that his record of devotion and service to Elizabeth would convince her that this was no sinister plot involving Mary.

Old Margaret Lennox, meanwhile, was making heavy weather of her recall to London. Her first letter of explanation was written from Huntingdon on 3 December to Leicester. She excused her delay by the fact that her mules were 'ovrlabored ... bothe croked and Lame wth ther extreme Labor', and that floods had forced her to leave the road and hindered her progress. She too underlined the feelings of the young couple, 'Nowe my Lorde', she wrote 'for the haystie Marryage of my sonne After that he had Intangled hym-selfe so that he coulde have nowe other.' Also, pointing out, she had not broken her promise to the Queen, for she had not been within thirty miles of Sheffield or Chatsworth. That same day she wrote a short note to Burghley sending a copy of her letter to Leicester and asking him in the name of friendship to help her.

Still on her way to London, Margaret Lennox wrote to Burghley on 10 December, saying again that she had not disobeyed the Queen's orders, that the marriage was the chance result of the couple's affection which there had been no stopping and that she herself was a poor and aged widow. It was all rather lame.

By 12 December Fénélon reported that the Countess of Lennox had just then arrived at her house in Hackney and that she was expected at Court the following day, adding that she very much feared the Queen's rage and the prospect of the Tower.

The Earl of Huntingdon was entrusted with the enquiry into the whole affair;[13] he was no friend to any of the parties and could be counted on to smell out any dark international plots had there been any. Whilst the enquiry was going forward, Margaret Lennox was confined to her Hackney house with her son Charles and his new wife Elizabeth.

Walsingham, Secretary of State, wrote to Huntingdon on 22 December giving him detailed instructions on where to begin his enquiries.[14] Servants were the obvious weakest point for, being hired, their loyalty was doubtful, and true to this principle

Walsingham instructed Huntingdon to start his enquiries with one of Charles Stuart's servants. His comments on this are interesting. Wenslowe was the unfortunate man's name; for four or five days before his examination he was to be committed to 'some close and strait custody'. He was to be warned that punishment would follow if he did not tell all he knew, for 'some kind of persuasion cunningly used may, perhaps, breed such fear and deep conceit in him to utter such truth as otherwise may hardly be drawn out of him'. Unfortunately it all has a horribly modern ring: methods have not changed. Like most State enquiries this was particularly thorough. Lady Lennox's secretary, Thomas Fowler, was closely interrogated but no connection with the Queen of Scots or Bess was found. This is likely to be the truth, for Bess had certainly learnt a lot since her last trouble over Catherine Grey. If there had been any collusion between the two Countesses, it had been by means of the Duchess of Suffolk as go-between, and she was never questioned. No international conspiracy was found; indeed there was none.

The Earl made a plea to Burghley on Lady Lennox's behalf exonerating her of any charge of dealing with Mary when she was in the area.[15]

But I must be plain with your Lordship. It is not the marriage matter nor the hatred some bear to my Lady Lennox, my wyfe, or to me that makes this great ado and occupies heads with so many devices; it is a greater matter, which I leave to conjecture, not doubting your Lordship's wisdom hath foreseen it.

What was that 'greater matter' Shrewsbury wrote of? It was perhaps the story which was being passed around of the old Countess's plan to have kidnapped the young Scottish King. We shall never know if there ever was such a plan in Lady Lennox's mind when she left London for her trip north in that November. It may have been that the only plan she had was to marry her son Charles Stuart to Elizabeth Cavendish.

Nevertheless, 'greater matter' or not the old Countess had to stand some retribution and was put into the Tower for the third time in her life. From her prison she squawked:

Thrice I have been cast into prison, not for matters of treason, but for love matters. First when Thomas Howard, son to Thomas first Duke of Norfolk, was in love with myself; then for the love of Henry Darnley, my son, to Mary Queen of Scotland; and lastly for the love of Charles, my younger son to Elizabeth Cavendish.

There is no evidence that Bess was put into the Tower. As far as punishment was concerned the Countess of Lennox, since she was a member of the royal family, was considered the perpetrator. Perhaps Bess got off with no more than a dressing down from Queen Elizabeth, though by contemporary accounts this could be terrifying enough.

As if all this were not trouble enough, some of the Earl's servants were arrested on suspicion of carrying messages from Mary.[16] Alexander Hamilton, a tutor to the younger Talbot children, had been conveying letters for the Scots Queen. The suspicion that the Earl was lax in his watch over Mary was an obvious inference for Burghley and the Privy Council to make, and he was ordered to keep a closer charge over his prisoner. When the trouble over Elizabeth Cavendish was at its height, Shrewsbury made a proposal of marriage between his son Edward Talbot and Burghley's daughter, Elizabeth Cecil. The offer was quickly turned down by Burghley and he gave the reason that the Queen was suspicious that the Earl was over friendly with Mary and that he, Burghley, had confirmed this on a recent visit to Buxton. He feared that further suspicions might be aroused by a proposal of marriage between their two families. It must have seemed to poor Shrewsbury that nothing could go right for him. On 10 February 1575, he wrote to Burghley from Sheffield, telling him with some pride that Mary Talbot, Gilbert's wife, had just had a son.[17] In reply he received an immediate complaint from Queen Elizabeth, souring an otherwise happy occasion; strangers were not permitted at Sheffield when Mary was there. With pathos he excused himself, saying that only the midwife came, and he, with two of his children, christened the child. He ended his letter with news of an earthquake: 'My Lord ... the 26 February last there came an earthquake, which so sunk, chiefly her chamber, as I doubted more her falling than her going, she was so afraid. But God be thanked she is forthcoming, and grant it may be a forewarning unto her.' This was a very severe tremor, felt over a large area of the Midlands and western England; books were thrown from library shelves, pots to the ground and people from their beds. It may well have been taken by Shrewsbury as an omen for the Scots Queen but it could also have been interpreted as a warning to the hard-pressed Earl.

'MY JEWEL ARBELLA'

1575-1578

The birth of a child to Elizabeth Lennox was an event waited for with anticipation by Bess and the old Countess Margaret Lennox, but by Queen Elizabeth with a certain sourness. Some time before the winter of that year old Margaret Lennox was released from the Tower with her presumption purged. On 17 November she wrote to the Scots Queen from Hackney, 'I yield your Majesty my most humble thanks for your good rembrance and bounty to our little daughter,'[1] and Elizabeth Lennox, also at Hackney, added a message of affection. The little daughter was Arbella and this is the first mention of the grandchild who was to cause so much trouble and heartache to Bess.

Arbella's grandfather, Mathew Stuart, had been Fourth Earl of Lennox. On his death the earldom would have passed to Lord Darnley, his eldest son and Mary's husband, but Darnley died before his father and the title went to Mary's only son and child by Darnley, James VI of Scotland, and the earldom merged with the Scottish crown. Then in April 1572 James granted the title to his uncle Charles and therefore at her marriage, Elizabeth Cavendish became Countess of Lennox. Later the title became a prize to be fought for by Bess on her daughter's behalf, not for the sake of the title itself but for the lands which went with it.

But the complications caused by Arbella's birth went further than an earldom, for her father Charles Stuart shared with Mary Queen of Scots the same royal grandmother, Margaret Tudor, who was the older sister of Henry VIII; therefore any children of Charles would be considered as heirs to Elizabeth's throne and their claim would be as strong as that of Mary, the Scots Queen. Charles Stuart was a sickly lad and not considered likely to live for many years

– there was no need to consider him in the succession. But his marriage transformed the situation.

The birth of Arbella rather detracted from Elizabeth's unique policy of teasing her Council and Europe as to her intentions over a successor. Had Arbella been a boy then Elizabeth would have had to accept the child as her heir, but a girl was a different matter and meant that the whole question could be shelved. Her sex, whilst mollifying for the two Queens, must have been something of a disappointment for Bess and Margaret Lennox who had hoped for a more definite answer to the succession problem – an answer which would have been to their advantage.

Human relationships are notoriously unpredictable, and Fénélon's comment that Bess would lose her friendship with Mary through her alliance with Margaret Lennox was founded on sound French logic. This, however, was not the way it worked out. For a time Mary was suspicious of Bess, then either Bess's considerable charm, or the fact that this Lennox marriage was not part of some deep international plot, caused the Scots Queen to welcome her once more, although they never again shared their former close relationship. There must have been an injunction placed on Bess by the Privy Council not to see Mary. On 1 May the Earl of Leicester told Shrewsbury that the Queen had relented and was 'well pleased that the Countess of Shrewsbury should have access to Mary Queen of Scots, preferring her to pass the time with Lady Shrewsbury than with meaner persons'.[2] By this time Bess had been forgiven by both Queens. Indeed there was a spirit of forgiveness in the air, for Lady Lennox, during her time in the Tower, made for Mary a little square of braid-stitch, which is listed in the Chartley inventory of Mary's belongings made in 1586. Mary thought sufficient of this small gift to have kept it for eleven years. After her release from the Tower old Lady Lennox began writing to Mary in affectionate terms, signing herself 'Your Majesty's most humble and loving Mother and Aunt. M.L.'

Even though Bess was perhaps disappointed that Arbella was a girl, she had every reason to congratulate herself on pulling off the marriage of her daughter Elizabeth. She had avoided the discomfort of the Tower and this can only have been because of her relationship with Queen Elizabeth. It cannot be called friendship, for that would not have been permitted between Queen and subject, but there was a bond between the two women which had spared Bess the full blast of royal disfavour. Elizabeth understood that Bess was not intending to undermine her authority and could count on her loyalty without question. Elizabeth had said 'there is no Lady in this land that I better love and like'; Bess had counted on this, sailed very close to the wind indeed, and the risk had paid off.

Cut off in Derbyshire, Bess needed all the influential friends at Court that she had. Her half-sister, Elizabeth Leche, had married Anthony Wingfield who was one of the Queen's Gentlemen Ushers with apartments next to the Office of Revels in the old Hospital of St John of Jerusalem; perhaps Bess had got him the position. Her cousin by marriage, Mary Scudamore, was a Gentlewoman of the Queen's Bedchamber, another useful connection for Bess. Lady Cobham, another distant connection of Bess, was also in attendance on the Queen and used by Bess as a line of communication from her Derbyshire wilderness. Her sons Henry, William and Charles Cavendish could keep the Queen's attention on Bess when they were at Court; and by her marriage with Shrewsbury, Bess had increased her circle of relatives with the addition of the Earl's children. Gilbert Talbot, married to Bess's daughter Mary and a close friend of her son Charles, was a supporter of Bess even in the days of the great quarrel with Shrewsbury. Gilbert was often at Court though constantly in and out of favour with the Queen for he was a difficult man inclined to fall out with anyone. One morning, walking in the tiltyard where the annual accession-day jousts were held in November, Gilbert, looking up, saw the Queen at a window still in her night clothes; Gilbert was embarrassed and Elizabeth possibly not at all, although later that day she told the Lord Chamberlain of the incident, adding that she was ashamed.

It was the custom of Elizabeth's Court that gifts were presented to the Queen at New Year. Birthdays were not celebrated and Christmas was solely a religious festival. In 1584 the value of gifts to Elizabeth was over £800 for that New Year; and it was typical of her economy that whilst she was pleased to receive the presents, her own in return were not as costly. Nevertheless, the right choice of gift for the Queen and the value of it, was a reflection of the giver's indebtedness and thanks to his monarch, or his hopes of bounties yet to come. The business of assessing the correct balance between what would be expected and what would be considered suspiciously extravagant was a delicate matter. Particularly so for Bess at New Year 1576 and she relied on the advice of her friends at Court. Anthony Wingfield saw Lady Cobham and Lady Sussex, who putting their heads together and taking hints from the Queen came up with the suggestion that rather than a mundane gold cup or present costing £40 which anyone might have given, a cloak would be far more acceptable. Wingfield went further than that for he suggested something more impressive; a travelling outfit of cloak and safeguard, or outerskirt. The cloak was to be of satin in a peach or watchet colour (light blue) embroidered with flowers and lined with 'sundry colours', made up with gold spangles and silks; 'these fantastical things will be more accepted than a cup or jewel', recommended Wingfield.[3] He was right of course. Queen Elizabeth was fond of dress, particularly of 'fantastical things', for she had to shine above all others in her own Court. Another New Year, 1577 or 1578, Elizabeth Wingfield told Bess that the Queen had never liked a gift so well as that which Bess and Shrewsbury had just given. Again it was fine clothing, and the Queen was reported as saying, 'That good couple show in all things what love they bear me.' Of course the Queen was perfectly correct, there was none more loyal.

Year after year, Bess used the ingenuity of her friends and her own, to contrive pleasing gifts for the Queen. One year it was a kirtle or skirt and a doublet in yellow satin, embroidered all over with short 'staves of purled silver', lined with black sarcenet and a matching passmain. Another year she gave a gown of tawny satin laid with lace of Venice gold and gold buttons. By 1578 the cost of the gifts had risen from £40 to £100 and by 1590 Bess was employing Mr Jones, the Queen's own tailor, to make up the gowns and cloaks. But by 1601 Bess had lost interest in the matter, for all she gave was a purse with £40 of gold pieces in it, needing no great ingenuity as in earlier years. By then her son William had taken a lot of the responsibility on his own shoulders and his own gifts reflect Bess's former generosity.

Although Gilbert Talbot could be counted as an ally of Bess, Shrewsbury's heir Francis was never a supporter of hers, nor was

Henry Talbot, the Earl's youngest son, though neither of them actively opposed her. With the exception of these two sons, Bess managed to keep a good relationship with Shrewsbury's family. His daughter Catherine had married Henry Herbert, Second Earl of Pembroke; Catherine was on particularly close terms with her stepmother and could be counted on to support Bess at Court. That Bess in return was not deaf to appeals from her step-children is shown in a letter she received from Catherine written 23 March 1575. Catherine and her husband Henry were about to visit their Welsh estates and she asked Bess to use her influence to persuade Shrewsbury to let her sister Mary go with her. Although the bearer of the letter was Sir George Saville, Mary's husband, who was happy to let his wife go, Shrewsbury's patriarchal attitude precluded the trip without his approval. This was where Bess came in; neither Mary, her husband nor Catherine were sufficient to push Shrewsbury to say yes and it fell to Bess to provide the persuasion.[4] That summer poor Catherine, who had been ailing for some time, became ill and in July Pembroke took his wife to Spa in Flanders, in a desperate search for a cure for the malaise, the Queen lending them one of her best ships to make the journey to Antwerp. Returning to England, Catherine lingered on for a time; on her death she was buried in Salisbury Cathedral in May 1576.

Only the month before Catherine was buried, Charles Lennox died. His declining health may have been the cause of the reconciliation between Margaret Lennox and Mary, the Scots Queen. Mary and Margaret had a twin purpose to the same end. Mary wished to leave the succession to the Scottish throne in safe hands, and Margaret wanted to ensure that her son Charles Lennox should be included in that succession. Mary, believing that she had the divine right and authority of a reigning Queen, made a will putting Charles Stuart in the succession and admitting the right of Elizabeth Lennox to the earldom. It is not hard to see the influence of Bess behind this move, but Bess was a realist and it is doubtful if she believed that Mary could actually enforce her wishes. Nevertheless the will might come in useful later. After a mere eighteen months of marriage Elizabeth Lennox was left a widow with her only child Arbella, and although legally the earldom of Lennox and the estates in Scotland and England should have belonged to her, the power and authority to bring this about lay with the Queen Elizabeth and the rulers of Scotland.

In June of 1576 Bess made a visit to Court. Her main purpose was to persuade the Queen to press the claim with Scotland for her daughter's earldom. This apparently was the first visit Bess had made to Court since the trouble over the Lennox marriage. If the Queen had felt any dissatisfaction with Bess over the matter then all was forgotten and forgiven, for her reception at Court was warmly gratifying, perhaps because Bess was sponsored and supported by Leicester. Bess made her base at Leicester House in the Strand which had been placed at her disposal and Leicester wrote a reassuring note to Shrewsbury that he had never seen the Queen 'make more of any body than she have done of my Lady'. But it was not a visit from which Bess got any results; her request to move Mary to Buxton for a short visit was not granted; and although Elizabeth wrote to the Scots Regent pressing the claim for the Lennox lands and title it brought no result: Elizabeth's influence in Scotland was as ineffective as Mary's.

The Scottish government and Mary's son James VI argued that when Charles Stuart died the title and lands returned to the Crown of Scotland to be awarded where merited. As Mary had abdicated the Crown to her son James, then the earldom was his to dispose of. That Elizabeth Lennox's claim was supported by the English Queen and the disowned Queen of Scotland only ensured its rejection by the current Regent. To stall further attempts he gave the title to the next heir, the old Bishop of Caithness, childless, unmarried and without heir.

For a time, Arbella was referred to by her mother as 'Comitessa', and the painting of Arbella aged twenty-three months, still at Hardwick Hall, is titled 'Arbella Comitessa Levinae'. This charming portrait was made in the autumn after her father's death and shows a chubby-faced child with blue eyes and a serious expression. The only concession to childhood is the doll she holds, otherwise all emphasis is on the fact that this is the portrait of the Countess of Lennox. Round her neck hangs a gold chain from which depends a miniature countess's coronet. Her clothes, richly embroidered and trimmed with gold and pearls, are fitting for the rank of countess. Poor Arbella Stuart, she lived her life as she started it, under the restrictive disadvantage of her royal blood.

Soon enough, Elizabeth Lennox and Bess had to forget these ideas of grandeur; instead of 'Comitessa' Bess referred to the child as 'my Jewel' or 'my dearest jewel'. And old Margaret Lennox was left to use her influence in the only direction she could. Mary, in a draft will dated February 1577, did what Bess and old Margaret wished: 'I give', she willed, 'to my niece Arbella the earldom of Lennox, held by her late father; and enjoin my son, as my heir and successor, to obey my will in this particular.'[5] But the order was worthless.

The Lennox lands were divided between Scotland and England: Margaret Lennox, who was having a difficult time making ends meet, had been left to support Elizabeth and Charles out of the English estates – by marrying Charles to Elizabeth, she had added to her dependants. For four years immediately after the marriage old Margaret Lennox was paying Bess £500, which is likely to have been the repayment of a loan.[6] But there had been trouble over a dowry for Elizabeth, for since the marriage had taken place without Shrewsbury's prior approval, he did not see why he should provide anything. This provoked a disagreement with Bess who 'by brawling did get three thousand pounds'. But Elizabeth never saw this money, which was handed over to Arbella many years later.

Bess and the Earl continued to lobby the Queen and the Privy Council to press the Scottish Regent to release the Lennox lands in Scotland. They knew perfectly well who would have to support Elizabeth and Arbella if no funds were provided. That summer the Earl of Leicester was at Buxton for his health, conveniently near to Mary's place of imprisonment. Gilbert Talbot acted as host since Shrewsbury was tied down with his prisoner at Sheffield, and used the chance to press the Lennox case, extracting a promise from Leicester to do what he could when he returned to Court. Leicester also accepted an invitation to visit Bess at Chatsworth.

When Bess created Chatsworth she had in mind just such occasions for entertaining visiting statesmen. The house, as far as Bess was concerned, was not completely finished. From early January that year, plasterers and glaziers were at work at what appears to have been completing apartments for Leicester's visit.

Blackstone for overmantels was quarried and Thomas Accres, who was to serve Bess as master mason through the rest of her building operations, including the completion of Hardwick Hall, was working for her for the first time. Sawyers cut timber for wainscoting and doors; wallers and masons completed what seems to have been a courtyard or garden walls. This was not a major building operation but improving or completing what had not previously been finished. Shrewsbury complained that Bess was hindering his own building works by employing so many men. The intensity of the preparations rose to a pitch on 8 June when the construction work was replaced by more domestic laundering from 10 June to 8 July – the likely period for Leicester's visit to Chatsworth.[7]

Robert Dudley, Earl of Leicester, was then in his forties; a fat puffiness of middle age had taken over from his youthful good looks, which had attracted Elizabeth when she first came to the throne. His visit to Buxton was a success; a friend told Bess that he had wished he had stayed three weeks longer, though the rich living gave Leicester a nasty boil on the calf of one leg and he returned from Chatsworth carried on a litter. This was clearly a time when Leicester was in Elizabeth's favour and when the Queen wrote to Shrewsbury thanking him for entertaining her favourite, she composed a skittish letter prescribing a facetious diet for Leicester which could have been taken as a play on Shrewsbury's constant requests for an increase in diet money for Mary. Elizabeth thought better of this teasing note and sent a more prosaic letter instead.[8]

Shrewsbury would not have taken the Queen's jest in good part, for the high cost of keeping Mary, and Elizabeth's meanness in the allowance was a constant headache to him. In September 1575, when Elizabeth proposed reducing the diet money to £30 per week, he protested. He said that he had accepted £52 when Mary came to him, which was less than half what Elizabeth had been paying Knollys: 'I demanded not great allowance nor did stick for anything, as all men used to do.' In her own mind Elizabeth was acting reasonably. After all, she had ordered the household to be reduced from thirty to sixteen and she could argue that the cost of keeping had thereby gone down. To Shrewsbury this was ingratitude and he hinted many times that Elizabeth was asking too much of him and that she had gone too far. These pinpricks from his monarch, the constant strain of watching over Mary, and his troublesome gout combined to make him short-tempered and testy. Shrewsbury deserves sympathy. He had been given a task for which he received no material thanks; in fact it was costing him money, and it was arduous. The fact that he guarded Mary for sixteen years without serious mishap is testimony to his devotion to Elizabeth and to his ability. It had become a costly and a fretting worry that took its toll of his nerves. In July 1575 Gilbert told Bess that his father was 'constantly pestered with his wonted business and is very often in exceeding choler of slight occasion, a great grief to them that loves him to see him hurt himself so much. . . . Truely Madame I rather wish myself a plowman than here to continue.'⁹ In October that same year Gilbert witnessed another outburst when Shrewsbury behaved unreasonably at Sheffield Castle over the cost of new bed linen; the strain of guarding Mary and the expense was on his mind, causing him to quibble over a penny or so on linen costing twelve pence a yard. Gout too was making him irascible, his letters were full of complaints about his 'old friend gout', letters which are all but unreadable. Indeed he knew they were practically illegible: 'Excuse my evil favoured writing to the Queen's Majesty, for by reason of a great ache which had vexed me in the wrist of my right hand a long time, I am able to write no better.' It has been said with truth that the pain Shrewsbury suffered four centuries ago conveys itself very vividly to the twentieth-century reader faced with Earl George's holograph.

These were the nagging discontents which were the root of the trouble between Bess and her husband that summer of 1577. Shrewsbury was unreasonable and Bess replied to his testiness in an unsympathetic manner. In turn the Earl would feel resentment against Bess added to his resentment against the Queen. It is doubtful if Bess had time that year to give as much thought to the Earl and his problems as she should; with Chatsworth to prepare for grand visitors, with the problem over the Lennox title and the ever-present Scots Queen, she had her own worries.

Their differences notwithstanding, the task of keeping Mary still had to be undertaken. Whilst the Earl was complaining to Gilbert about Bess, Mary was diverted by having her portrait painted whilst she was at Sheffield that August.

By the late 1570s Mary's position had become unique: she had no power, she must have realised that her days were numbered and that eventually Elizabeth would solve the intractable problem by having her beheaded. Yet Mary was a dowager Queen of France, ex-Queen of Scotland and the mother of James VI. For a long time she had been worried about the influence of the Regent Morton over her son. Early in the spring of 1578 Morton was deposed in a bloodless revolution and James, although not quite thirteen, was invested with the government of Scotland. From Mary's point of view only good could come from this, but her satisfaction was short-lived, for Morton staged a comeback and Scotland was not freed of his machinations until he was beheaded in 1581.

The sudden death of Margaret, Countess of Lennox, on 9 March 1578 at the critical point of Morton's deposure, and within a few hours of dining with Leicester, deprived Mary of one of her most influential friends. From the enmity of five years earlier had grown a useful intimacy: 'This good lady, thank God was on the very best terms with me, since the last five or six years,' she told the Archbishop of Glasgow.[10] If Mary's judgement of the passage of time is correct then they made up their differences before the marriage of Elizabeth to Charles Stuart, in which case old Lady Lennox had certainly been lying to the Queen when she had said that she would never forget the murder of her son, on being forbidden to go nearer than thirty miles of Mary in 1574. Mary's loss of her powerful and important friend was in some measure counterbalanced by close and unpolitical friendships nearer at hand. Bess's grand-daughter, Elizabeth Pierrepont, had been taken into Mary's retinue in 1571 when she was aged four and Mary had treated the child as if she had been her own daughter. That she was fond of Bessie Pierrepont is certain; a letter addressed to her from Mary in 1583 was endorsed 'To my well-beloved bed-fellow'. And it concerned a black silk dress which Mary was making for her. It may have suited Bess to let her granddaughter be on such intimate terms with Mary; she could keep in touch with her intrigues. It was not without its dangers, for Bessie fell in love with Mary's secretary Nau and wanted to marry him, and in 1581 Elizabeth Pierrepont and her father were under suspicion of being Catholic recusants because of her friendship with the Scots Queen.

By August of 1577 Gilbert was telling his father, when asked why Bess was not at Sheffield, that he thought the Earl preferred her out of the way.[11] His father had been unreasonable again over one of Bess's grooms, Owen, whom the Earl wanted dismissed. Reasonably, Bess said that she would do as he wished if he would tell her why; cavilling in his answer, he would only say that it was for many reasons. Anyone in Shrewsbury's state of mind generates their own problems, which multiply unwittingly. Gilbert, in a long letter to Bess written that fatal summer of 1577, told of a conversation he had had with his father at Bolsover which was continued as they returned to Sheffield on horseback. Shrewsbury had been glad to discuss his disagreements at length. They amounted to trifling matters which had become magnified out of all proportion in his troubled mind. There had been a recent occasion when Bess's embroiderers had been locked out of Sheffield Lodge by the Earl's steward and right-hand man John Dickenson; perhaps an error, certainly a misunderstanding. The Earl grumbled on about her groom Owen, and said some cruel words against the embroiderers; then of Bess, 'I was forced to tell her, she scolded like one that came from the Bank.' There had been a dispute and Bess had taken herself off to Chatsworth. Gilbert told his father that she had gone that morning, and reported the reaction of Shrewsbury word for word to Bess: '"What", quoth he, "is she gone from Sheffield?" I answered, "By nine of the clock". Whereupon he seemed to marvel greatly and said, "Is her malice such she would not tarry one night for my coming?"' and then Shrewsbury became concerned about what his household would think of Bess's sudden departure.

As father and son rode home to Sheffield that summer afternoon, the Earl became more reasonable and Gilbert was able to tell him something of Bess's sentiments. 'My Lord', he said to his father, 'when she told me of this her dear love towards you, and how your Lordship had requited her, she was in such perplexity as I never saw woman.' 'I know', replied the Earl, 'her love hath been great to me: and mine hath been and is as great to her: for what can a man do more for his wife than I have done and daily do for her?' Gilbert, finding his father in a more conciliatory mood continued his advocacy of Bess, which he described to her thus: 'At your departure, I said your Ladyship told me that you verily thought my Lord was gladder of your absence than presence. Wherein I assure your Ladyship he deeply protested the contrary; and said, "Gilbert you know the contrary; and how often I have cursed the building at Chatsworth, for want of her company by her going away."' Gilbert obviously felt that his step-mother should return to Sheffield whilst his father's mood of conciliation lasted, and enticing Bess with his little son George, then aged two-and-a-half, he added, 'George rejoiced so greatly yesterday at my Lady's coming home, as I could not have believed if I had not seen it.' In another letter dated 1 August he added a postscript, 'George is very well I thank God, he drinketh every day to Lady Grandmother, rideth to her often, but yet within the court; and if he have any spice, I tell him Lady Grandmother is come and will see him; which he then will either quickly hide or quickly eat; and then asks where Lady Danmode is.'[12]

Ten days later, little George was dead. Shrewsbury reported his distress to Burghley on 12 August:

> Whereas it pleased God, yesternight, a little before supper, to visit suddenly my dearest jewel under God, next to my soverign, with mortality of sickness, and it has pleased God to take that sweet babe from me – he surely was a favoured child – I thought it rather by myself than by common report you should understand it from me, though it nips me near. .... I doubt not my wife will show more folly than need requires, I pray your lordship write your letter to her which I hope will greatly relieve her.

Bess took the loss of her grandson badly; Shrewsbury telling Walsingham of the sad news wrote,

> ... my wife (although she acknowledges no less) is not so well able to rule her passions, and has driven herself into such a case by her continual weeping as is like to breed in her further inconvenience, and being desirous to prevent the same by my persuasions (she being now at Chatsworth and not able to come hither) I am desirous to go to her for a while.

He asked for permission to join Bess at Chatsworth, taking Mary with him.

The guarding of Mary had become so demanding that Shrewsbury was not able to leave her, even for a few days. There had been another alarm; Mary's name had been connected with Don John of Austria, an illegitimate brother of Philip of Spain. Don John was a spectacular figure with ambitions worthy of the later Napoleon; ambitions which thoroughly worried the Privy Council. He planned to subdue the Spanish Netherlands, then in revolt, invade England, Scotland and Ireland, marry the Queen of Scots and restore the Catholic faith to the islands. He made some headway with his plans in the Netherlands but died in 1578, before he could carry out the rest of his plans. There was never any suggestion that Mary encouraged Don John, but Shrewsbury was ordered to keep a closer guard on his prisoner.

Once more Shrewsbury trundled Mary across Derbyshire for a brief visit to Chatsworth in September. The Earl was prepared to put up with all this disturbance to go to Chatsworth to be with Bess, rather than that Bess should move to Sheffield. The death of George, their grandson had apparently brought them together again.

But Bess and her reconciled husband were not allowed to enjoy their mutual consolation for long. The whole matter of the Lennox inheritance was brought into focus again by the death of the old Countess on 9 March 1578. Anticipating the event, Shrewsbury wrote to Burghley on 4 March, requesting his interest in the wardship of Arbella (Burghley was Master of Wards).[13] This was a prudent move, for had the wardship been granted out of the family, Bess and her daughter Elizabeth would have lost all influence over Arbella and any lands she might have been able to claim. On 17 March Bess thanked the Queen for awarding the custody of the child to 'her poor daughter ... notwithstanding that there were divers means used to influence her highness to the contrary'. Again Bess reminded the Queen of the claim for the Lennox earldom, which with the dowager's death had now become of prime importance. In granting the wardship, the Queen was following her usual policy of seeming to be generous at no cost to herself; there was nothing in it for Elizabeth Lennox or Arbella.

The old Countess was buried at Westminster with the full panoply of a state funeral; Heralds Clarenceux and Garter; the Lord Treasurer and the Earl of Leicester; six banners above the corpse, all preceded by a great banner. Her tomb was elaborate, although now overshadowed by that of her daughter-in-law, Mary Queen of Scots. The Lennox estates in England were claimed by the Scots

Regent, but as he would not give up the Scottish lands, Elizabeth saw no reason for parting with those in England. She replied saying that the cost of the funeral and the payment of debts would not be covered by the value of the English lands, which she then took over herself. For good measure she reminded the Scots that they were holding lands which rightfully should have gone to the young Countess, and that Arbella was the legal heir to the earldom. In that respect Bess could not have asked Elizabeth to put the claim more clearly; and yet whilst she was willing to poke the Lennox claim at the Scots, saying that 'Her majesty finds it very strange that any disposition should be intended of the earldom to any other to the prejudice of the young lady,' Elizabeth found nothing strange in her own intention to deprive that young lady of her English inheritance.

Elizabeth Lennox was left penniless, suggesting again that the Shrewsburys had given no dowry. In her attitude, Queen Elizabeth was displaying some logic, for by withholding the Lennox lands she was forcing Bess and the Earl to provide for Elizabeth Lennox what they should have properly provided as dowry in the first place.

Fate was determined to deprive Arbella of what little she was entitled to. It was as well that she had such a powerful and determined champion as Bess, but even she was partially defeated by the superior forces of the Crowns of England and Scotland. The Lennox jewels had been left to Arbella by the old Countess, and were to be held by Thomas Fowler, the executor of her will, until Arbella became fourteen. In September 1579 Mary, the Scots Queen, issued a warrant ordering Fowler to hand these over to Bess. But Fowler had departed to Scotland with the jewels which eventually found their way to James VI.

By Bess's persuasion, Burghley and Walsingham prevailed on the Queen to provide something for the support of the Lennoxs; the young Countess received a pension of £400 a year and Arbella £200.[14] It says something for Bess's determination that she was able to get anything at all, for although a total of £600 a year was a small sum to support a Countess, to Queen Elizabeth it was a large sum of money.

Pursuing the Lennox claim, Bess made a second visit to the Court in the autumn of 1578.[15] Leaving Derbyshire on 9 October, by the

11th she was at Dunstable where she had three or four hours' rest with her daughter Elizabeth, no doubt discussing their prospects. To avoid the plague the Court had moved to Richmond where Leicester found Bess a very good chamber and a little room in his own lodgings for which she was grateful. By the end of November her business was completed, for she was at Shrewsbury House, and by 24 December she was back at Chatsworth with the three-year-old Arbella before hurrying on to Sheffield. Bess commented that the child had 'endured very well with travel'. As the Queen refused to allow 'strangers' to stay under the same roof as Mary – even obliging Gilbert to move out of his father's house – Bess was forced to make the detour to drop her grand-daughter off at Chatsworth; possibly Elizabeth Lennox had come back also and was dropped off at the same time. Bess may have taken the little Arbella with her to Court, in the hope that the Queen might be influenced by seeing the small child. If this had been the case then the hope was wasted, for Bess was unable to move the Queen further than she had already gone and the claim for the Scottish lands was never likely to succeed.

At this point in her life, Bess had achieved a great deal. She was just turned fifty and still possessed of robust health. Her children were marrying and having families of their own, the dynasty was taking a step forward. It was a time of her life when perhaps Bess might have expected to be able to sit back a little and to let the next generation take over some of the responsibility. This, however, was not to be the case; it would have been impossible for Bess to foresee in 1578 that her greatest struggle was yet to come, when she could lose most of what she had built up, when she would need the virtues of patience and perseverance which she so admired in Penelope and the virtue of liberality in Lucretia. Bess could never have seen that it was Mary who would be the cause of her coming trials and tribulations and that the Scots Queen, who had been her friend in the past, would become her spiteful enemy.

'THE
OLD SONG'
1578-1580

Although by the 1580s Henry Cavendish had been married for over twelve years, he had no heir: for Bess, with her ambition of dynasty, this was a setback. So far she had built on the assumption that Henry and his heirs would continue the Cavendish line and live on at Chatsworth which was entailed to Henry. Faced with this problem, Bess took no chances and somewhere about this time William, her second son, assumed the mantle of inheritance. William was knighted in 1580; in March 1582 he married Anne Keighley – no doubt the usual arranged marriage. Anne was the daughter of Henry Keighley of Keighley in Yorkshire, where William's father had been lord of the manor before 1540.[1] After their marriage William and Anne lived with Bess at Chatsworth. For some time Bess had been exercising some sort of occupancy of Hardwick Hall, her father's old estate: before her marriage to Lennox in 1574, Elizabeth, her daughter, had addressed a letter to Bess at Hardwick; in 1577 Bess thanked Shrewsbury for sending timber to Hardwick though she would have preferred it to be at Chatsworth. On 2 June 1583 Bess bought Hardwick outright in William's name for £9500 with the intention that after her death this should be his estate and home.[2] Bess's brother, James Hardwick, who inherited his father's lands, had died bankrupt in the Fleet Jail some time just before April 1581. His financial crash was another of Bess's worries and one which could so easily have brought disaster to her as well. James Hardwick's career was a mournful contrast to that of his sister.

Her brother's sad and dramatic death must have affected Bess, although she probably expected something of the sort. It is quite remarkable that James, who started his life with so much more material benefit than Bess, with the advantage of the Hardwick estate which he estimated brought in a revenue of £341 in 1570, should have lost everything, whilst Bess, who started with nothing, gained her brother's lands and a great deal more. Later Bess complained that 'the Earl would not give her money to purchase the land of Hardwick her brother deceased'. But indeed the poor Earl was unable to had he wished, for his money was running out.

By the early 1580s George Talbot, Sixth Earl of Shrewsbury, was financially embarrassed. It was assumed that he was the wealthiest nobleman in England and by appearance this may have been the case. But the keeping up of that appearance and behaving as custom and his rank demanded was costing Shrewsbury more than he could afford. The main source of his income was from land, under the able stewardship of William Dickenson, his right-hand man. In the haphazard way of Elizabethan magnates, Shrewsbury was building up the embryo of an industrial empire. His lead-works and iron-hearths were scattered about Derbyshire and Herefordshire, and to carry his heavy products to London and northern European ports he had his own ship called *The Talbot*[3] in which Hawkins had a share. This was not a conscious investment in shipping and export; the sea was simply the only way to carry loads conveniently from Hull, and his ship could return with the spices and wines which his household demanded. With an eye on the profit to be gained from adventurous speculation, *The Talbot* became a privateer and in July 1583 captured a pirate in the Channel. Prior to January 1582 it had voyaged to Newfoundland and Spain; in 1583 there was a proposal to join Carliell's expedition to Newfoundland, and Shrewsbury contributed £100; the expedition fell through but *The Talbot* sailed for Newfoundland nevertheless. A year later Hawkins sent Shrewsbury a bill for £72 – it had been an unsuccessful venture. But the profits of trade and privateering comprised only a very small percentage of Shrewsbury's income and the mining and refining of minerals was only a means of getting an additional quick return from land.

Acting generously, as the honour of his position demanded – and Shrewsbury was very touchy about his honour – he provided estates for his younger sons and dowers for his daughters. Francis Talbot, his heir, was deep in debt and likewise Gilbert found it impossible to live within his means; Bess too was taking sums averaging £2500 each year and Henry Cavendish, his son-in-law was finding his income insufficient. Henry had gone off to the Dutch wars in April 1574[4] with a recommendation from Leicester and '500 tall men', most of them drawn from his own estates. England was fighting Spain's armies in the Netherlands led by Don John. The Spanish Ambassador reported that Henry was a rich young man who knew nothing of war, echoing almost the very words used by Leicester in his recommendation. Henry arrived in the Netherlands with the rank of captain and by July he had been promoted to colonel; he had also arrived with insufficient money and had to borrow. The cost of this expedition and the support of his five hundred men may have been the cause of Henry's debts: In 1582 he had to sell lands at Hardwick-in-Ashby in Nottinghamshire which had come to him from the Talbots when he married Grace and which Bess bought for Charles Cavendish. But in any case Henry was leading an expensive life outside his military adventures. He was returned to Parliament in 1572 and for six consecutive elections up to 1597, sharing the honour with Henry Talbot from 1584 to 1588. By 1584 Henry Cavendish was £3000 in debt, but his borrowing had started at least nine years earlier when he raised a loan of £300 in London. And on top of all this Shrewsbury had the cost of keeping Mary. Shrewsbury's letters in the early 1580s are full of complaints that the Scots Queen's diet money was either not enough or not paid at all. Thomas Baldwin, his London Steward, was asked in February 1581 to enquire the going price of plate as he might have to sell some to pay his creditors. By November he was thinking of selling *The Talbot*, and complaining to Baldwin that Bess was pressing him for money 'the old song'.

Before Shrewsbury had realised that his commitments would outstrip his assets he had involved himself in building Worksop Manor in Sherwood Forest. Bess has sometimes been wrongly credited with the building of Worksop, although she may have been responsible for bringing Robert Smythson, the most ingenious architect of his time, up to the Midlands from Longleat. Shrewsbury's father, the Fifth Earl, had started a house on the site but had died when it had hardly begun. Using what existed of the unfinished work, Shrewsbury built a house which was in every way more magnificent and larger than any other in the Midlands. It boasted the fairest gallery in England, 224 feet long, and what it lacked in the advantage of an elevated site it made up for in its stupendous height. The compulsion for Shrewsbury to build such splendour came from the spectacular progress of Elizabeth through the Midlands in 1575, and the prodigality of the entertainment at Kenilworth which made such an impact on Midlands gentry and notables. This was on Shrewsbury's doorstep and although he was equipped with many castles and manors he lacked a suitable modern mansion to entertain his Queen. The lack was emphasised by the visit of Leicester and Burghley to Chatsworth in June and July 1577, and Bess and the Earl were well aware that Chatsworth was entailed on Henry Cavendish. But the building of Worksop had probably started long before the two statesmen came to Chatsworth – before Shrewsbury realised he was running out of money. In August 1577 Shrewsbury told Burghley, 'I have sent Greves a platte of a front of a lodge I am building, which if it were not for troubling your lordship, I would have your advice thereon';[5] this could have been a reference to Handsworth at Sheffield which he was building, or to Worksop. When the Earl wrote to Bess in October 1580 he scrawled across the cover, 'I pray you send me Accres as soon as you can for I may spare him no longer.' Accres was a mason, skilled at carving architraves and overmantels. He was working at Chatsworth in 1577 and was obviously there again in 1580, but Shrewsbury could spare him no longer for he wanted to finish the interior embellishment of a building – probably Worksop – and he wanted to take the Scots Queen to his new mansion. Mary was at Worksop in June and again in September 1583; by then Shrewsbury had stopped his building for he had not the money to complete it and Elizabeth would never have let Mary go there with workmen about the place. Worksop was not completed until 1585 when the balustrading round the roof was put up and the overmantels in the gallery installed – by then Shrewsbury was rid of Mary and could find the money to finish his house.

Bess must have had a hand in giving Shrewsbury advice and help over the building of Worksop; after all, she had been carrying out work at Chatsworth for years, could lend Shrewsbury her best workmen and tell him where to find the best architect for the 'Platte'. The architect for Worksop was Robert Smythson, who was

later responsible for many houses in the Midlands, including Hardwick. Smythson was working for Thynne in the building of Longleat in the 1570s; and Thynne was an old friend of Bess. He may
have responded to another request from Bess, this time for the loan
of a cunning architect. It would not have deprived him of Smythson's services for he needed only to provide plans, elevations and
major details, leaving Shrewsbury's master mason Giles Greves
with the responsibility of translating the drawings into a building.
Apart from this indirect involvement, Bess would have had no part
in the building of Worksop.

It must have seemed to Shrewsbury that his whole family were
clamouring at him for money to pay their debts, whilst he was
becoming insolvent himself; Shrewsbury's position was unenviable.
His attempts to get the Queen to increase Mary's diet money rather
than reduce it was one way in which he could try to stop the erosion
of his wealth. In 1578 Shrewsbury had tried several times to get
to Court to explain to the Queen personally what his grievance
was, but Elizabeth forestalled this by supplying no relief jailor and
refusing to allow Mary to be left unattended.

To add to his nurtured grievances, Shrewsbury was having difficulty with tenants.[6] There had been serious trouble as early as 1575,
when Gilbert reported that the tenants of the Peak Forest, 'thos
leude fellowes of the Peak', had walked to London to present their
case against the Earl. It is difficult to be certain what their grievance
was about; it may have been compounded of a number of things;
certainly enclosure of traditional grazing on common waste was one.
In May that year Shrewsbury defended himself in a letter to Burghley about 'a great barren ground which has been enclosed and let
out. A complaint has been made to the Queen as though I were
a great wrongdoer.' Shrewsbury's honour had been touched again.
John Kniveton, in a letter to Bess written later, gave the traditional
landowner's view: 'they shall have more commoditie than they had
or could have if the Forrest should lie open to be used by them
as they desired.' In May of 1579 the tenants were marching again,
this time not only from the Peak but from neighbouring Ashford
and Glossopdale, the latter under four ringleaders, one of whom
was named as Otewell Higginbotham. Gilbert Talbot met the party
just beyond Barnet 'but could not reason with them'. Shrewsbury

can only have been upset when Gilbert reported that the Queen was under the impression that he was making £3000 to £40000 a year out of the Peak and Leicester had to intervene to put the Queen right about that rumour.

These tenants were ordinary simple villagers who had held their tenancies-at-will for over sixteen years and who left their farms and holdings to walk to London to present their complaints to their Queen. It took them time and it cost them money. Admittedly these troubles arose in the slack of the rural year between sowing and harvest; nevertheless they must have been provoked by a great feeling of injustice which was directed against the Talbot bailiff, Nicholas Booth, and not against Shrewsbury or Bess. Enclosure was unpopular with Elizabeth and her Privy Council; it caused the sort of peasant unrest of which troublemakers could take such advantage. In the Shrewsburys' case the danger was multiplied by the possibility of Mary's supporters taking advantage of the hiatus. On one reported occasion the frustrated tenants were roaming dangerously round Sheffield. The Queen and Privy Council tended to take the side of the tenants, to bring stability to this area of disorder. The trouble may have stemmed from Shrewsbury's need to increase his income and his bailiff's over-eagerness to screw higher returns, although no unrest was reported from other Talbot estates. The grievances of the Glossopdale tenants were said to be due to a revaluation of their holdings and consequent higher rents; rents indeed so high as to astonish the Privy Council. After making their complaint the party hung about waiting for a verdict, refusing to return to their homes; the four ringleaders in consequence were imprisoned briefly. These simple people, in making their complaint, were risking victimisation by taking on so great a prince, and yet remote as the Queen may have appeared, she was accessible: she heard their cause and relieved their distress against a powerful landlord. Shrewsbury's honour yet again had been impugned. He felt rejected by his sovereign and his wife; life at Sheffield must have become almost intolerable to the Earl.

The situation at Sheffield had become so disquieting to the Privy Council that in November 1581 they sent Robert Beale, the Clerk of the Council, who was also brother-in-law to Walsingham, to make a full report. There were rumours at Court of the disagreement between Bess and the Earl; Mary had taken a nasty fall from her horse in August 1580 when leaving Sheffield for Buxton – she had fallen heavily on some steps and injured her back and was full of complaints about her health. Beale's main purpose was to question Mary on the correspondence she had been exchanging with the King of France about acceding her royal title to her son James. Mary had written to Elizabeth and explained that she had been ill almost constantly for the last three years and felt that she would not live out the winter; it was time she did something for her son.

Beale arrived at Sheffield on 11 November and saw Mary the next day; his visit lasted three weeks and during that time had many interviews with the Scots Queen which got him nowhere. Mary was setting the scene and playing the part. The most bizarre exchange which Beale had with Mary took place on 23 November when, as he entered her chamber, the candles were suddenly blown out. Beale had to carry on his conversation in total darkness. Mary, surrounded by her weeping women, told him in a strange faint voice that she was dying. Beale was nonplussed but Bess not at all: she had known her far worse and said so. In her opinion Mary was only putting it on. Always a good judge of character Bess was probably correct. The gloomy conversations with Mary were accompanied by depressing talks with Shrewsbury, who was suffering a bad attack of gout which gave force to his complaints about Mary's diet money. He explained that he was paying out £700 to £800 annually in serv-ants wages to look after Mary, and that he was expected to provide pensions when they left his service which would cost his estate £300 a year.[7] His sons Gilbert and Francis had to be maintained in separ-ate establishments as the Queen would not let them share the same roof with Mary. Finally 'he always spent £1000 over the shoulder' even before the allowance was reduced. In return all Shrewsbury requested was the lease of a fee-farm worth £200 a year – 'He desired this only for the preservation of his honour, which he esteemeth above all things'. Shrewsbury once more displayed his wounded honour which troubled him more than gout. Beale could make little of his visit and wrote many pages of reports which brought no relief to Shrewsbury, but Mary was allowed a coach and six horses to ride in Sheffield Park.

Beale left Sheffield early in December, leaving behind a depressed

household. The gloom was further increased by the death of
Elizabeth Lennox on 21 January 1582. Elizabeth had made her will
five days earlier when she was already 'sick in body'.[8] Hopefully she
left the lands, which the Queen had given her, to Arbella, and to
strengthen the hope she left 'her best jewel set with great diamonds'
to the Queen. She asked the Earl of Leicester, Sir Christopher Hatton, Burghley and Walsingham to continue their good will to her
'smale orphant'. And she thanked Shrewsbury for being a generous
father to both her and Arbella, reminding the child to repay the
kindness later, leaving him her little gold salt. To Bess she left her
white sables, and sadly to her brothers and sisters gifts for the following New Year which she would never live to see. Concluding
with gifts to her servants she committed Arbella to Bess, leaving
the rest of her money to her daughter to be held by Bess until Arbella
became sixteen in 1591. She signed the will with a shaky hand and
five days later died. No doubt Bess was responsible for the main
terms of the will, but the repayment to Arbella of her mother's
money is interesting; Arbella did not get this until she was eighteen-
and-a-half and it totalled £3360. The money was what could be
called Elizabeth's dowry, which she probably never received, for
Shrewsbury had fallen out with Bess over this. Elizabeth Lennox
was interred in the Talbot vault at Saints Peter and Paul, the parish
church of Sheffield – one of four of Bess's decendants permitted
to lie there, the others being George Pierrepont her grandson in
1573, Charles Cavendish son of Sir Charles in 1594 and finally
Mary, her daughter, in 1632.

Shrewsbury wrote to Walsingham the evening of Elizabeth's
death, 'The poor mother taketh her daughter's death so grievously
and so mourneth and lamenteth that she cannot think of aught but
tears.'[9] But the household was not so far upset as to let him forget
to ask Walsingham to remind the Queen that Arbella was now altogether destitute. This appeal was followed by another letter to Walsingham from Bess seven days later on the same subject and another
to the Queen from William Cavendish; the pension of £400 awarded
to Elizabeth Lennox ended at her death and Bess wanted this for
Arbella. To say that the seven-year-old child was destitute was an
exaggeration, for she had £200 already, paid each year by the Queen.
Bess had another go on 6 May; she wrote two letters that day on

the same topic, one to Burghley reminding him bluntly and tactlessly that Arbella was related to the Queen and entitled to financial support, the other to Walsingham pointing out that Arbella was a nice child and deserved the Queen's bounty. None of these supplications brought any result.

It is significant that Bess was addressing her appeals to Walsingham and Burghley and not, as she would have done a year or two earlier, to Leicester. Leicester's marriage to Lettice Knollys had been inevitably revealed to Elizabeth in the late summer of 1579. and their son Robert was born in 1580. Leicester had fallen from favour and there was nothing to be gained for the Shrewsburys from that quarter.

Shrewsbury was by this time a sick man and unable to act reasonably, a fact probably recognised by the Queen and her Privy Council. And whilst his marriage was disintegrating under his unwitting impulse generated by the 1572 deed of gift, at the same time he was grappling with the problem of financing Mary's costly keeping, and fretting about expenditure, his family's debts and the Queen's ingratitude. He suffered yet another setback in the summer of 1582. Plague was raging in London and – cruel fate – it caused the death of his eldest son Francis Talbot. He died leaving no heirs and a great many debts. Shrewsbury, with his usual misunderstanding of Bess, claimed that her alienation started from Francis's death; he imagined that Bess made Francis her enemy because he stood between Gilbert and her daughter Mary; once Francis was dead, he reasoned, Bess had no further use for him, for her grandchildren would be Earls of Shrewsbury. Misunderstanding and misunderstood, Shrewsbury must have felt as if the whole world was ranged against him, and yet his troubles were almost entirely of his own making.

A burden not of his own making, however, had been added to his duty as Lord Lieutenant responsible for law and order. Philip of Spain and the Pope had increased their pressure on England, not only by the war in the Netherlands but by Jesuit infiltration. Whilst many Catholics welcomed these missionaries there were more who, although sympathetic, felt that such action would be counted treason and in this they were right. Shrewsbury had the unenviable duty of searching out the Jesuit priests and their hosts and handing his prisoners over to justice. Father Edward Campion, one of the first of these invaders, was welcomed to Derbyshire by one of the Pierrepont family; one of the Foljambes was put under house arrest; the Fitzherberts at Norbury in Derbyshire were adamant Papists and Sir Thomas spent the last thirty years of his life imprisoned rather than recant; the Babingtons of Dethick, also in Derbyshire, were too closely involved for their own safety. These were all Derbyshire worthies and friends of Shrewsbury; the Foljambes and the Pierreponts were related by marriage to Bess. Yet it was part of Shrewsbury's unpleasant duty to his Queen to hound and imprison these recusants, an unsavoury duty he cannot have relished.

In contrast to Shrewsbury's financial decline, Bess was obviously prospering, which caused the Earl a great deal of chagrin. He had no doubt from where her prosperity came – her 'old song', as he termed it, was where he laid the blame. Bess's extravagance, to his way of thinking, was the cause. After Bess had regained control of her lands in 1572, she embarked on a policy of purchasing blocks of land, mainly in Derbyshire, to provide suitable patrimonies for William and Charles, which Shrewsbury had been unwilling to provide under the terms of their marriage settlement. So that she could keep control of her lands and at the same time to prevent Shrewsbury claiming back all, the purchases were made in the names of nominees, William or Charles and sometimes other members of her family; in all the transactions she retained a life interest. By 1584 she was said to have bought lands for William at a cost of £15,900, whilst Charles was apportioned only £8800-worth: a total of £24,700 invested in land over a period of twelve years, bringing in an income of £1500.[10] It is impossible to arrive at completely accurate figures, for the Earl exaggerated her investment and Bess tended to minimise it; the figures given are those which Burghley accepted. The income which Bess received from her original estates had risen by 1584 to a total of about £2500 annually. Where then did Bess acquire the capital to make all these purchases between 1572 and 1584? Admittedly Bess was a brilliant manager, but the figures involved are so enormous that something more than brilliance must have been employed. In the later dispute, when Shrewsbury alternated bellows of accusation against Bess with laments that she had taken his money, it becomes impossible to know when he was telling the truth. However, it can be said with certainty that Bess did get a great deal of money off Shrewsbury over those twelve years, though probably no more than should have been her due under the marriage settlement had Shrewsbury not altered the terms.

Burghley's later notes hint that the 'great sums of money' which the Earl was let off paying to William and Charles by the 1572 deed amounted to £20,000 each. Therefore by acting as she did Bess might have claimed that she was only taking her due. Shrewsbury did not realise, until it was too late, what Bess's dynastic ambitions were about; what she was unable to get under the terms of the settlement she would get in her own way. Had Shrewsbury not altered the terms of the settlement he would have had Bess as a dependable ally; instead he found her ranged against him and she was formidable. As Shrewsbury said, 'they have sought for themselves and never for me', and he could not understand why.

Bess showed wisdom in not relying on Henry and his wife Grace to maintain the honour of her dynasty, for they failed Bess in this; they had no children. Henry, however, had a host of bastards and he was remembered over a hundred years after his death as 'the common bull of Derbyshire and Staffordshire'. To have won such a reputation his performance must have been remarkable.[11]

By this time, Bess had written Henry off as a waste of her money, and her ambitions were fully transferred to her second son William. She gave him an allowance by passing on the income of the Western Lands in 1584 which exceeded £700;[12] sales of wool in about 1580 brought in £100 and went straight to William. Bigger sums of money paid to him in this period, sums such as £1000 and £750 sent by the Mansfield carrier, were to be used for buying land. The money paid to William in Bess's rough accounts for 1579 to 1584 is considerable but does not indicate more than that William was acting for his mother and taking over some of the responsibility of running the business as far as she allowed him to. On frequent visits to London he was taking and returning with bags of money, used for unspecified purposes, except that it can be certain that Bess was making sure that Shrewsbury could not get his hands on it. By then William had become responsible for the annual problem of the

Sir William Cavendish, c. 1540, who died in 1557, Bess's second husband and the father of her children.

Sir William St Loe, Bess's third husband who died in 1565.

Sir William St Loe in his ceremonial armour which he had made at the Royal Armoury, Greenwich, 1560.

George Talbot, 6th Earl of Shrewsbury and Bess's fourth husband, who died in 1590. The portrait is dated 1580, when he would have been fifty-three.

Hardwick Hall (east front) in 1781, from a watercolour by S. H. Grimm.

The front entrance and porter's lodge at Hardwick Hall.

ABOVE Chatsworth about
1680, after a third floor had
been added. This illustration
is a detail of a late
seventeenth-century painting
by R. Wilson.

LEFT Embroidery at Oxburgh
Hall. The knotted serpents
are taken from Gesner's
Icones Animalium, the
inspiration for the Cavendish
knotted serpent emblem. The
work is likely to have been
done by Bess herself.

LEFT Mary Queen of Scots. This is the so-called 'Sheffield' portrait at Hardwick Hall and is certainly a posthumous painting of her.

RIGHT Arbella Stuart, Bess's granddaughter, painted by the unidentified 'C.V.M.'. The portrait was painted in 1589, when Arbella was thirteen-and-a-half years old.

South Wingfield Manor. One of Mary Queen of Scots' prisons and a property belonging to Shrewsbury. The illustration is from a watercolour by S. H. Grimm.

Earl of Devonshire 1576. Æ. SVÆ. 2

Queen Elizabeth.

TOP LEFT Henry Cavendish, Bess's eldest son, who married Grace Talbot.

TOP RIGHT William Cavendish, 1st Earl of Devonshire, Bess's second son, in 1576 when he was twenty-two. This portrait is possibly by Cornelius Ketel.

RIGHT Mary Talbot, (although entitled Queen Elizabeth) wife of the 7th Earl of Shrewsbury, and Bess's youngest daughter. By the dress, this portrait was painted around 1600, when she would have been about forty five.

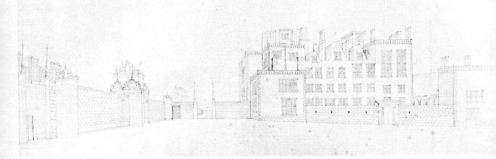

TOP Owlcotes House, identified from a survey map of 1688.

MIDDLE Old Hardwick Hall: a seventeenth-century drawing from a scrapbook at Audley End.

RIGHT The High Great Chamber at Hardwick Hall, from *Vitruvius Britannicus*, 1835.

LEFT The Long Gallery at Hardwick, where Sir Edward Bronker interviewed Arbella over her secret marriage plans with Edward Seymour.

BELOW The last flight of ceremonial stairway at Hardwick Hall, leading up to the State Apartments.

RIGHT Bess of
Hardwick: a portrait
probably painted around
1590, after the death of
her fourth and last
husband. The portrait is
thought to be a copy of
a vanished original by
Rowland Lockey.

BELOW Bess's effigy,
approved by herself,
from her tomb in Derby
Cathedral.

Queen's New Year gift – paid for by the Earl – responsible of course to Bess and not left to his own initiative. His wife Anne, on her visits to London, made the journey loaded with bags of coin for William to use on his mother's behalf. Although William was obviously enjoying prosperity from Bess's bounty and was now married, he still had no establishment of his own; apart from needing accommodation in London, which he probably rented, he and Anne lived with Bess, which must have been a constraining influence for them both. It was perhaps Bess's intention that they should live on at Hardwick and she at Chatsworth, but Shrewsbury was to drive Bess out of Chatsworth, and until Bess built Owlcotes in the 1590s William and Anne had no permanent home and he must have been at the beck and call of his mother in all things.

Charles Cavendish, on the other hand, had his own home at Stoke Manor just four miles north of Chatsworth, perhaps too close for Charles's taste.[13] Stoke had been one of Bess's earlier purchases in 1573 and although the estate remained in his possession it was not where Charles preferred to live given other alternatives. In 1581 Charles married Margaret, the daughter of Sir Thomas Kitson of Hengrave in Suffolk. There had been a previous attempt to marry him off to Lord Paget's niece, which had come to nothing when Shrewsbury refused to provide £1000 for the betrothal. Shrewsbury had not been let off scot-free, for Bess asked for a settlement of £5000 when Charles and Margaret married, but the Earl only managed £1500. Their only son William, later Duke of Newcastle, was born in 1582. The same year Charles was knighted and by July Margaret was dead. Of all Bess's sons Charles was the most attractive and yet he is the one about whom we know the least. Where William had a justified reputation for meanness, Charles was generous; where Henry ran up huge debts, Charles never seriously overspent and as far as can be known he was never unfaithful to either his first wife or his second, Catherine Ogle. He was a firm and lifelong friend of his brother-in-law, Gilbert Talbot, who, when in financial trouble, sold Welbeck Abbey and Bolsover to him. The friendship with Gilbert landed him in quarrels and in one instance he was seriously wounded in the thigh; Charles was said to be 'always at his elbow'. He had a great appreciation of music and was patron of the madrigalist George Wilbye, who dedicated a book of airs to him; his skill and taste in architecture is demonstrated by the little gothic castle at Bolsover which he started building in 1612 but never saw finished (he died in 1617). Dependable, trustworthy, sincere, one would like to know more of him.

In the gathering Shrewsbury dispute, Gilbert took Bess's side against his father and this may have been because of Charles's influence. William of course was tied to his mother in all things, whilst Henry, out of favour, used random opportunities to snipe back at his mother. Once Bess had made up her mind on a course of action there was no stopping her, but it was Shrewsbury who unwittingly began the trouble. Many times he must have marvelled at what a hornets' nest he had stirred up. Honest, jealous of his honour, devoted to his Queen, perhaps not over bright, his only weapons were rage and choler. He never was a match for Bess.

8

'NO GOOD AGREEMENT'

1580-1584

Reports of the rumbling discontents of Shrewsbury and his Countess had reached Court by the Spring of 1579. In a letter to his father dated 15 May, Gilbert Talbot passed on a hint which had been dropped by Leicester 'that there was no good agreement betwixt my Lord and my Lady'.[1] Leicester then explained that the Queen was likely to be disturbed about Mary remaining with the Earl if there was any suggestion of friction in the household. Here was a royal rebuke for Shrewsbury; for the sake of his honour he could not allow Mary to be taken from him.

By the time the hint was dropped the differences had been buried for the moment. Possibly the Queen had heard stories about the flare-up at Sheffield in June 1577 which both Shrewsbury and Bess forgot in their common grief over the death of their grandson, little George Talbot. By June 1580, Shrewsbury's letters show an affection contradicting any reported discontent: 'My own Swete hart,' he wrote, and signed himself 'yr fethul husband.G.shrewsbury'. He then added a postscript concerning Marmyon, a gentleman servant in Bess's establishment. In the disaccord between master and mistress it had become impossible to avoid taking sides and in doing so Marmyon had become the target of Shrewsbury's displeasure. Feeling that his position had become too precarious, Marmyon wrote to Sir Francis Willoughby asking to be taken into his household: 'Methinkes Wollaton Howse should not be without a Marmyon.' Unfortunately this is another letter giving only the day of the month, 28 October, and no year; however Marmyon got his job with Sir Francis, for the building accounts for the new Wollaton Hall show Mr Marmyon receiving £40 for his master's use in September 1584. Marmyon's letter was written between 1580 and 1584, the most likely year being 1582, for the Shrewsburys had parted by June 1583. This is the nearest date which can be achieved for the description of the tumult within the walls of Sheffield Castle which Marmyon gave in his letter to Sir Francis: 'I am sorry with all my heart to see my Lady in such danger and that she taketh my departure in so ill sort. That house is a hell and her lady-ship being furnished with few, or rather not one about her which faithfully love and honour in deed, the sequel is in doubt to breed afterclaps and she suspects no less.'

Another brief glimpse of the strife is given in a letter written by Frances Battell, one of Bess's gentlewomen, and sent to Lady Pau-let, the wife of the Marquess of Winchester. It is dated 23 March 1584 at Chatsworth, some nine months after the Earl had parted from Bess. Frances had been victimised by Shrewsbury who 'gives out hard speeches of her to her great discredit if it should be believed by her friends. . . . The cause of her lord's hard dealing with her is that the Scottish Queen cannot abide her. For how can she abide her when she is with all hatred bent against her mistress [Bess].' This letter was passed to Burghley and is endorsed in his hand 'xj Aprill 1584'; why and how it reached him is interesting speculation for there is in it a paragraph in which Frances reports Bess's answer to the question of what would happen if the 'Scottish Queen should be Queen of England'. None save Bess dared answer this one and she replied 'that it war better that the Scotyshe Queene were hanged befor that tyme shoulde com to pas' – a good patriotic reply and one which Bess's friends wanted Burghley to know about, for another endorsement on the letter shows that it came to Burghley by one of 'Mistress Wynckfield men xjth daye of Apryll' (Mrs Wingfield was Bess's half sister Elizabeth). Frances ended her letter saying, '. . . but if my lord continues his hard speech of her . . . she cannot abide it any longer'; this refers to his persecution of one of Bess's gentlewomen – how much worse the situation must have been for Bess. Also it is significant that it shows the Earl being influenced by Mary's attitude to Bess.

Bess and Shrewsbury were still able to make up their differences for the sake of a united appeal to authority.[2] Bess's nephew John Wingfield had married the Countess of Kent without the Queen's permission; his bride was Susan Bertie, the widow of Renald Grey,

Earl of Kent, and the marriage has the aspect of being managed by Bess, the inveterate matchmaker for all her family. On 6 February 1583 Shrewsbury wrote to Walsingham from Sheffield asking him to appease the Queen's displeasure in the matter of this marriage, and the following day Bess wrote a similar appeal from Sheffield: this is their last recorded date of living under the same roof. Their parting, if the account is true, shows something of Shrewsbury's peculiar state of mind. In May or June of 1583 Bess left Sheffield for Chatsworth on some matter, as she so often had done in the past. Shrewsbury showed 'not the leaste myslyke' at the parting, ' but with manie faire wordes and promyses assured her that he wolde in a few daies sende for her againe.' Despite her many appeals, Shrewsbury never did send for her again; furthermore he stopped paying her allowance of £800 per year from that moment. A curious farewell, and it was not an account he ever denied as untrue.

With Bess out of his way, Shrewsbury engaged in recruiting support for himself amongst his own family, which had been weakened by Gilbert's defection to Bess.[3] His two younger sons, Henry and Edward Talbot had been sent to France with Thomas Baldwin in 1582 after they had completed a year at Oxford. Shrewsbury wrote to Baldwin on 2 July 1583, giving instructions that as the two boys had returned from France they were to be sent to Sheffield and that 'when they come they are to be stout with his Countess'. They arrived at Sheffield bringing with them a letter from Leicester telling Shrewsbury pointedly to make up his differences with Bess: 'she ys your wife and a verrye wyse gentlewoman'. That month Shrewsbury wrote to Baldwin again telling him that the dispute was to be settled by arbitration. Shrewsbury's only ally was Henry Cavendish, his son-in-law, who sided against his mother out of spite. The Earl was almost completely isolated and it must have been tempting to discuss his problems with Mary, who in her increasingly desperate situation would have been happy to fish in these very troubled waters.

Shrewsbury had become unreasonable in his attitude towards Bess; his persecution of her following their parting was no more nor less than a mania. However it is important to try to understand his point of view, no matter how unreasonable it might be. The whole dispute turned on Shrewsbury's interpretation of the 1572 deed of gift; a clause stated that Bess could not sell land without his agreement and he claimed that Bess had done just that – an accusation which she denied – thus breaking the clause. Shrewsbury reasoned that the deed had become void. Believing this to be the case, it was perfectly logical of Shrewsbury to take the rents and revenues from Bess's lands on the principle that they had now reverted to him. As far as Bess was concerned it was difficult to prevent this diversion of her rents and the position of her tenants became difficult, for not knowing who would triumph, they risked further troubles by denying rents to one side or the other.

Understandably the greatest resistance came from the old St Loe estates, which owed no allegiance to Shrewsbury. A warrant dated 26 July 1584 instructed an unnamed bailiff to ensure that the tenants of the late Sir William St Loe in Somerset and elsewhere paid their rents to the Earl and not to the Countess at 'their utter most perrill'.[4] This was intimidating and it was from the western lands that the greatest resistance against Shrewsbury came, as he later realised. It was a perilous position for any tenants unlucky enough to be trapped in the dispute and the greatest peril raged round Chatsworth where Bess had taken her household.

At Ashford, on Chatsworth's doorstep, Charles Cavendish had been attacked by a party of the Earl's servants led by Nicholas Booth and had been compelled to take refuge in the church and 'forced to take to the Steeple', where he hid for an uncomfortable twenty-four hours. Charles suffered another inconvenience when the walls round his pastures at Stoke were demolished and even some of his servants were wounded. In the park at Chatsworth an innocent servant of Bess was set on by the same Booth and others, receiving two wounds to his head. Richard Stubbs, another of Bess's servants was peacefully carrying out his duties for his mistress and had settled down in his room for supper at an inn in Uttoxeter, when he had 'his chamber door broken open upon him', but this time the troublemakers were shut in the Town Hall for the night by the constable. Tenants had their beasts impounded by the Earl's servants because they had already paid their rents to Bess and were not paying twice over. The countryside round Chatsworth, by the end of 1584, had become uninhabitable for supporters of Bess – thanks to Booth who, it was said 'rideth upp and downe the countrey with half a Score men in a lyverie . . . havinge dagges gonnes and apointed in warlike sorte'. At Chatsworth windows were broken and the iron bars guarding them reported torn out. No one who supported Bess was safe; the situation of her tenants had become intolerable.

In July 1584 Shrewsbury rode over to Chatsworth from Sheffield to assert his ownership. He took with him forty mounted men and demanded entrance, which naturally William Cavendish refused, ' with halberd in hand and pistol under his girdle'. From Shrewsbury's point of view William had committed an offence. Not only had the situation become unbearable for the tenants, it had become intolerable for Bess as well; she left Chatsworth for Hardwick Hall. On 26 July Shrewsbury wrote to Walsingham complaining that Bess had carried off furniture and goods from Chatsworth to William's house at Hardwick. To the offence of armed resistance had been added that of robbery; the Earl complained to the Privy Council. In August the local justices were ordered to find out what had been removed and to take bonds of William Cavendish to appear before the Council to explain his action in refusing Shrewsbury entrance to Chatsworth. For this 'insolent behaviour' William was sent to the Fleet Jail, where his uncle James Hardwick had died only a year or two earlier.

Certainly it was dangerous to be a tenant at Chatsworth that year, but there is nothing to suggest that Bess or her sons were in any physical danger, and Henry's involvement was notably lacking. Mary Talbot was at Chatsworth in late June and was pregnant at the time; she would hardly have been staying with Bess had there been any physical danger. The Earl's harassment was confined mainly to servants and tenants, and was caused by the Earl's bailiff Nicholas Booth. As early as 1579, this man had shown his enmity towards the Cavendish brothers when he reported them as being responsible for stirring up trouble amongst the Glossopdale peasants – a story utterly unlikely at a time when Bess was as concerned as Shrewsbury that the tenants should be peaceful.

In going from Chatsworth to Hardwick Hall, the only house available to her free from the Earl's influence, Bess must have moved into comparative squalor. There is no record of any work being carried out before her arrival there in 1584. The house was a substantial building, comprising a large hall, the usual offices, and it probably boasted a gallery forty-five feet long – likely enough one of James Hardwick's extravagances. Nevertheless it fell far short of what Bess had been accustomed to at Chatsworth. The rank of a Countess required a large number of attendants; more than James Hardwick's house would have provided for. The earliest reference to building work at Hardwick is in July 1587, when Bess had been there three years and had already started building an east wing to the house, an extension so haphazard as to suggest that it was a hurried piece of planning with little thought.[5] In that summer of 1584, when Bess was forced to move there, she must have been living in some discomfort.

There is nothing to show that Bess took any active part in retaliation against her husband. Her letters written during this troubled period, and reports of her conversation, all show her distress and wish to return to Shrewsbury as a dutiful wife. Shrewsbury on the other hand used every means to keep Bess away from him. On the Queen's instructions, Leicester had acted as mediator between them when he visited Buxton in June 1584[6] as the Earl's guest; he called in at Chatsworth briefly on his way back to the Court at Richmond. In a letter to Shrewsbury dated 26 June he tried to get him to see reason.

I found my Lady in very great grief ... and turning all the blame from herself, charged divers with evill offices done betwixt you. ... She protested all innocency towards your Lordship and craving nothing but to be charged with some particularities, which she never yet could be. Thereupon I was so bold to tell her the same things which I heard of; that she should overshoot herself as well in unmeet speeches as otherwise among other things. I said it was reported she should threaten your Lordship that she could harm you if she listed, which I did marvel at that so wise a woman could do to her husband. To this she answered very calmly, 'I think there is no man able to say it of me neither had I any thought to deal with him in that way,' sayeth she, 'both myself and my children are made now to be the chief instruments of ill service towards the Queen's majesty and in all matters cast upon them, which I hope will not be proved. As for my lord husband, God forbid I should use any such speeches against him and so deemeth therein to me to be free from any such intention.'

In this reported conversation with Leicester, Bess has been given the Earl's comments and she was the injured party. She felt that Shrewsbury had been unreasonable towards her; he had accused her of misdeeds not stating what these were. Again these are the actions of a man under stress; Bess is willing to return to Shrewsbury and he will not have her back. In the same letter, Leicester mentioned that he met Gilbert Talbot in the gallery and was taken to a bedchamber where Gilbert's wife Mary was resting. Gilbert had been forbidden by his father to visit Chatsworth, another unreasonable action even though Mary was there expecting a child. Gilbert explained this to Leicester, who tactfully pointed out to Shrewsbury that Gilbert's visit was only a short one to see Mary and that he joined Leicester to return to Richmond that night.

Shrewsbury's reply to Leicester's reasonable letter thanked him for reporting his wife's 'undutiful proceedings, being very glad you have found her shameless answers what I most truely told you thereof and looked no other'. Indeed the Earl looked for no other and could not see what was under his nose, for her replies were the opposite of shameless and her conduct completely dutiful.

Whether or not they realised it, the Queen, Leicester, Bess and Gilbert, were dealing with a sick man; in September the year before, Gilbert had noted of his father that he had a 'swellinge wch he sayde he thoughte none but himselfe did know'. Shrewsbury had been pushed too far in the service of his Queen and his actions had become inexplicably unreasonable to those attempting to deal with him. Impatient, irascible, unreasoning, racked with gout so acute that often he was unable to stand up, and a sick man, the Earl was past fifty and tired of the stresses of guarding Mary. He only wanted to be left alone in peace and that was impossible. It is likely that Bess realised all this, for her constant request was for Shrewsbury to allow her to return.

Mary, the Scots Queen, no doubt also desiring nothing more than peace, was drawn into the vortex. In the winter of 1583 and the spring of the year following, Mary involved herself in the possibility of marrying Philip of Spain. Her negotiations were of course secret, or supposedly so, but in fact very little of what went on was hidden from Walsingham who maintained his own network of spies and informers. It is not known if Philip took the proposal seriously but

if he did not, then Mary did; by April 1584 her emissary was at
Bordeaux travelling on this very matter.[7] There was a simple way
to stop Mary's chances of marrying anyone by compromising her
reputation, and the only prominent figure who could be associated
with Mary in such a rumour was of course Shrewsbury, for no one
else had access to the captive Queen. Where the rumour came from
will never be known; it may have been Walsingham. But whoever
started it, the story went round that Mary had been having an affair
with Shrewsbury and that there had been a child; one rumour said
two children. Knowing the Earl's state of health and also that of
Mary, the story becomes ridiculous, but those points were not
known to the multitude who picked it up and improved it. The
rumour got back to Mary in February 1583 by way of the French
Ambassador De Mauvissière and in reply she complained to him
that the calumnies were to prevent her marriage with Philip and
that they were generated by William and Charles Cavendish. She
was careful then not to implicate Bess as she could easily have done.
The rumours were common talk in inns throughout London; they
could have been started by anyone. It was impossible to know who
was responsible and Mary, locked away in Derbyshire, was the last
person likely to have been able to name the author.

Baldwin, the Earl's London steward and Copley, one of his bailiffs, tried to deal with the lies in a court action before the Recorder
of London. In September 1584 Walmsley, the landlord of an inn
at Islington, had been telling his guests at table 'that the Erle of
Shrowsbury had gotten the Scottish Quene with child, and that he
knew where the child was christened'. Meredith Hammer, the vicar
of Islington, was another witness 'who had delt as lewdlie towardes
my Lord in speeches'. But this interlude which injured Shrewsbury
in his tender honour, and which upset Mary, was only a small part
woven into a larger canvas of intrigues, plots and counter-plots,
which are impossible to disentangle at this distance of four hundred
years.

In November of 1583 the Catholic threat of invasion by Philip
was brought into sharp silhouette by the discovery of plottings to
depose Elizabeth and invade England; plots which culminated in
the final tragedy to Mary; and the Babington Plot. The first of these
conspiracies to be uncovered was the Throckmorton Plot, which

in November brought the arrest of Francis Throckmorton on suspicion of carrying letters for Mary in connection with an invasion by
Philip of Spain. It was all perfectly treasonable stuff and Throckmorton was beheaded. Mary's own plottings were so shot through
with informers that she must have wondered who her friends really
were. Of one thing she could be certain, that Charles and William
Cavendish, as firm Protestants, were not numbered amongst her
supporters; naming them as the source of the rumour did her no
harm and of course it would irritate Bess.

At this distance of time it is possible to see the rumpus of Shrewsbury's supposed intimacy with Mary in its correct perspective. It
was a minor move of little importance carried out on a tapestry of
major intrigues and plots. Shrewsbury over-reacted and likewise
Mary, but one can understand their feelings of outrage; the Earl's
cries and shouts of offended honour have echoed down to us. But
the reason for this sub-plot in major plottings has not been echoed
so clearly. Shrewsbury naturally accused Bess of the slander, as one
would expect, though there is nothing to show that she was involved.
To have been writing to Shrewsbury, to the Queen and to Walsingham, asking to be restored to her husband's side and at the same
time defaming him with false slanders would have been self-defeat-
ing and two-faced. This was not one of Bess's faults. It would have
been completely out of character for Bess to involve herself in
two-faced subterfuge.

Shrewsbury was indeed behaving irrationally. He was engaged
in taking away Bess's revenues claiming them as his own and at the
same time he cut off her allowance of £800: what did he expect
his wife to live on? He never gave an explanation. For Bess the situation had become almost insupportable; there is one letter which
demonstrates her feelings dramatically and it is one of the very few
which give away her emotions – she was not a woman able to pour
out her feelings in letters as was Arbella, her grand-daughter. Bess
wrote to Walsingham in April 1584[8] when she must have been at
Chatsworth. It is a strange appeal from a hard-pressed woman. She
asked that her sons should have permission to seek their livings in
some other place and that care should be taken of their deer, saying
at the same time that the unfolding of her strange miseries would
but trouble him. 'For herself she hopes to find some friend for meat

and drink and so to end her life.' Not the sort of letter one would expect to read from a woman pursuing a personal vendetta of hatred against her husband, as she has been portrayed, but rather from one who is perplexed by the unreasonable attitude of Shrewsbury.

In the strife which led up to the parting, and eventual breakdown, of the Shrewsburys' marriage, the Earl accused Bess of many faults and in August 1584 he told Leicester that he detested her. Nevertheless we can take his word for it that in an argument Bess would give more than she received. In 1577, on that ride back from Bolsover with Gilbert, Shrewsbury had said that 'she scolded like one that came from the Bank'. This was said when he was in a more reasonable state of mind and it can be taken as true. Later when his mind was clouded with venom he said of her that she 'called him knave, foole and beast, to his face and hathe mocked & mowed at him with words and gestures' which could only come 'from a heart replenished with deadly malice and hatred'. This latter taunt was not the truth for there is no evidence to show that Bess bore Shrewsbury any malice. Time after time Bess said that her only wish was to be reunited with Shrewsbury and that she would do nothing 'but it shall be for your honour and good'. Her only rebuke was in recalling an occasion when 'she had been separated before the servants openly made an exclaimation of her to her own face, coming from the Chapel'. Harsh, uncompromising words fell all around and Bess, provoked by Shrewsbury's unreason, would have answered sharply: in this she was no different from the Queen whose language, when she was roused, could equal that of anyone.

After Bess had been abandoned by Shrewsbury and not invited back again, he referred to her as his wicked and malicious wife who was a woman of base parentage and that she had used slanderous speeches and sinister practices to dishonour him. Of his marriage he said no curse or plague on earth could be more grievous and that he was ashamed of his choice of such a creature. But these were the rantings of a confused mind and he produced no evidence to support his wild accusations; his former love and adoration, even admiration, had turned to bile and choler, perhaps caused by the venomous tongue of his captive Queen. William Overton, Bishop of Coventry and Lichfield, wrote to Shrewsbury in October 1590, only a few weeks before the Earl died; the Bishop was even then trying to bring about a reconciliation between man and wife. He summed up Shrewsbury's pig-headedness by saying with truth 'if shrewdness and sharpness may be just cause for separation I think that few men in England would keep their wives for long, for it is common jest yet true in some sense, that there is one shrew in all the world and every man hath her'. Overton was a man who married twice and was respected for his extravagant hospitality and the good repair in which he kept his episcopal house at Eccleshall. (In fact the expense of his living caused Overton to borrow from Bess in the 1590s.)

In all this complicated strife, Arbella was caught up; indeed she may have been the cause of the Scots Queen's new hatred of Bess. It was possible that Arbella could succeed to the throne after Elizabeth and there was Mary, another Queen, a captive under her grandmother's care; the danger of being a Queen at all might have occurred to the child. To keep her grand-daughter as free as possible from the effects of the turmoil Bess let her stay with Mary Talbot where at least Arbella would have the companionship of the small Talbot grandchildren: Mary born in 1580 to whom the Scots Queen was godmother, Elizabeth born 1582, and the baby John born in 1583 but who had died before the end of that year. There had been a proposal, by the Earl of Lennox, that Arbella should be betrothed to Esmé Stuart. A marriage between them would have settled Arbella's claim to the throne, but Esmé who had fallen foul of the complicated politics of Scotland, had fled the country and died in 1583.

A more serious piece of matchmaking for Arbella on Bess's part was with Leicester's 'Noble Impe', his son Robert by Lettice Knollys.[9] A move which, had the Queen heard even a hint, would have brought trouble to the ambitious Leicester. In March 1583 Lord Paget told the Earl of Northumberland, 'The Queen should be informed of the practice between Leicester and the Countess for the Lady Arbella.' The news had even come to Mary's ears by March the following year, no doubt by way of Mauvissière who lost no chance to pass to Mary what she least wanted to know; for in a letter to him dated 21 March 1584, she asked him to pass the news to the Queen saying 'that nothing has ever alienated the Countess from me more than the vain hope she has conceived of setting the

Crown on her grand-daughter Arbella's head, even by marrying her to the Earl of Leicester's son, divers tokens have been exchanged between the children ... and their portraits have been exchanged.' Mauvissière received many instructions from Mary for messages to be passed on to Elizabeth, but as he was the Ambassador of France and not Mary's, he chose not to involve his country in Mary's profitless intrigues. However, all the hopes of Bess and Leicester ended when Robert died on 19 July 1584 and was buried in the Beauchamp Chapel of St Mary, Warwick.

After the death of Leicester's son Robert, Shrewsbury must have written a letter of condolence which has been lost; Leicester's answer has not, but it is unfortunately undated.[10] Obviously upset and at the same time touched by Shrewsbury's thoughts, he still had time to discuss the Earl's problems and attempted to calm down his indignation and chagrin. William Cavendish, he said, had been no more than foolish to take anything from Chatsworth; children often are, he suggested. But what seemed worse to Leicester, having just lost his own son, was Shrewsbury's grudge against Gilbert; Shrewsbury was lucky indeed to have a son at all and should make up his disagreement. The Earl could not leave his problems alone and even that letter from Leicester was answered by another in which he called Bess and Mary 'nethar barrell bettar hering of them bothe', adding for good measure, 'I doo deteste her mother.' Even in his polite letters of commiseration his paranoia would not let him leave Bess alone.

Mary began to add her venom to the attack on Bess, because as she had said in that letter to her false friend Mauvissière on 21 March, she had been alienated by Bess's hope of the Crown for Arbella. Mary had become extraordinarily bitter. Bess, who had the gift of inspiring great loyalty in friendship, had the contrary gift of inspiring great hatred in her enemies. In that same letter Mary hammered away with acrimony and all for Mauvissière to pass on to the Queen.

Had I been her own Queen she could not have done more. ... I had the certain promise of the Countess, that if at any time my life was in danger or if I were removed from here, she would provide the means of my escape and she herself would easily avoid danger and punishment in so doing. She made her son Charles Cavendish, swear before me that he would live in London, particularly to be of service to me in passing on all that happened at Court and that he would keep two strong geldings ready especially to carry speedy news of the death of the Queen who was ill at the time. ...

Mary went on with more treasonable revelations against Bess. Obviously one must look behind this letter for Mary's motives.

First reports of the rumour of the intimacy between the Scots Queen and Shrewsbury were sent to Mary, predictably by Mauvissière, who was involved with intrigues on behalf of his master, the King of France – they were using Mary for their own ends. Mary wrote to Mauvissière on 2 January 1584 asking him to deny the rumours as strongly as possible.[11] Three days later, on 5 January, she sent another letter secretly to Mauvissière – and a copy went straight to Walsingham for Mauvissière's secretary, Cherelles, was in Walsingham's pay. In this secret letter Mary reveals herself as the inventor of the later rumour crediting Bess with spreading the Mary/Shrewsbury scandal, 'You will have somewhat understood by my aforesaid letters, *my intention of involving indirectly the Countess of Shrewsbury.*' Whilst Mauvissière was unwilling to follow most of Mary's requests, there were some he acted on when it suited his purpose and it suited him to add Bess's name to the scandal story. Mary continued her interesting revelations in the letter: 'For I have already in writing such acts and practices of her and hers to reveal, in which the Earl of Leicester and others of his faction are deeply involved, that if the Queen of England once has knowledge of them, I do not think she can ever tolerate them. ...' Mary, although a close captive, was storing up a venomous bomb to use against Bess.

The 'acts and practices' of which Mary wrote were contained in a letter which has come to be called the 'scandal letter'. It was addressed to the Queen and undated; it had nothing to do with the Mary/Shrewsbury scandal, but concerned the Queen and Bess. A lot of time has been wasted on speculating as to when it could have been sent; it is likely that it never was. By the contents it has been dated May 1584, but this is obviously wrong for Mary said in the secret letter dated 5 January that she had already put the revelations 'in writing'; in any case since the letter was possibly never sent the dating has little significance. It has been suggested that this letter was intercepted by Burghley and never given to the Queen because the contents were too indelicate, but this is nonsense. Burghley was anxious to be rid of Mary and if the letter had come into his hands in Mary's lifetime he would certainly have passed this compromising evidence to Elizabeth, who would not have believed the venom and it would have strengthened Burghley's hand in dealing with Mary. It is far more likely that the letter was written shortly before 5 January 1584 and kept by Mary and that it was found amongst her possessions when she was beheaded in 1587 and thus came into Burghley's hands – he did nothing with it because Mary was by then dead. What Mary had to say may have seemed indelicate to Victorian historians but in Elizabeth's time it would have been no more unseemly than today. Mary was displaying Bess as disloyal to Elizabeth and she would not have been believed, but there is a touch of truth in some of what she wrote and it must have been based on Court gossip passed on to Mary by Bess.

In the letter, Mary quoted Bess as telling her that Elizabeth had made Leicester a promise of marriage in front of one of her ladies-in-waiting and that 'she had slept with him an infinite number of times with all the familiarity and licence as between man and wife', but, Mary continued Bess's supposed conversation with the Queen, 'you are not like other women and it was stupid of everyone to have negotiated your proposed marriage with the Duke of Anjou, for had the marriage gone through you would never have given up your freedom to take new lovers as you pleased and you were not able to satisfy yourself with Mr Hatton and another man.' Mary showed Bess as portraying the Queen as a raging nymphomaniac; then she went on to reveal Bess as telling her that Elizabeth not only took a foreigner, Simier, as a lover, but gave him state secrets. Simier was the Frenchman who came as envoy for the Duke of Anjou; even the Duke was brought into the account. Having taken Simier as a lover, Elizabeth then let his 'master, who you found at your chamber door one night when you were in your night clothes ... enter your chamber where he stayed nearly three hours'. Bess advised Mary to let her son James become Elizabeth's lover; it would be to her advantage, and here she reported Bess as laughing loudly at this. Shooting her poisoned arrows with every sentence, Mary ranged on to the Queen, 'You took too much pleasure in exaggerated flattery, such as that none dared to look you full in the face because it shone like the sun and when on her last visit to Court, she and the late Countess of Lennox dare not look at each other when addressing you, for fear of bursting into roars of laughter. ...' Bess, she added, had said that 'she would never return to Court to attend you, for anything in the world, because she was afraid of you when you were in a rage, such as when you broke her cousin Scudamore's finger, pretending to all the Court that it was caused by a fallen chandelier. ...' Bringing a touch of reality, Mary recalled that when Bess was negotiating the marriage of Charles Cavendish to Lord Paget's niece, Elizabeth had stopped the match because she wanted Paget's niece for one of the Knollys boys, claiming him to be a relative. Bess, said Mary, had protested violently about this and accused Elizabeth of carrying off all the heiresses in England. These stories which Mary told were too fantastic to be believed and it was just as well for Mary that she never used the letter.

In the writing of the 'revelations', Mary was showing just how desperate her situation had become. She knew that as long as she lived, she would be regarded as a threat to Elizabeth and in the end it would be her survival or Elizabeth's. If Philip invaded England successfully and Elizabeth was as a consequence deposed, then Mary would rule in her place. By supporting Philip in his plans, Mary was indulging in treason against Elizabeth; if she was discovered her days would be over – she would lose her head. When Mary wrote the 'scandal letter' she was using her venom against Bess, but greater dangers overtook Mary and her hatred of the Countess became of little significance in her desperate struggle for survival.

Mary was allowed to visit Buxton some time in July, a treat she always enjoyed; it was to be her last. With a presentiment of her fate, she scratched a Latin verse on the window glass of her bed-chamber at the Hall: 'Buxton whose fame the milk-warm waters tell, Whom I perhaps shall see no more, farewell.'[12]

By now the Privy Council had decided to remove Mary from Shrewsbury's keeping. This presented some difficulty, for Shrewsbury was a member of the Council, although unable to attend, and they hesitated for fear of offending him; the request must come from the Earl himself. It must have been obvious to the Queen and her councillors that Mary was using the dissension between the Shrewsburys for her own ends. Mary had asked for an enquiry into the rumours of the Mary/Shrewsbury affair and it was difficult to refuse when Shrewsbury was making the same request. In thanking Elizabeth for giving her permission, Mary threw another name into the pot; Topcliffe, she said, was involved in spreading the rumours as well as the Cavendish boys.[13] The fogs and mists of history swirl round Bess's part in all this intrigue; occasionally they clear and give a glimpse of just how difficult it had become for her. This Topcliffe was one of Bess's supporters and a firm Protestant, therefore a target for Mary's slander; seemingly too he had an enemy in Shrewsbury, for one of the Earl's servants, George Bentall, was involved in an affray with Topcliffe near Temple Bar in January 1585.

In July, before the rumpus at Chatsworth, Shrewsbury had applied for the Queen's permission to visit Court; he had the problem of his marriage to discuss and to ask to be relieved of Mary's keeping. It was no easy matter to leave Sheffield, it was not something to be done on the spur of the moment for a relief jailor had to be found first. Sir Ralph Sadler, Chancellor of the Duchy of Lancaster and a specialist in Scottish affairs, arrived at Sheffield on 25 August to take over the charge of guarding Mary. Shrewsbury stayed just long enough to remove the prisoner to Wingfield, which she had last visited in 1569, then he was on his way to the Court at Oatlands by the seventh of that month.

Bess also had good reasons to be at Court and in London that summer, and she had no duties to delay her. The enquiry into the Mary/Shrewsbury rumour was about to be held and it is likely that she had been summoned to attend; also her son William was in the Fleet Jail following the Council's verdict after the Chatsworth fracas in July.[14] Bess got to London and the Court before Shrewsbury. On 25 August, she wrote a short letter to the Earl from her lodgings in Chancery Lane – conveniently near the Fleet Jail. It was another appeal to be allowed to return. 'My Lord, how I have tended your happiness ... my life would have been adventured for you ... notwithstanding what I have suffered ... hatred must grow of something and how I have deserved your indignation is invisible to me. ... I trust you will quieten my heart, receiving me into your favour, for only you can do it. ...' – Bess levelled no accusations or blame at her husband. By the time Shrewsbury arrived at the Court at Oatlands in September he found Bess had already been well received and he must have written this admission with some chagrin to his brother-in-law John Manners on 24 September: 'I have been well received by the Queen and Council.' He wrote, 'My wife has come to Court and finds great friends. I try all I can to be rid of this troublesome burden.' That was his only known reaction to Bess's affecting letter.

In agreeing to hold the enquiry, Elizabeth was in something of a quandary, but this was nothing new – she usually found an ingenious way round such perplexities. The Council must have been aware that neither Bess nor her sons were responsible for spreading the rumours; Walsingham had Mary's letter where she stated her intention of implicating Bess; but to stop the Scots Queen obtaining any more advantage out of the story something had to be seen to be done. It would have been unfair to ask Bess to admit to what she was not responsible for, and a way was found round the dilemma which was more or less satisfactory to all parties.

It has been wondered why the Council should have occupied themselves with so small a matter when on the larger scale there was a very real danger of invasion and the future of England was at risk. But the Mary/Shrewsbury affair was bound up in the whole Catholic threat and the result of the enquiry was discussed as far away as Italy. Let it be remembered that Bess was Elizabeth's very loyal supporter and could be counted on to do what was required. Shrewsbury's honour and his wild unpredictable reactions made his co-operation impossible. Bess was the only person able to get the Council out of their predicament.

In December of that year Bess, with her two sons Charles and William, went on their knees before the Lords of the Council to declare of the rumour 'that it was a false and malicious invention', furthermore they denied on oath that they had ever said it and a written declaration was signed stating 'that the Queen of Scotland had never, to their knowledge, born any child or children since she had been in England.'[15] All utterly true and certainly not a confession of guilt. Mauvissière, naturally, was a witness and reported the event to Mary, who had to be satisfied, likewise the Earl who probably was not, for he denied the scandal at length on the epitaph of his tomb in Sheffield Cathedral.

Mary, locked away at Sheffield with Sadler, was still dropping hints of the 'revelations' she could make if she wished. On 20 October Sadler wrote to Walsingham, 'She sayeth she can and will charge the said Countess withall, which she will first disclose unto her Majesty only.' But time was running out for Mary and she knew it. Every move she made was blocked by Walsingham or Burghley. One of her secretaries, Gilbert Curl, had made an association with Shrewsbury's London steward, Thomas Baldwin, which was very foolish on Baldwin's part, for on 20 September Curl sent him a semi-coded letter. The principal names were substituted by trading merchants and the whole had the appearance of being to and from merchants: Mary was 'the merchant of Newcastle'; Elizabeth 'the merchant of London'; Shrewsbury 'the 'merchant's factor', whilst Bess, appropriately enough, was 'the pedlar'. The meaning of the note was a request to Baldwin to find out where the 'merchant of Newcastle' was to be sent next, a simple enough enquiry and one which perhaps could have been sent openly. However, the letter was intercepted and in Walsingham's hands almost as soon as despatched; cunningly Walsingham watched and waited for Baldwin to compromise himself, then struck and Baldwin was in the Tower almost before he knew what had happened. In January the following year Shrewsbury wrote to Walsingham asking for Baldwin's release but the Earl's steward fades from the scene and was being sued for £100 by Gilbert Talbot in 1597.

Baldwin was just one example of many, for Shrewsbury's household was riddled with informers for both sides – his earlier strict caution had lapsed after Bess was banned from his house. It was now time he was rid of the burden of Mary and for her part she would never find a fairer nor more concerned jailor; it had been a difficult task for Shrewsbury and had cost him more than the Queen deserved to expect. He had done his best.

Shrewsbury's break with Mary was not to be clean-cut for there was the problem of finding someone to take over the thankless task of looking after her. Although Elizabeth accepted Shrewsbury's resignation, Mary continued to board out in his mansions. In November Sadler was told by the Queen that he was officially taking over from Shrewsbury who was giving up the duty due to 'his decayed health and weak state of body', and that he was to take the Scots Queen to Tutbury. 'The merchant of Newcastle' was bound on a voyage to Tutbury and so moving out of the life of 'the pedlar' for ever.

The last four years had been the most trying of Bess's life but although now in her late fifties she was bearing the strain remarkably well. Notwithstanding all her efforts, her marriage with Shrewsbury had broken down with his health. Mary, who had been Bess's friend, had used Shrewsbury utterly to her own ends and had influenced him even to alienating the Earl from his Countess; but Bess had not been completely friendless for she had had and still enjoyed the support of the Queen and her Privy Council. She could console herself with the thought that she had done everything in her power to prevent her marriage disintegrating and she would continue to ask for a reconciliation.

As Mary moved out of Bess's life, so the 'revelations' she had threatened became less significant. The Council had counteracted the venomous attacks and rendered Mary harmless for the moment; but the Scots Queen's poison had already done its work on Shrewsbury in stiffening his resolve to be rid of Bess. The final break-up of their marriage was caused by the great Catholic menace, of which Bess was as much a victim as Baldwin in the Tower.

THE FALL
OF THE LEAF
1584-1590

By 1584 the Earl was possessed with a blind obsession that Bess was a problem and so must be removed from his life. However, he had not reckoned on the close association between Bess and Queen Elizabeth. The Queen never approved of disharmonies in marriages and Bess certainly never wished to be parted from her husband. If the Earl had been capable of giving rational thought to his troubles he would have realised that he could not win his case.

Bess, too, regarded Shrewsbury as something of a problem but she possessed infinitely more patience than her husband. During her visit to Court in the summer of 1584, she must have discussed the matter with the Queen, so that when Shrewsbury was received at Oatlands on 18 September, a decision had already been reached by Elizabeth and her advisors that an end would have to be made to Shrewsbury's unreasonable animosity. The dispute had already caused enough disturbance to those running the nation's affairs – the matter would best be settled by appointing a powerful commission of enquiry. It is likely that Shrewsbury welcomed the enquiry when he heard of it, for so far had his power of reasoning deserted him that he supposed he would be vindicated. He should have taken a hint from Leicester who, acting as the Queen's spokesman, wrote in August: 'God forbid, for it is heavy in the sight of God to seek separation between man and wife. God hath joined them together and without good cause, no man can separate them.'[1] But Shrewsbury was incapable of seeing the warning.

The commission of enquiry was composed of the Lord Chancellor and two chief justices. Walsingham wrote to Shrewsbury advising him of the first meeting of the commission to be held on 23 December; both sides were instructed to appoint council and submit their evidence. The latter instruction to the Earl hardly seemed necessary, for he had been bombarding the Queen, the Lord Treasurer and Walsingham with letters purporting to demonstrate Bess's perfidy ever since the idea of the commission had been put to him.

Both sides based their case on the 1572 deed of gift. Shrewsbury's attempt to discredit the document was patently weak; he shifted his ground from his first allegation that it was a forgery, to an even more preposterous suggestion that he thought when he signed it that the deed was for the benefit of Bess alone and not William and Charles Cavendish, forgetting for the moment the cash settlement he had got out of paying to the two boys by his making of the deed of gift. Shrewsbury's wild charges and weak case were obviously disbelieved by the commission. His estimate of the total sum of money spent by Bess on purchasing land in the twelve years since the date of the deed was a wild exaggeration. Furthermore he claimed that Bess had pestered him for money whenever he was sick and the lands bought with this money extracted over his sick-bed should rightly be his. Bess on the other hand showed that the purchases had been made by William and Charles with their own money and that they were still in debt as a result; she claimed that the total sum was not nearly as high as that put forward by her husband. Somewhere between the two points of view lay the truth and Bess's case was more believable than Shrewsbury's.

Whilst the commission was digesting the conflicting evidence, Shrewsbury made his way to London to be on hand when what he believed would be a victory for him was to be declared. He was at his Chelsea house in March and April 1585; it made a convenient base to lobby those at Court whom be believed to be his friends, but who must have found his obsessive vituperation of Bess a tedious distraction. A letter to the Queen raked up all his old complaints, told her that he was unable to attend Court due to colic and the stone, then asked leave to return to the country. Bess was tactfully out of it all, living quietly in Derbyshire, patient and persevering.

Shrewsbury was summoned to the Court at Oatlands on 24 April to hear the result of the commission's enquiry from Walsingham. His temper would not have been improved by what he heard, which amounted to a complete vindication of Bess; Shrewsbury was to cease his quarrel with Bess and to take her back into his house; William and Charles were to keep all the lands purchased within the last twelve years and Shrewsbury was to hand back £2000 from rents he had seized; Bess was to keep all the lands made over to her by the 1572 deed of gift; and Shrewsbury was to drop all legal suits against the Cavendishes and Bess's servants. For the sake of his honour, Bess was to pay Shrewsbury £500 a year. But it was a severe reprimand for him.

The verdict clearly shook the Earl; a week later he meekly wrote to Leicester from Chelsea confirming that he would abide by the Queen's decision but had hoped for a better reward for his sixteen years of service and devotion. He felt bitter, but worst of all his honour had been wounded again – he had become his wife's pensioner.

Three months later Leicester remembered to write to Bess telling her of the verdict. In July he wrote again telling Bess that the Queen had not forgotten her promise of leases of lands in the Peak Forest – obviously offered in compensation – but that he would have preferred that these had gone to Shrewsbury and she to keep her £500 per annum – a far better solution which would have salved Shrewsbury's honour, but not one the Queen preferred. By then the Earl had decided that Leicester and Walsingham had favoured Bess against him and that the result of the enquiry was unjust and he went back on his promise to do as the Queen commanded; he was exhibiting his accustomed unreasonable behaviour. He kept none of the terms of the Queen's order; the £2000 was not paid over; he did not take Bess back into his house, notwithstanding her several requests; he did not let Bess or her two sons enjoy their lands in peace and continued to displace their tenants; neither did he drop any of his legal suits against the Cavendishes or their servants. Shrewsbury ignored the Queen's order completely; it was just as though the commission of enquiry had never taken place.

By the autumn of 1585, Bess and the Cavendishes were telling Walsingham that Shrewsbury was continuing his harassment. The letter which went to the Earl as a consequence brought a reply containing almost no sense at all and a great deal of abuse of Bess, and a similar reply went to the Queen which could not have pleased her majesty. On the same day, 23 October, Shrewsbury also wrote to Bess and this letter must qualify as one of the most vituperative ever written by a husband to his wife, every line was vitriol: 'The faults and offences which you have commited against me which no good wife would do, are admonitions sufficient for all men to be advised within their marriage.... Your fair words ... though they appear beautiful yet they are mixed with a hidden poison.'[2] In the reading of the letter Bess must have wondered if Shrewsbury had not gone completely out of his mind. The only verdict must be that the Earl was suffering a mental breakdown and that he was a very sick man. A conclusion which the Queen, Leicester and Walsingham had obviously reached.

Irrational though Shrewsbury was, he showed great ingenuity in his excuses to the Queen as to why her command was not being obeyed. Having been ordered to cease all his legal suits, he persisted in continuing one against Henry Beresford, arguing that his charge against the man of 'Scandalis Magnatum', was outside the controversy and was too serious a cause to be dropped.

The truth of the matter was that Shrewsbury, unable to take any revenge on Bess, chose this way to embarrass his wife. In taking rents from the disputed lands the Earl had met a certain amount of resistance from the old St Loe estates in Gloucestershire and Somerset, where the tenants were, naturally enough, confused. A letter to Shrewsbury from a tenant of these distant estates written in March 1585, tactfully understood that there was 'some brake' between the Earl and his Countess; there was also a dispute about to whom the rents should be paid.[3] Leases at Chew in Somerset had been granted to Henry Beresford and Peter Bisse; Beresford was a firm supporter of Bess, but Bisse had fallen three years behind in the payment of his rents, owing Bess about £250. It is understandable that Bisse should have supported the Earl particularly as Shrewsbury was prepared to overlook the debt; in return Bisse heard Beresford say that he knew that the Earl had raised twenty thousand men in revolt against the Queen. Furthermore, said Bisse, this had been said on the hallowed ground of Tormarton churchyard about Michaelmas 1584. It was an easy way for Bisse to settle his debt and it cost Shrewsbury nothing.

The whole story was of course a pack of lies. Anyone with the

wealth and power of Shrewsbury could buy witnesses to say whatever was required. Another witness was found to support Bisse's
evidence and the innocent Beresford was caught up in the Earl's
dispute with Bess. Shrewsbury's claim that the case was nothing
to do with his quarrel and that he was suing Beresford for damages
for having spread a great scandal of an army raised against the
Queen, was not believed by the Privy Council, and Bess and her
sons pressed the Court for the case to be dropped.

After what must have been for Beresford an agonising period of
two years, his case was heard at York assizes in March 1586 before
Mr Justice Clench. The members of the jury had been picked by
the Sheriff, who was related to Shrewsbury, every member was
bribed by the Earl and by the time Bess's legal adviser got to York
he found every attorney had been engaged by Shrewsbury and none
was able to act for Beresford. Beresford was found guilty and
ordered to pay Shrewsbury £1000 damages.

The verdict presented the Queen and her Privy Council with a
problem, for they were aware that the case had been trumped up,
and since the charge had only been indirectly aimed at Bess they
had not been prepared to upset the Earl by preventing the hearing
or reversing the verdict. Justice Clench submitted a report of the
case on the orders of Sir Christopher Hatton, but his remembrance
of the event only three months earlier was vague. However, the
Master of the Rolls made a stay of execution in collecting the
damages and none were paid. Old Beresford, for his devotion,
became a favoured gentleman servant of Bess, favours which descended to his son Richard. This case gives a fine picture of where
the influence of Shrewsbury and Bess lay when it came to a fight.
Shrewsbury could command complete territorial allegiance in
Yorkshire away from Somerset or Derbyshire where Bess's strength
was; but Bess could countermand the result by her influence at
Court. It had been a power-game played out by the Earl with no
consideration for the puppets involved. It was a lesson Bess never
forgot, and it must have required a great deal of trust in Bess on
Beresford's part to believe that all would end well.

Shrewsbury's flagrant disregard of the Queen's command resulting from the first commission of enquiry, posed problems for her
advisers. Anyone less exalted would have been sent to the Tower

until he came to his senses, but this was no way to treat the Earl Marshal of England. As the Earl's harassments continued, so Bess pressed Walsingham for something to be done; her position was no better than before the enquiry. By the end of November 1585 the decision had been made that Bess's allegations should be investigated, this time before Walsingham and Burghley. Commissions were sent out to Sir Francis Willoughby of Wollaton in Nottinghamshire and John Manners of Haddon in Derbyshire, to take proof of the allegations from both sides.[4] The choice was fair; Willoughby was a supporter of Bess and Manners was brother-in-law to Shrewsbury. The allegations were heard at Ashford in Derbyshire on 12 January the following year; William and Charles Cavendish gave evidence for their mother and Shrewsbury appeared in person to support his case. The whole business was gone through all over again and most of the same evidence re-used – nothing was really any different. The result of the commission's work was sent up to Walsingham and Burghley. Before publishing their verdict and to see if the Ashford commission had frightened Shrewsbury into obedience, Walsingham asked Charles Cavendish for a true account of Shrewsbury's conduct. Charles's answer, dated 25 March 1586, showed that nothing had changed; Shrewsbury was still obstinately refusing to do what had been commanded. On 8 May the Queen made an order at Greenwich before Walsingham and Burghley which effectively commanded Shrewsbury to do that which he should have done by the order of the Queen's first commission. An exception was made in that he was permitted to sue William Cavendish for the return of the hangings and plate which Shrewsbury said had been taken from Chatsworth.

This time the Queen's order brought a partial result, for although Bess reported in May that the harassments continued, she stated that £850 of the £2000 had been paid to William and Charles; otherwise Shrewsbury had shown no obedience to the Queen's order.[5] On 9 June Bess wrote another letter to her husband, humbly asking to be taken back as his wife. By the twelfth of that same month the Earl was at Chelsea and attending Privy Council meetings. He was in a peculiar mood and he accused Walsingham of favouring Bess and then asked him to have his wife banished from the Court. The Earl regarded the result of all the enquiries and commissions as unjust and openly accused Bess of influencing the Queen, Burghley and Walsingham against him. Shrewsbury continued his stay in London and attended Privy Council meetings until early October. Gilbert Talbot was also in town but carefully avoiding his father.

It was one thing for the commission to reach a decision and the Queen to make orders, but it was quite another to bring the obstinate Shrewsbury to Bess's welcoming side. During the months the Earl was in London, following the latest order, great pressure was brought on him to conform in his marriage. The result of this persuasion was waited for by many with curious speculation. Shrewsbury's recriminations against Bess had been so violent and vitriolic and his vow never to have Bess under his roof again so firm, as to involve his honour. Roger Manners, an Esquire of the Body, in a letter to his father, the Earl of Rutland, on 8 July, reflects some of the Court interest in the battle of wills being fought out. Manners added a postscript to his letter giving the latest news in this interesting debate: 'The warres contynue betwixt the Erl of Shrewsberie and the Contes. The Contes is humble in speach and stowte in actions, wherby she giveth the Erl greater advantage than her wise frends wolde wishe.' But only the day before Shrewsbury had written to the Queen complaining of his treatment at Court and the 'cunning devices of his malicious enemy', his wife. During the days which followed, Shrewsbury must have been given a great deal of advice by the Queen and her Council. Bess held all the trump cards. She actually wanted to return to her husband and in all this the Queen and her advisers were behind Bess; no wonder Shrewsbury complained of his treatment at Court.

Ten days after Roger Manners had written to his father, another letter was sent by Thomas Scriven giving Rutland more up-to-date news:

It is given out that her Majestie hath reconciled the great Erle and his wief, which was solempnely don in her Highnes prescence when the Lord Treasurer used som large speach in comendacon of the most gracious and christian acte. And so we nowe say, the Erle and she loveingly together will shortely into the countrey and make it appeare to the world that all unkindnesses arre appeased. Thus may your Lordship see that things desperate arre often times recovered, and no man's hart so strong which a woman cannot make wofte. It cannot but be a presage to a generall peace thoroughout Christendom.

It looked as though the Earl had capitulated at last – the main cause being that he was bound by the enormous sum of £40,000 to end all discord with Bess – even his honour had a price.[6] On 20 July, Roger Manners told his brother John, 'The peace betwixt your great Earle and his wife is made by her Majestie as greatly to the honour to the Contes as may be.' Manners was giving credit to Bess who had been incredibly forbearing. But more was to be needed of her, and the Queen for that matter, for the obstinate Earl was more intractable than they suspected. Manners continued his account 'and if it be not to his honour and liking, there is none to blame but himself'. Not only was Shrewsbury bound over to keep the peace but every item of the terms of the Commission held the previous year were upheld and in the troublesome matter of living together, Shrewsbury was to take Bess with him to Wingfield Manor and from there to Chatsworth or any other of his houses. Shrewsbury told Walsingham that he had been driven to accept the terms – not a good omen to their hopeful reunion. The Earl was to be allowed to have returned to him the items of hangings, plate and furnishings which William had carried off to Hardwick, and accordingly submitted a list of the missing articles on 1 August. Shrewsbury overplayed his hand again, and his claim became farcical by the inclusion of bed sheets made seventeen years before, which Bess said were, of course, worn out. Many of the articles of plate, she claimed, had been gifts and so were hers by right, or had been pawned 'for necessity' and would be returned when her money was paid over. Bess too overplayed her hand and found reason for deleting every item from the Earl's list; it would have been more tactful to have left Shrewsbury something of his claim. Bess ended her answer with the true comment, 'The parcels above demanded by the Earl are things of small value and mere trifles for so great and rich a nobleman to bestow on his wife in nineteen years', concluding that she had given him far more in the way of gifts during those years. The demand for the return of plate and furnishings plainly riled Bess; she was losing her habitual forbearance.

The answer to Shrewsbury's tiresome demand provoked a letter to which Bess replied on 4 August. Hers was a reasonable letter asking what new offence she had committed – obviously Shrewsbury's letter had been another of his vitriolic numbers. Humbly she asked forgiveness for what offence she knew not. And Shrewsbury's reply inevitably was up to his usual unreasonable standard. Bess was trying hard, but the good that the Queen thought she had worked had lasted no longer than seven days. Further efforts were made to patch up the reunion of this impossible husband with his willing wife but to no effect. The government had other matters on its mind at Fotheringhay Castle and the Shrewsburys' problem was put aside for the moment. Bess probably returned home to Hardwick Hall and her programme of enlarging her father's old house.

Bess was now aged about sixty and was in good health apart from occasional touches of rheumatism. The strain of the last four years had been considerable yet she was possessed of remarkable stamina and except for the regrettable moment when she had rejected with impatience the Earl's request for the return of hangings and furnishings, she had shown little sign of the stress she was undoubtedly under.

Although Shrewsbury had not carried out the terms of the agreed reunion, it is unlikely that he forfeited his bond of £40,000. The Earl claimed that Bess had not returned the furnishings and hangings, which she pointed out were either worn out, sold or pawned – therefore he reasoned, Bess had broken the terms and not he. The Queen, recognising Shrewsbury's unbalanced state of mind, may have hesitated to press the matter of the bond to be of good behaviour. It is surprising that at this time, when England was facing a very real threat of invasion by Spain and the further threat of Catholic insurrection, the Court and all the Queen's men should have spent so much time and energy trying to bring Bess and Shrewsbury together again. The fact was that both Bess and the Earl had rendered Elizabeth enormous service in keeping the Scots Queen for sixteen years and further, Bess had always shown unswerving loyalty to Elizabeth, so that the least the Queen could do was to support Bess. Although Shrewsbury continued to bleat that he merited some reward for his devotion to the Queen, he never recognised that his reward lay in the gentle way the Court dealt with him in his obstinacy, using no force but only patient coercion – notwithstanding his flagrant disregard of the Queen's orders.

Shrewsbury had one more duty to perform for his Queen and without doubt one of the most unpleasant. Mary the Scots Queen had become involved in one final plot to assassinate Elizabeth and proclaim herself Queen of England; this has come to be called the Babington Plot after the name of the principal conspirator, a Catholic, Anthony Babington, whose family came from Derbyshire and were well known to Bess and Shrewsbury. How much of Mary's implication was provoked by Walsingham's agents is another story; to involve Mary uncompromisingly in treason was an indirect way of bringing about her end. Mary had gone to Fotheringhay Castle in Northamptonshire as a prisoner and there her trial took place. The story has been told many times and, on the evidence given, her guilt seemed unquestionable. Her trial was presided over by the Lord Chancellor with the Privy Council and thirty-six judges in attendance.

As Earl Marshal, Shrewsbury had to be at the trial. He stayed at Orton Longueville near Peterborough, a mere sixteen miles from Fotheringhay, the home of his son Henry Talbot. The trial was also the reason for suspending attempts to reunite Bess and her husband; with the exception of Queen Elizabeth and Bess, all those involved in that hopeful endeavour were present in the court room at Fotheringhay on 11 October when Mary's trial opened. By the end of October the drama of the trial had shifted to the Star Chamber in London and back again to Fotheringhay in early February of 1587. Whether or not Shrewsbury trailed after the court cannot be certain; he was certainly at Orton Longueville on 1 January. Even had Shrewsbury wished to keep to the terms of his reunion with Bess, his duties as Privy Councillor and Earl Marshal would have prevented their co-habitation at that time.

On 7 February Shrewsbury was back at Fotheringhay for the final act of the macabre drama being played out around Mary. The 8th February was fixed for her execution and as Earl Marshal it was Shrewsbury's unpleasant duty to signal Mary's end to the executioner ready with the axe. Shrewsbury raised his baton of office, at the same time turning his face away from the awful scene taking place before him. Three sickening blows with the axe were needed before Mary's head was cut from her body. The executioner holding up the severed head streaming with blood cried, 'God save Queen Elizabeth!' 'So let all her enemies perish!' replied the Dean of Peterborough. One solitary voice alone responded 'Amen!' – it was that of the Earl of Kent. Mary's servants were hurried out of the hall and locked in a chamber. But one faithful attendant still remained: Mary's Skye terrier was found crouching under her garments saturated with her blood, too terrified to leave what remained of his mistress.

With this bloody business out of the way and notwithstanding the storm clouds gathering over Europe, the Queen and her advisers were able to think again about bringing the Shrewsburys together. The Earl returned to Court and attended Privy Council meetings in March. His visit was likely to have been the result of a summons from the Queen. Bess was also in London at the same time. On 6 April the Queen had a conversation with Bess's daughter, Mary Talbot, the wife of Gilbert. The Earl was present and Gilbert reported the scene: 'The Queen then commanded her to say what her mother desired of my Lord, which she did, whereat my Lord grew impatient and spoke of his great offence against her.' Mary was not provoked by this interruption and replied that she could not answer back Shrewsbury in front of the Queen but all she wished was that her mother should be taken back again by the Earl. Mary added that Shrewsbury's behaviour was causing 'the utter destruction of her old distressed mother'. Whilst this conversation went on, Shrewsbury was spluttering away in the background. Immediately after the exchange with Mary, the Queen had an hour's talk with Shrewsbury, and Mary Talbot was sent for several times; no doubt the Earl was made fully aware of his duties for the result of this royal persuasion was Shrewsbury's capitulation. A reconciliation was forced on Shrewsbury and he was to be required to take Bess from London to Wingfield Manor where they were to 'keep house together'; he was to allow Bess £300 yearly and provisions for housekeeping; he was also to drop all legal suits for the return of plate and furnishings.[7] What persuasions the Queen had used on the obstinate Earl will never be known, but they must have been formidable.

'Since then', reported Gilbert, 'my Lord has been at Chelsea with my Lady and promises never to hear anything he dislikes about her without sending her word and receiving her answer, and that if she behaved well he would make all her causes his own and all his friends hers.' Bess moved into the Chelsea house with her husband but notwithstanding all her willingness the atmosphere could only have been chilly; what powerful persuasion the Queen had used might have moved them together, but it could never alter the Earl's obsessive hostility.

Bess and her reconciled husband left London at the end of Easter week about 22 April, for Wingfield. The manor had been chosen because it was neutral ground; it belonged to Shrewsbury, but Bess, by the marriage settlement, had a life interest. The Earl's stay at Wingfield was of the briefest; he was at Sheffield Lodge by 26 April, but back at Wingfield again when he examined a suspected Catholic priest on 16 May. In his report to Walsingham on the examination of the recusant, he added a postscript to the effect that he had been at Wingfield with Bess, as Henry Talbot could confirm when he next visited Court. Shrewsbury was indeed conforming, but it had taken nearly four years for all the power of the Queen's Court to bring this about. His honour and his obstinacy had been finally forfeited.

The peace, if peace it was, did not last long. Shrewsbury's visits to Bess became fewer and fewer and she reported to Burghley on 6 October that his conduct was becoming a matter of complaint. Shrewsbury had not been to see her more than three times; he had withdrawn the promised provisions and she had not sufficient fuel to make a decent fire.

For the remainder of that year, Bess divided her time between Wingfield and Hardwick. The Earl retired to Handsworth Manor at Sheffield to console himself with Mrs Eleanor Britton, a lady of his household, who, whilst giving comfort to Shrewsbury, gave a great deal of trouble to his heirs after his death, for she indulged in long and expensive litigation with Gilbert over gold and jewels which she claimed his father had given her. The only other complaint against Shrewsbury's companion of his late years was from William Dickenson, the Sheffield bailiff, in 1586 when he reported that she had put so much wine and spirit in some venison pasties that they had broken up on the way to Sheffield; she may have been as generous as she was consoling.

Shrewsbury by 1588 was taking deliberate measures to avoid Bess; indeed his efforts became ridiculous. Nicholas Kinnersley, the steward at Wingfield, wrote to Bess on 5 November that year reporting that Dickenson, the Earl's man, had been at Wingfield questioning the servants as to where Bess was and when she had last been to Wingfield. Kinnersley told Bess that a boy had come from Sheffield late one night and had talked to the stable hands. From these mysterious comings and goings, Bess had to draw her own conclusions.

In the main Shrewsbury left Bess alone and ceased his harassments; his time was spent chasing suspect Catholics in Derbyshire, although a letter, again from Kinnersley, indicated that he had attempted some mischief at Wingfield. Kinnersley told Bess in April 1589 that she need have no worries about the safety of Wingfield; her orders would only be obeyed if confirmed a second time by one of her recognised men.

In September of 1589, Shrewsbury bought the Barley estate and with it Bess's dower from her first husband, then worth about £100 a year.[8] The Barley estates were adjoining the Earl's lands at Dronfield outside Sheffield and near his guild lands in Chesterfield; from that point of view the purchase was a wise one and it included the Barley lead mines. The price paid was £8000 but the estate was so encumbered with debts by Peter Barley as to make it a doubtful bargain. In working out the details of the estate years after Shrewsbury had died, Gilbert found that the debts totalled £7000 and he noted on the bottom of the page, 'Queer what a dear purchase Barley is'. Peter Barley was not entirely to blame for the run-down, for the estate had never recovered from the plunderings of wardship long before.

No determined attempts were made by the Queen to bring Shrewsbury to heel again. Indeed the Queen had a great deal more to worry about than her obstinate Earl; intractable though Shrewsbury was, Philip of Spain was proving infinitely more difficult. In December 1589, after the might of Spain's Armada had been broken and Philip's hopes of invading England had sunk for the moment with his ships, the Queen found time to write to 'her very good old man'.[9] Charmingly she asked after Shrewsbury's health, 'especially at this time of the fall of the leaf', and hoped that he was not too much touched with gout. Then came the point of her letter, she asked him to let Bess see him from time to time 'which she hath now of a long time wanted'. Bess's patience was unlimited; even after all the humiliation, the trials, the tribulations, she would still have gone back to Shrewsbury if he would have permitted it.

Bess's attitude was not dictated by convention. She clearly believed that those who had been joined together in the sight of God should not be put asunder; it is doubtful if by this time she had any love for her husband but perhaps a fondness and certainly a belief that she could be of help to him.

By 1590 Shrewsbury was aged sixty-two but he must have looked more than his years. He was practically unable to use his hands so bad had become his gout, his legs were so affected that he was unable to stand without help and he suffered from other unspecified maladies. It must have been a source of irritation to him that Bess, although about the same age, kept in such good health. He lived on at Handsworth nurturing his obsessive hatred for Bess. A letter to Shrewsbury from London written in February of that year told him of a rumour that Bess was planning to spend the summer in London: 'My Lord, if you could find the means she might bring all her train with her young and old; and in like case that they should not come down again to your country at all, I would think it the better for your Lordship.' The writer was certainly echoing Shrewsbury's thoughts. Another letter written on 12 October the same year, from the Bishop of Lichfield and Coventry, could have given him no pleasure as the good Bishop urged him to take Bess back again. But by the time he received the Bishop's homily he may have been past caring for in five weeks he was dead. At seven in the morning of 18 November 1590, at Sheffield Manor, George Talbot, Sixth Earl of Shrewsbury and Bess's fourth husband, died.

There is no record of Bess's comment or reaction to the news of her last widowhood; she would have been sorry to hear of his death. It would have been no occasion of joy to her whatsoever. No doubt she would have wished to have been at his side as a dutiful wife; the fact that he prohibited this would have saddened her. Throughout the last difficult years she had never condemned her husband and her conduct had been almost beyond reproach.

Shrewsbury was buried at the parish church of Saints Peter and

Paul at Sheffield on 13 January 1591. The delay of eight weeks between his death and funeral allowed Garter Herald to organise the ceremony and the body was, by custom, embalmed. Shrewsbury's funeral was more sumptuous than 'was ever to any afore in these countrys: and the assembly to see the same was marvellous both of nobility, gentry and country folks and poor folks without number'. Three people lost their lives by the fall of two trees that were burnt down, which seems an improbable accident, but nevertheless the coroner was paid a fee on 13 January for one who was accidentally killed at the funeral. The impressive tomb erected above the Shrewsbury vault had been designed and made during the Earl's lifetime; likewise the epitaph composed by Fox the martyrologist some years previously but under the Earl's supervision, for it omits all mention of Bess and dwells at length on his innocence of any improper association with the Scots Queen. The date of his death was left blank and remains so to this day; as the Earl had foretold, his executors would forget to insert this detail. So passed from Bess's life a man not well endowed with intellect but with great obstinacy, and who once adored her, but who allowed the strains of office to distort his reason and turned his love to an obsessive hatred. He had a touching devotion to his Queen and should be remembered for the great service he rendered in acting as Mary's jailor for sixteen thankless years, a service in which he had been supported and helped by Bess.

`ARBELLA WAS MERRY'
1590 -1591

There is nothing like a will to bring out the worst in a family and the will of George Talbot, Sixth Earl of Shrewsbury, was no exception.

Dated 24 May 1590, the year in which he died, it showed none of the unreason which he had previously displayed – perhaps the relinquishing of his strenuous duties and his retirement to the charms of Mistress Britton had enabled Shrewsbury to recover his mental balance before he died.[1] The will made no mention of Bess, but this is understandable; she was provided for at his death, under the terms of their marriage settlement. Her portion would have been one third of the Earl's total disposable lands which he held at the time of the marriage which she would have for her lifetime only; thereafter they would pass to Shrewsbury's heir, Gilbert Talbot. The Sixth Earl appointed his younger sons, Henry and Edward Talbot, as executors of his will, but they declined the office and Bess was made sole executrix, a move Shrewsbury would not have approved. Almost immediately this was revoked and Gilbert appointed in her place. Thereupon, although previously Bess's ally, Gilbert became her foe.

During his life, Bess had been unable to get any supporting allowance from her husband and after his death she was faced with the same problem; she was unable to get her widow's portion from Gilbert. It was the same story told under a different title. This was an age when, if rights were not claimed, they were lost by default. Bess had no option but to pursue those rights until she got them and this was the cause of her quarrel with Gilbert.

Gilbert was probably unable to give Bess what she was demanding. Shrewsbury had left debts, Gilbert had large debts himself and the debts of his late brother Francis were still unpaid, while Eleanor Britton was claiming lands and cattle, as well as gold plate and jewels. From Gilbert's point of view, if everyone would be patient and wait, then all would be settled; he played a stalling game.

Lord Burghley had been appointed a supervisor of the will by Shrewsbury. It was the job of the supervisors to see that the terms of the will were carried out by the executors. Bess wrote to Burghley from Wingfield on 11 April 1591 complaining that she was not getting her dowry, and mentioning Gilbert's unkind treatment. Three times the matter had been discussed with Gilbert or his representatives and three times some agreement had been reached, but three times Gilbert had failed to carry out the agreed terms. She told Burghley that she felt Gilbert was taking advantage of her willingness to help. The matter was finally settled and sooner than other items connected with his father's will – Gilbert, like his father, was no match for Bess. Gilbert had a contentious nature; he challenged his brother Edward to a duel in 1594 and there was a famous quarrel with the Stanhopes over the weir on the River Trent – it was better to have Gilbert as a friend than an enemy, but it was infinitely worse to have Bess as a foe. It was a very long time before she forgave her son-in-law for their differences over Shrewsbury's will.

The death of her husband released Bess from the possibility of any further harassment and eventually she was free to use all the properties which came to her under the marriage settlement. Wingfield Manor; its iron works, smithies and glass works; Bolsover Castle and its coal pits; the parks of Alveton in Staffordshire, Shirland in Derbyshire and Over Uden in Yorkshire for their pastures. Bess was free to exploit the timber and minerals which had come to her in addition to the rents from these properties, which in the mid-1590s totalled £2500 annually; further revenue would have come from entry fines and manorial courts. The total revenues from her Talbot lands must have been around £3000 annually – no wonder Gilbert Talbot stalled over parting with such an enormous sum.

But the exploitation of her estates was only one facet of Bess's enterprise. In the year before Shrewsbury died, Henry Cavendish went on a remarkable journey to Constantinople[2] and although he was out of favour with Bess he may have gone on this difficult trip at Bess's bidding. With pepper at 3s (15p) the pound in the late 1580s (later in 1601 Bess paid 5s 6d (27½p) the pound), plainly there was scope for trading in spices and other eastern imports. Leaving England on 28 March 1589, with three servants and a friend, Richard Mallory, Henry sailed to Northern Germany, avoiding the battlegrounds of the Netherlands, and went due south by waggon averaging thirty miles a day until by way of the Brenner Pass he reached Venice on 3 May. Henry's manservant Fox kept a journal of this remarkable trip but unfortunately he gives no hint whatsoever of the purpose of the journey and one is left guessing. On the trip south through Germany they had stayed at Augsberg, the home of the banking family Fuggers, and may have made some contact for Bess. Venice was not approved of at all:

The gentlemen be merchants and very rich and therefore proud. They have wives but for fashion's sake, for they prefer a common courtesan before their married wives. . . . These men love this sweet sin so well that they term them most virtues that I think to be most vicious, but why should not the citizens be like the city, which is a most foul stinking sink. . . .

This, coming from a servant of Henry, whose promiscuity was notorious, was a quaint comment.

From Venice the party took a small vessel round the coast to Dubrovnic, the little walled Venice of Dalmatia. Here the party stayed with Mr William Robinson 'an Englishman, a man of many words but slow in performing, for time hath so altered the man that he is become a Slovenian in nature but a very kind fellow in his fashion'. At Dubrovnic they prepared for the trip across land to Constantinople by way of Sofia. Only twenty years ago Dalmatia was wild enough, with neither roads nor inns: in 1589 it was no different. Hardened travellers as they were, this part of the journey was undoubtedly the worst. On 25 May the night was spent in a hen roost; the 26th on benches; the next night in a cart. Meeting two Turks by the way, they were attacked with whips for being Christians and had a hat stolen. They arrived at Constantinople on 16 June with some relief, a relief tempered by the fact that the town had been all but destroyed by fire only two months earlier. After a stay of fourteen days they returned by way of Poland taking rather longer than the outward journey, arriving in England towards the end of September.

The purpose of this long journey remains a mystery. The 1601 inventory of Hardwick, however, shows a number of Turkish carpets which may have been brought back by Henry and his party, and two carpets still in the Long Gallery today date from the sixteenth century: one, a Persian woven for the Shah Abbas, was commonly placed beside his throne and on it a black cheetah. But if this was a trading venture on Bess's part, then it was a venture that failed to bring any return. It was perhaps her first and last attempt at foreign trade and she contented herself thereafter in developing her own estates.

Chatsworth, once a bone of contention between Bess and Shrewsbury, now became one of her stations of residence; she moved about her estates as the business directed, from Hardwick to Wingfield, to Chatsworth and back to Hardwick. The peregrinations of the Dowager Countess and her court were directed by the need to settle legal disputes, to buy lands, to pay her taxes and to establish a right to occupation. Nevertheless of all her properties, the only house she could call her own was Hardwick Hall. Chatsworth for all its magnificence was entailed on her 'bad son' Henry and was hers only for life while Wingfield was of course Talbot property. With Henry Cavendish disinherited as heir, William became her favourite and Hardwick had to be rebuilt in a style and manner suitable to the dignity of the dynasty.

The remains of that first Hardwick built by Bess still stand within a few hundred yards of her second building and must surely be one of the great mystery ruins of England. It is incredible that Bess, who was responsible for the magnificence of Chatsworth and later the new Hardwick Hall, which is one of this country's most brilliant architectural expressions, could have conceived such a hotch-potch of a house as the old Hall. There was no architectural concept; the window mouldings on the east wing differ from those on the rest of the house; part of the exterior is rendered, part ashlar-faced; the roof of the centre portion is gabled and slated and the two wings were flat; the building lines are not parallel and there is no attempt at a balanced elevation anywhere. How Bess, one of the most competent women of her time, came to erect such a conglomerate mess of a building will remain a qualified enigma.

A partial explanation lies in the fact that Bess was forced to live at Hardwick before she was ready; it was Shrewsbury's intransigence that made her move there in 1584. At the time the house would have been as her brother James had left it, a four-storey block of a house with a transverse hall – and the concept of a transverse hall (a hall running across the full width of the house, rather than medieval fashion along the length) was not a discovery of Bess's; it was a matter of living convenience and requirement. If James was the originator of the Hardwick which Bess moved into in 1584, then it suited James to have such a hall and it was convenient for Bess to incorporate the same feature in her later new Hardwick. Although James's Hardwick boasted a large hall and a small gallery it was not big enough to accommodate Bess, her entourage and her son William and his wife who were still without an establishment of their own. The house had to be enlarged but Shrewsbury was then taking the revenues from Bess's lands; she had no money to pay for an extensive building programme.

After August 1586 when the Earl had been forced to pay back to Bess the rents which he had wrongfully seized, it was a different matter. Bess could afford to extend the old Hardwick house. By July 1587, which is the earliest account of any building work at old Hardwick, the central three-gabled block was being reconstructed and reroofed.[3] Bess was probably living in a three-storey east wing which had been constructed to contain what may have been intended as State apartments. The roofing completed, she moved back to occupy a rather mean bedchamber on the first floor of the old main block – there were still no obvious apartments for William. With the house in this condition of cramped disarray, Bess's visits to London may have been welcome breaks, but harassed by Shrewsbury and yet able to bear the discomforts of the building programme at the advanced age of sixty, Bess was showing remarkable toughness and perseverance.

Early in 1588 a new wing at the west end of the house was started. This contained the kitchens and brought the building right to the edge of the cliff on which the house stood, a fact which later gave Bess a lot of expensive trouble to prevent this end from slipping down into the valley. Above the kitchens were William's apartments; above these another set of chambers and set on top of all the 'hill great chamber', giving a breathtaking view across the wide sweep of the valley to the distant Derbyshire hills hiding Wingfield and Chatsworth.

The hill great chamber was panelled with a large diamond-patterned wainscoting up to a height of nine feet, framed with fluted pilasters which have now found their way into the dining room of the new Hardwick. Above the panelling, a two-storeyed series of moulded plaster arches breaking up the severe vertical lines were finished with a fine classical plaster cornice; the whole room dominated by a vast overmantel of Gog and Magog. If it still existed this hill chamber, with its perfect proportions of space, would have been one of the most exciting rooms in Europe and must have given the impression of being suspended above the hills and valleys of Derbyshire.

But Bess still had an inadequate house and in the same year that the west wing was completed she added a fourth floor to the east wing to provide another great chamber, which was called the 'forest great chamber' after the plaster frieze of 'forest folk' which decorated it. At the same time she built a block on the north face of this east end to complete a suite of state apartments complementary to the new great chamber. When all was finished the old Hall had been equipped with a range of state apartments on the top fourth floor comprising the forest great chamber, withdrawing-chamber and three bedchambers with the long gallery beneath – an unorthodox and bizarre arrangement, also very inconvenient. Bess herself moved into a bedchamber on the cold north side of the third floor of the new east wing. Another inconvenience was that her withdrawing-chamber was on the next floor up.

As a concept in living the whole must have been as uncomfortable as it was unsatisfactory; the planning had been haphazard as her funds and predicament dictated; no architect had been employed to produce such an indifferent building which was the creation of spasmodic need, directed by Bess, working with her clerk of works David Flood and relying on experienced masons. Yet the proportions of the hill great chamber and the decoration in it, together with the decoration of the forest great chamber and its leather hangings decorated in gold, show a higher standard than was employed at the new Hardwick and was only a little less sumptuous than Chatsworth: the result of letting her old plasterer from Chatsworth, Abraham Smith, translate her ideas. Bess was an organiser delegating to craftsmen who could create what she wanted. The old Hardwick was a conglomerate mess because Bess employed no architect: there had been no one to convert her thoughts into orderly architecture and she was quite unable to do this herself. However, before the old Hardwick was finished Bess had plans for a new Hardwick drawn up by the architect and mason Robert Smythson.[4]

Smythson must have been consulted about the new Hardwick at some point late in the year 1589 or early 1590. He probably supplied the plans, elevations and details in the late summer of the latter year. The only certain date is when the foundations and cellars of the new Hardwick were dug by twenty labourers in four weeks starting 4 November 1590. It has been suggested that Bess started her new Hardwick when Shrewsbury's death released revenue to pay for the project. This was not so, for Bess was unable to get all her settlement revenues until the quarrel with Gilbert had been sorted out. Shrewsbury died on 18 November and the foundations were begun two weeks earlier, and Bess must have consulted Smythson months before; the site had been measured, surveyed and plans supplied before Shrewsbury fell ill. Furthermore, Bess's average annual expenditure on building the old Hardwick from 1587 to 1590 was £340, which was only increased to an annual £345 from 1591 to the full finishing of both buildings in 1598.[5] For Bess this represented only a small part of her income and she was never dependant on Shrewsbury's money to build the new Hardwick. The new Hardwick was the result of the necessity to provide a suitable mansion for her dynasty and nothing more.

Whilst Bess had been closely involved in her struggle with Shrewsbury and then providing herself and her family with accommodation, England had drifted into a more serious war with Spain, had defeated Philip's Armada and had restored some stability to Europe.

With Mary's execution, political problems in England had been simplified; the possibility of a Catholic succession on Elizabeth's death had been ended. Unless mischance intervened, the succession was now assured on James who was certainly no Catholic – but Elizabeth refused to acknowledge this. It is true that there was another potential candidate in Bess's grand-daughter, Arbella Stuart, but it is doubtful if Elizabeth ever seriously considered her, though she used the possibility as a bargaining lever when it suited her. Mary's end may have simplified matters nationally by removing a rallying point for dissident Catholics, but Mary had willed her English succession to Philip of Spain who was determined to claim that succession by invasion from the Spanish Netherlands. A half-baked plan of conveying the army across the Channel by means of a massive Armada of ships sent from Spain occupied the resources of Spain and her monarch for two years before its ill-fated end was achieved – the only Spaniards to land were those wrecked on the unfriendly and distant shores of Scotland and Ireland. Whilst the hopes of Philip and Catholic Europe were centred on invasion, expatriate Englishmen at Philip's Court were assuring him that all good Catholic Englishmen within the country would rise and revolt against the Protestant oppression. This of course was plain wishful thinking and what Philip wanted to hear – it was far from the truth. Shrewsbury had been involved in rounding up suspect Catholics in Derbyshire, resulting in some of his friends being locked away; he was also responsible for raising the local musters of amateur troops. These activities alone would have been evidence in landlocked Derbyshire that there were dangers all around: the Catholic menace could not be ignored. Nevertheless Bess pushed ahead with her haphazard building programme at Hardwick. At the moment when Spain's Armada was being burnt, blown out of the sea and washed up on foreign shores, Bess was having trees felled in Pentrich woods to provide timber for her roofs and was making ovens in the kitchens of her new west wing overhanging the cliff edge. Plainly she was confident that Philip's armies would never march through her estates.

It is likely that Shrewsbury was as confident. The Elizabethans never seem to have considered the possibility of defeat; their optimism was boundless. By the time he died the old Earl could congratulate himself on having done his duty, as he saw it, towards his Queen. And his honour, again as he saw it, was intact, even though he had

moved Mistress Britton into his establishment. However, Shrewsbury did have certain worries on his mind and in the autumn before
he died he poured out his concern to a confidential servant,[6] who,
whilst writing down his words, also noted his gestures and emotion
in relating this confidence. Shrewsbury feared that Arbella would
bring trouble to his family because of Gilbert's domination by his
wife Mary, Bess's daughter; as he spoke his old obsession returned.
Mary and Bess would use Gilbert to their own ends, was his fear,
but as long as he lived he would block their devices. His forecast
was partially right; Arbella never brought any trouble to Gilbert
but she gave a great deal to Bess; that alone would have delighted
Shrewsbury had he foreseen it.

Exactly where Arbella was when all the trouble with Shrewsbury
was exploding is not clear. She could hardly have been accommodated at Hardwick after Bess had been forced to move from Chatsworth, for there was no room. It is likely that she was living for
periods with one or other of her Cavendish aunts and uncles, and
the uncertain upbringing of this orphan must have contributed to
her later insecurity. After the death of Leicester's son, no further
projects for Arbella's marriage had been undertaken by Bess. It had
been noted in 1587 that King James of Scotland could do worse
than marry his cousin Arbella, but this was none of Bess's doing.
James was aware of the inherent dangers should Arbella marry an
ambitious husband prepared to promote her claim to the English
throne.

During the summer of 1587, when Bess and Shrewsbury had been
momentarily reconciled and had returned to Wingfield, Arbella was
at Court, staying in London with Mary Talbot. No doubt many were
anxious to catch sight of the only Princess of royal blood, now aged
twelve and for so long shut away in Derbyshire – Bess and her
family were attracting most of the attention that summer. Charles
Cavendish wrote to Bess, giving his mother detailed news of Arbella's
reception by the Court, 'My Lady Arbella hath been once at Court,
her Majesty spoke to her but not long and examined her nothing
touching her book; she dined in the presence.'[7] Afterwards Burghley asked Arbella and her uncle to dine and Charles, sitting next
to Burghley, overheard favourable comment made to Raleigh about
Arbella. Then Burghley dropped his voice and said something in

Raleigh's ear which Charles could not catch, but he caught Raleigh's reply when he said 'it would be a happy thing'. Were they perhaps discussing a possible husband for Arbella? Bess must have wondered at this when she read her son's letter, and yet the matter was out of her hands, she had problems enough of her own. Undoubtedly the Court was looking Arbella over and speculating on her future. Arbella's accomplishments were a credit to Bess, for notwithstanding her mere twelve years, she spoke French and Italian, played instruments and wrote with a very fair hand; all necessary attainments for a lady of the Court. The Queen approved of what she saw in her old friend's grand-daughter and, again playing politics, commended Arbella to the French Ambassador telling him that she 'would one day be even as I am'. Arbella was taken in by this comment, but Bess who knew the Queen too well would have realised that it meant little or nothing. Nevertheless Charles's report could only have given Bess pleasure; Arbella's first visit to Court had been a success.

With Arbella's return to Derbyshire, her luggage was sent after her along with Bess's; a list of silver dated 21 August 1587 which was mainly Bess's showed 'Plate sent from London to the Country.... Plate of my La Arbella: one bason & ewer, parcel gilt; two beer jugs with covers; one great bowl with cover, gilt; two livery pots, parcel gilt', and a small number of silver spoons, plates and three plain white candlesticks. It was not a great deal for a royal Princess, but Bess was having trouble with Shrewsbury over her own silver and could spare little for her grand-daughter.

Arbella's earliest surviving letter to Bess was written in February of the year following that first Court visit: 'Good lady grandmother, I have sent your ladyship the ends of my hair, which were cut the sixth day of the moon on Saturday last and with them a pot of jelly which my servant made.' The letter hints at magic rites, this was a common indulgence; the Church encouraged a belief in the power of prayer, the State supported the Church, and yet sickness and sudden death were disasters which the Church, for all its beliefs, was impotent to prevent and doctors as helpless. Small wonder if Bess indulged in a little harmless magic as a double insurance.

That year of 1588, when Spain's ships were sailing arrogantly towards England's shores, Arbella returned to Court, again staying with her aunt Mary and Gilbert Talbot. Bess was not with them, being occupied with her roofs and ovens at Hardwick; perhaps as well, for fourteen years later this visit was recalled, when Arbella insisted on taking precedence over all others of the Queen's suite, resulting in a right royal rebuke at Greenwich and her being ordered from Court.[8] Bess would not have been pleased.

There were to be no more visits to Court for Arbella for some time. The fault was hers: perhaps she had been brought up by Bess and her aunts to demand more at Court than was her due. Spoilt she may have been, for she was moved from one household to another, from her uncle Charles to her aunt Mary to her uncle Henry, leading a semi-royal existence with no companions but her younger cousins. In November 1588 she was at Wingfield attended only by servants: Nicholas Kinnersley the steward wrote to Bess on the 5th of that month in some desperation, 'My Lady Arbella at 8 o'clock this night was merry, and eats her meat well; but she went not to ye school these six days: therefore I would be glad of your Lady coming' – clearly things were getting out of hand.

The choice of a husband for Arbella was not debated by Bess at this time although others could not leave the subject alone. In December 1588 James was seriously proposing the Duke of Lennox. The possibility was discussed, and James was reminded that Arbella had never been given the Lennox jewels left to her by her mother. It took three attempts by the British Ambassador to learn the truth about these, and the truth was that James had them; claimed, he said, in recompense for legacies from the old Countess of Lennox which he had never received. But James had other matters on his mind: he was getting married to Anne of Denmark, a wedding by proxy in their separate countries in August 1589. Anne was detained by witchcraft on her voyage to England and turned back – she suffered a terrible storm which was thought to have been caused by evil spirits and James had to sail to Denmark to fetch his bewitched bride. A strange pair they made. Bishop Goodman, a confidant of James, said of them, 'The King of himself was a very chaste man, and there was little in the Queen to make him uxorious.' James had not inherited his mother's hot nature.

Arbella's disgrace at Court in 1588 would have caused considerable irritation to her grandmother. Bess knew Court life too well and was probably tired of the small intrigues and smaller talk, but to Arbella it was life – the masques, dances and ceremonies she would have missed at an age when she was tasting such pleasures for the first time. Bess was landed with the problem of a mewed-up teenager when she had least need of it. Arbella's trouble at Court was something which could be dealt with between Bess and the Queen personally and would have to wait; the girl would come to no harm by her deprivation. At the time Shrewsbury was Bess's main preoccupation and worry and after this problem was solved and his subsequent death she became involved in the creation of the new Hardwick, the ultimate expression of her achievements.

Robert Smythson, 'architector' of Wollaton Hall 'and divers others of great account', was the most ingenious architect of his time, who excelled in composition of neat plans and exciting innovation. For Bess he was the obvious choice to produce the plan for her new Hardwick. It was an age which delighted in devices, and in the plan of her new house Bess obtained just such a device – it was based on a double cross and in every way unlike any house previously built, or for that matter any which were built later. As at the old house, the hall was transverse; in a building of this size it was the most convenient way to accommodate such a feature, the walls being high enough to take the large end windows needed to light such a hall and the two-room depth of the building taking care of the ninety-five-foot length. Bess's apartments were conveniently on the warm south side, well away from the smells of the kitchens and the noise of the hall, and the chapel was on the same floor: if she wished, Bess had no need to leave that first floor for weeks on end, for everything was conveniently where she could reach it without going upstairs or down.

Yet for all its size, the new Hardwick had only six principal bed-chambers. On its own it was not a large house, it relied on the accommodation provided by the old Hall close by, a building which was slowly completed as the new Hall was finished. The old Hall was complementary to the new, an inconvenience which one hundred years later was to save it from being rebuilt, for the first Duke of Devonshire chose to indulge his own skill in architecture by pulling down Bess's Chatsworth and rebuilding on the same foundations.

Thereafter Hardwick became the secondary residence of Bess's Cavendish descendants, occasionally lived in but in the main the repository for furniture and pictures regarded as too old fashioned to be used in other mansions. By desultory neglect Bess's Hardwick was preserved and is the only one of her buildings to survive; it is also the least altered of all the great Elizabethan 'prodigy' houses.

Hardwick Hall, its turrets topped with great stone coronets above Bess's initials E.S., makes a dramatic and romantic skyline and proclaims itself as Bess's creation; within the house the overmantels repeat the same message in variations struck between the arms and supporters of Cavendish, Hardwick and Talbot with occasional reference to the marriages of her children. It is the story of Bess's life told in heraldry and there is but a single reference to Arbella – Hardwick was built for Bess and her dynasty, not for Arbella.

During the early stages of the building of Hardwick, when the old house was barely habitable and the new was no more than four walls, Bess chose to live more comfortably at Wingfield only twelve miles away where she could keep an eye on the work. She was there in April 1591 and possibly she had Arbella with her.

Within twelve months of the foundations being dug, the walls were up to the second floor and there the work stopped: Bess had urgent reasons for being in London for an extended visit. That October of 1591 John Rhodes, a master mason from Wollaton, signed a contract with Bess for all the remaining exterior stonework for the new house, and a dwelling for him to live in was found and enlarged.[9]

By November the old Hall was completely glassed except for six windows on a stairway. David Flood the clerk of works was superseded by Bess's household priest, Henry Jenkinson, and the day-labourers were reduced to a minimum necessary for maintenance. Thus Bess could leave her building programme ticking over whilst she was away. Rhodes and his men were left to quarry and cut the ashlar ready for the next storeys; John Balechouse, whose Flemish name gave difficulties (he was often simply called John 'Painter' after his craft), was left to pay the carpenters sawing the joists and beams for floors and the lead boards for the roofs; and Jenkinson was to pay the few day-labourers. The new Hardwick was left in capable hands with work being prepared ready for starting up again on

Bess's return. The household staff at the old Hall was reduced to barely a dozen and Bess left for London at the end of the third week of November taking her personal servants, her sons William and Charles and their wives and Arbella with her.

'SOMEONE VERY DESIROUS'
1591-1593

Bess's visit to London was the result of several urgent matters. In the forefront was the trouble with Gilbert over her marriage settlement and his father's will – Gilbert was intending to take his case to a London court. Arbella's possible marriage was business which the Queen wished to discuss with Bess and there may have been a summons for Bess to visit Court. These two reasons apart, the visit suited Bess for she wanted to buy hangings for her new Hardwick, and silver and gold plate to replace what she had been forced to sell during the time of her difficulties with Shrewsbury. Now in her mid-sixties, it was unlikely that she would ever again make the journey to London – Bess wished to see her Queen for the last time.

Her retinue totalled about forty: with her went Sir Charles, Sir William Cavendish and their wives with their servants; Arbella and her lady-in-waiting, Mrs Abrahall; Jane Kniveton, Bess's half-sister, as lady-in-waiting; Mrs Digby, also a lady-in-waiting, then about six months pregnant and probably newly married.[1] It is likely that Arbella, Mrs Abrahall, Jane Kniveton and Mrs Digby all travelled in Bess's coach, a huge lumbering, unsprung vehicle, which would have pitched and rocked about from rut to pothole on the unmade roads; the coach was little more than a covered cart and the most uncomfortable way of travel ever devised. It is likely that Sir Charles's carriage followed, for it was used in London and that would have carried the other ladies who likely enough swapped places during the journey as families do when they have a great deal to talk about. The rest of the cortège followed more comfortably on horseback. It was no easy matter for Bess to move to London for the eight months the visit lasted; for one thing there was only a small staff at Shrewsbury House in Chelsea village, their destination, and she had to take with her all necessary staff for the protracted visit, including cooks, a bottelier and her clerk of the kitchen. The whole project must have taken a great deal of preparation and organising: the revenues from the Western Lands had been diverted to Edward Whaley, the Chelsea steward, so as to build up funds to finance expenses; furniture was sent in advance by waggon; and forty sheep with two fat oxen were driven up from Bess's Talbot estate of Bittesby in Leicestershire to feed the household.

To lodge all the retinue in the Chelsea house there had to be alterations. The gallery was boarded over, partitions put up and the stables converted to a dormitory. Loads of bricks and sand, timber and boards had to be ordered and the conversions completed before Bess arrived. In the event they were not approved, for within days of her arrival another load of bricks and sand was dumped at the house for more conversions. Vast quantities of wood for fuel were carried to Chelsea by barge and stowed in the cellars and finally fires were lit in time to air the house completely.

In effect Bess was moving the operational centre of her business empire from Derbyshire to London. The preparation of the house, although necessary, was only one side of the picture. Bess brought with her Timothy Pusey, her steward and business manager. Pusey had become indispensable to Bess and like Edward Whaley he had considerable legal experience. Bess had learnt a lesson from the unfortunate episode at York when Beresford's case had been blatantly rigged by Shrewsbury; she could afford to pay for the best advice and had assembled around her what amounted to a management board on which Pusey served as a key man. Both he and Whaley were going to have a great deal to do in London and they had to act quickly.

Of necessity, because of the heavy coach and the number of attendants, progress towards London was slow and took seven days. Apart from Pusey, they were in no great hurry and the fact that they were looking forward to the twelve-day Christmas festival at Court would have lent an atmosphere of anticipation and excitement, whilst for many of the servants it must have been their first visit to London. They went by way of Nottingham, Leicester, Market Harborough, Dunstable and Barnet; the clerk comptroller would have ridden on ahead to warn of Bess's coming, to order the church bells to be rung and to arrange accommodation for the night. Long before Bess's uncomfortable coach rumbled and creaked into view the curious would have been out to catch sight of the great lady on her way to Court. As the main party approached, the bells would ring out and the foreguard of Bess's retinue would pass in their light blue Cavendish livery. The rocking coach would follow, pulled by as many as six horses, the silver harness-buckles cut in the shape of E.S. gleaming as they went, and the watchers would have caught sight of the fashionable ladies within.

By country standards, the ladies may have been fashionable, but not fashionable enough for the royal Court. Almost the first thing Bess did after arriving at Chelsea was to spend over £50 on new clothes for herself and her ladies. This was followed by purchases of enormous quantities of gold and silver plate for the new Hardwick; purchases which continued throughout Bess's stay in London. Plainly she was suffering no shortage of funds.

Shrewsbury House in Chelsea was in what is now Cheyne Walk, near the Carlyle statue. It had been built about 1519, constructed round three sides of a court, and facing the river. This was only one of three London properties which the Talbot family owned, although Chelsea would not then have been thought of as being in London. Fields surrounded the village and open countryside lay between Chelsea and the city walls. For Bess this was convenient, for the livestock she had brought could be pastured, and as the stables had been converted the horses had to be put out to grass. The river at the doorstep was practical for carrying Bess to Richmond, to Greenwich or Westminster, whenever the Court was held at those palaces, and for bringing to the house the vast quantities of provisions needed. Almost the first visitor to call on Bess was her cousin Mary Scudamore, no doubt come to wish her well, to give the latest Court gossip and to discuss the problem of the Queen's New Year gift. This year it was to be another garment made up by Jones the Queen's tailor. She was followed by a procession of visitors: Lady Sheffield, Fulke Greville, Roger Manners and Anthony Wingfield, husband of Bess's half-sister Elizabeth. But more important was Bess's dinner with Sir William Cordell, the Master of the Rolls, on 4 January, which can only have been to discuss tactics to frustrate Gilbert Talbot in his attempts to prevent Bess getting her full marriage settlement. It is surprising that Bess could corner the head of the legal apparatus and discuss her problem, but this was one of the facts of Elizabethan Court life. Cordell was a personal friend of Bess and she had given him presents in the past: in 1590 a silver bowl had cost her nearly £10, and only the previous New Year she had given him a great standing cup, as well as deer pies from time to time. It was an acceptable practice and likely enough Gilbert was doing the same. In December Whaley had paid for the copying of a letter which Cordell had sent to Gilbert Talbot; Bess's friendship with Cordell was obviously useful.

Bess attended the Court for the great party of the whole year, the twelve days of Christmas. Ramsey, the Court jester, was given 20s (£1) for amusing her at New Year, and there would have been music, dances, banquets and masques; possibly a play by William Shakespeare. Arbella was allowed to attend for the first time since her disgrace three-and-a-half years before. In fact, as Arbella's marriage was to be discussed with the Queen, the girl had become one of the focal points of the visit.

Bess's London friends tended to fall into two categories. There were her old acquaintances, who were no longer involved in affairs of State, mostly widows like herself, such as old Lady Bacon, mother to Francis, First Viscount St Albans – an acknowledged eccentric who had a horror of plays and masques and was naturally a firm Protestant. Towards the end of her long life she was said to be 'frantic in her age'. In March she borrowed £50 from Bess for eight months. Old Lady Cheek, another friend of long standing, was the widow of Sir John Cheek who long ago had been tutor to Prince Edward; Lady Cobham was another familiar friend from the distant past. All called to pay their respects and to talk about old times together – and to borrow money. But these old friends apart, Bess's other circle of acquaintances comprised influential courtiers who could be of help to her – and whom she could help in return: for example, Admiral of the Fleet Lord Howard, with whom she had dinner in April 1592, and Lord Buckhurst, the Lord Treasurer, both of whom would have been able to lean in the right direction to aid Bess in the main purpose of her visit.

Pusey and Whaley had been working almost from the moment

that Bess arrived at Chelsea to prevent Gilbert Talbot bringing the case of his father's will in London. They followed a practice used by Gilbert's father over Beresford's case at York by engaging what must have been every attorney and serjeant in London, effectively preventing Gilbert from finding anyone to present his case. The cost was enormous: Bess spent £430 in legal charges of one form or another during that visit, an indication of how much was at stake. No avenue was left unexplored; it had occurred to someone that if the old Earl had been a Freeman of the City, then the case concerning his will could be heard without Bess as she was not then a Freeman. Whaley had answered that twelve months earlier by going through the Guildhall registers. Shrewsbury had been admitted to the Company of Clothworkers about 1562, and Whaley paid out 6s 8d (33p) to have Bess made a Freeman. Bess was drawing ahead of her son-in-law; and to make sure of the rules of the game Whaley bought 'a little printed book touching the customs of London and some other notes'.

So much energy and industry, not to mention expense, was not without reward. Gilbert was unable to bring his case in London and Bess made certain that it would be heard in Derbyshire in a Sheriff's court where she could be sure of the result. The law was a game which only the wealthy could afford to play – Bess had learnt that lesson from Shrewsbury and now used it to advantage against his son.

Meanwhile she also pursued her other business. She would certainly have sounded out the Queen on the possibility of getting an increased allowance for Arbella. Her grand-daughter was seventeen in 1592, old for a girl to be unmarried, and if to marry then she would need a dowry. All Bess had been able to secure was the continuation of the £200 granted when Elizabeth Lennox had been alive; she was quite unable to shift the Queen into paying more. There was also the matter of a husband for Arbella and this was certainly discussed. For some time Rainutio Farnese, a son of the Duke of Parma, had been rumoured as a possibility for Arbella, and it was he whom Bess discussed with the Queen in connection with Arbella's marriage. Politically, for the moment at least, it made sense and would save Elizabeth money; both expediencies would have recommended themselves to the Queen.

The war in the Spanish Netherlands still dragged on and Elizabeth was reluctant to spend more money on more men to support
the French. A marriage between Arbella and Parma's son would
bring the war to an end and stop the expense, but Parma's thoughts
on the matter had to be discovered first. On Walsingham's death
in 1590 Robert Cecil had inherited his secret service and with it
Walsingham's chief organiser, Thomas Phelippes. In October, just
before Bess arrived in London, Phelippes wrote to an agent telling
him that one of Parma's men had been informed that the marriage
was something to be thought about, and eight weeks before that
a secret agent had told Cecil that he was getting a portrait of Arbella
painted by 'Hildyard'. 'Hildyard' was the Court painter Nicholas
Hilliard, who would never have been involved without the Queen's
consent, but Arbella was then shut away in Derbyshire and unavail-
able for a sitting. Parma did not dismiss these overtures; there was
certainly someone in Flushing that same October who wanted to
see Arbella's likeness, for a double agent wrote to England 'touching
the Lady Arbella, I pray you send me her picture for there is someone very desirous to see it'.[2]

That was the state of the negotiations just prior to Bess's London
visit. The Queen through Cecil and his agents had put out a feeler
to Parma to see how he felt about a possible marriage between
Arbella and his son Rainutio and the plan had not been rejected;
rather it had been encouraged by the request for a miniature of
Arbella. This was another of the pressing reasons for Bess to be
in London that year. Hilliard would not have been able to produce
an acceptable likeness without seeing Arbella, which was reason
enough for Bess to take her grand-daughter to Court with her.

Some time during midsummer 1592, when Bess and Arbella were
enjoying themselves at Court, the miniature was painted by Hilliard. The clerk of Bess's household put the payment down in his
books, 'Given 27th of July to one Mr Hilliard for the drawing of
one picture, forty shillings. Given unto the same Mr Hilliard,
twenty shillings. Geven unto one Rowland for the drawing of one
other picture, forty shillings.' The payment to Hilliard of 40s (£2)
indicates a miniature; the 20s (£1), also to Hilliard, was the sum
Bess commonly gave when she was pleased with work well done.
Rowland was Rowland Lockey, who had served his apprenticeship

under Hilliard and was employed in his workshop; his payment of 40s is likely to have been for making a copy of what Hilliard had painted.[3] The payments were probably for the copy of a miniature of Arbella, as well as the original, which was to be sent to Parma.

However, these behind-the-scenes moves came to nothing. Parma died on 3 December 1592, just at the point when Philip of Spain was about to replace him for not prosecuting the war with sufficient energy. Rainutio without his father was a useless pawn in European politics and the shadowy agents in Flushing were called off. Arbella's miniature was abandoned with her marriage proposal – in the limbo of the Netherlands war.

Bess left no record of these negotiations and it cannot be certain what her thoughts were. She was doing what the Queen asked of her and marriage was seldom a romantic notion to Elizabethans; it was a duty and thus Bess would have looked on the proposal. Perhaps the prospect of Arbella as a European Princess was attractive, but after all she was an English Princess, which was better. At least marriage would have got her off Bess's hands and given Arbella an independent substance, but probably Bess was lukewarm about the whole thing though glad to be of service to the Queen.

Bess's extravagance on this last visit was astonishing: on clothes alone she paid out just over £300, but that included garments for Arbella and others in the household. For herself Bess's preference was black, a suitable tone for a widow of advanced years; black taffeta was bought by the yard and ell, and trimmed with black Spanish lace. 'Black velvet lace for your Ladyship's tuft taffeta kirtle' with fifteen yards of black boleine damask was enough to make Bess a complete gown and cost her £10. For Court visits, washed gloves and, the height of fashion, perfumed gloves and Spanish leather shoes. Bess was obviously enjoying herself, but the expenditure did not stop there. However, for the first time in her life she had no need to think of cost. Over £1200 went on gold and silver plate and nearly £200 on jewellery for the Court visits, including 'a pair of bracelets set with diamonds, pearls and rubies, twenty pounds', and 'five little jewels at 14s (70p) a piece . . . for an other little one of a bee 6s 8d (33p)' which could easily have been for Arbella as they sound too frivolous for Bess. Significantly, before the main extravagances, William was sent to pay off the debts and repossess pawned silver.

At Chelsea, in February, Bess's lady-in-waiting Mrs Digby had her baby. Bess gave her £4 and Arbella gave the baby 40s (£2); but Digby had to wait until December 1592 for Bess to give her £60 in full payment of her marriage money. There was a close relationship between Bess and Elizabeth Digby which went beyond that of mistress and servant. When she was sick, Digby had the attentions of Bess's own doctor and when Bess was ill, Digby gave Bess her physic; and 'payments to Digby' show her buying cloth for Bess's dresses. When Elizabeth Digby and her husband left in March 1595, Bess must have missed her, and she her mistress, for Digby was back again by Christmas 1596 and stayed with Bess until the day she died. Elizabeth Digby was the highest-paid of any servant at £30 per year; her husband John was a gentleman servant in the household. They lived at Mansfield Woodhouse in Nottinghamshire. He became Sheriff of the County in 1622 and was knighted in 1641; yet he was proud to wear Bess's livery, a gentleman servant who, like the others, saw no discredit in the service of a great lady.

In late January Bess bought silver plate from Sir William Hatton. Sir William was the son of Sir Christopher, who, although he had been Lord Chancellor, owed the Queen £42,000 when he died in 1591 and Sir William was now selling off items to pay his father's debts. In March Bess paid a dealer, Mulmaster, for two pieces of arras showing the story of Abraham; in April she paid the same dealer for another piece; but it was only in early July when she bought a fourth piece of the same series directly from Sir William Hatton that it is clear he had been selling through Mulmaster. It was no benefit to Bess for she still paid the same price, 14s (70p) the ell. These four hangings are in the state bedchamber at Hardwick today; in effect they represent the sinking fortunes of the Hattons and the success of Bess.

On that same July day Bess also bought from Hatton the seventeen hangings showing the story of Gideon which still hang in the Long Gallery at Hardwick. It has been suggested that the Gallery was specially designed to take these tapestries but this cannot be so for the dimensions of the room were already decided when the hangings were bought. Bess paid £321 for the lot and got a reduction of £5 to cover her for the cost of removing the Hatton arms. But this was not done until six years later when the tapestries were finally hung in the finished gallery and the cost of the replacement of the arms was only 40s 4d (£2.02), for she had pieces of painted canvas sewn over.[4] That spring Bess bought other hangings: Tobias tapestries for the Tobias Chamber; hangings of verderers and forest folk; cloth of gold and silver – all to garnish the chambers of the new Hardwick and most now vanished and decayed.

Bess's final extravagance was for a new litter. Like many Elizabethans, she found travelling by coach uncomfortable and in the past she had sometimes borrowed a neighbour's horse-litter, a more comfortable way of travelling. Early in the new year of 1592 she ordered one for herself. Usually a litter was no more than a chair on two shafts carried between two horses; Bess's new litter was magnificent and costly, upholstered in tawny velvet trimmed with a tawny silk fringe and finished with a deep fringe of gold like a pelmet, and to keep out the weather there were windows of tawny and gold parchment. Compared with her usual preference for clashing colours, the tawny and gold harmony would have been attractive to modern eyes. The final touch of luxury was a felt-covered footstool.

The first week in May, preceded by frantic buying of trimmings to brighten up old dresses, Bess and her entourage went to the Court at Greenwich for a three weeks' stay over the Whitsun celebrations. Bess and her personal party went comfortably in three boats, the new litter had a boat to itself and the servants followed on seven hired horses. Greenwich Palace had a more relaxed atmosphere than Westminster, the parties were better and it was preferred for that reason; years before, the Queen had informally sat on the floor on cushions and wiped a smut from Raleigh's cheek. There would have been no plays and masques as at Christmas but there would certainly have been dances, the energetic Galliard or for the less active the Parvan, imported from Spain, a stiff formal dance with curtsies and bowings as the men swept off their hats. And obviously Bess was impressed with the gardens at Greenwich for she gave the royal gardeners money, a generosity which later paid off, for in July on her last Court visit the gardeners brought fresh strawberries – one of her favourite dishes. The visit over, Bess returned to Chelsea on 21 May. The Bishop of Bristol lent his barge and only two hired boats were needed, but Bess had given £100 to found a clergy scholarship.

Whilst Bess and her family were enjoying themselves at Court, the main purpose of the visit was being carried out by Edward Whaley on his own, for Pusey would have been at Greenwich with Bess. Carefully, all loopholes were closed to Gilbert and the opportunity was used to enrol good titles to Bess's many properties, so that there could be no question of ownership after her death. By the middle of June the legal business was all but completed and Bess's purchases made, though the matter of Arbella's marriage may have still been under discussion, for Bess made a final visit to Court at midsummer. More clothes were bought and on 11 June, Bess with her retinue was installed at Greenwich for a visit which lasted until 19 July.

As might have been expected on Bess's last Court visit, she gave a shower of largesse to the royal household: to the buttery, the waiters at the buttery bar; to the pantry; to the cellar; even to the gardeners, a cook and the porter at the gate. She said goodbye to the Queen and sailed for the last time up the Thames to Chelsea in a fleet of six boats, leaving Arbella at Court. The Queen had forgiven Bess's grandchild for her behaviour nearly four years before; indeed if Arbella was to be of use to the Queen by marrying Rainutio, then she would have had to forgive her.

Bess finally left Chelsea for Hardwick on the last day of July, travelling comfortably in the new litter with a spare pair of horses; her carriage followed, then a waggon carrying gold and silver plate. The rest of the baggage was carried in nine hired waggons, whilst her retinue were mounted on forty-three hired horses. The return to Hardwick was a progress of triumph. Bess had frustrated Gilbert Talbot in his devious legal plots; she had secured titles on all her lands; Arbella was reinstated at Court and might soon be betrothed to the son of the Duke of Parma; Bess had spent a total of £6360 over the eight months of the visit, every penny wisely. Admittedly she still had a problem over Gilbert Talbot, but she was confident of overcoming that, it was only a small cloud. For the first time ever, Bess seemed to have no devouring worries. Now almost sixty-five, in the twilight of her life, provided she kept her health she could enjoy a few more years of living.

The party straggled out along the road to Dunstable where they spent the first night. Bells rang out and musicians played for the Countess that evening. At Northampton the next night, there were more bells pealing and more musicians in the hall; and the following day, using the convenience of her comfortable new litter, Bess left the main party and detoured to see Holdenby Hall in Northampton-shire, started in 1577 by the late Lord Chancellor Sir Christopher Hatton. The house was empty apart from a small staff and the housekeeper let Bess see the new building which would have given interesting comparisons with the work going on at Hardwick; Bess looked over the gardens and was on her way again. By evening she had caught up with the main party at Leicester and again there were bells ringing out and music to entertain the tired travellers.

The overnight stops which Bess made must have brought life to these small market towns. Without doubt Bess had become a legend in her lifetime. She was remarkably powerful and she travelled in style; it was not every day that such a retinue stopped overnight. Guards would have to watch the waggons overnight, parked in the street below the bedchambers. Repairs to the litter saddles and the carriage kept saddlers and smithies busy and the poor of the town-ships were given 20s (£1): it was an event to be remembered.

Just before Nottingham, Bess left the train to go on its way to Hardwick without her and spent a night with her daughter Frances, then a matron of forty-four, at Holme Pierrepont, a house which still stands, only four miles from Nottingham. Frances's daughter Grace was to marry George Manners of Haddon Hall, a neighbour-ing estate to Chatsworth – George was the son of Sir John and his runaway wife Dorothy Vernon – and from this marriage with Grace came the Dukes of Rutland. The match has the appearance of hav-ing Bess's hand in the making of it, and the family would have looked to her to use her connections and power to arrange her grand-children's marriages. It is beyond doubt that Bess discussed this match with Frances during the brief stay at Holme Pierrepont. The following day, Bess left her daughter for Wollaton Hall on the other side of Nottingham, the newly completed renaissance palace of Sir Francis Willoughby.

Bess would have wished to see this new building, the creation of Sir Francis and Robert Smythson, for which she had lent her master mason, Thomas Accres. Sited on the summit of a hill, it was impossible to miss and told all who saw it, shining out like an enormous lantern, that Sir Francis had built one of the wonders of the Elizabethan world. By comparison with the new Hardwick it was large and to Bess it may have appeared that the exterior was cluttered with too much decorative detail, for the outside of Hardwick is essentially uncluttered. As Bess mounted the steps to the main door, she might have reflected that the bright creamy Ancaster stone did not give such a successful impression as the warm tawny creams, occasionally veined with iron, of her own Hardwick stone. But architecture apart, there were other reasons for the visit. Sir Francis was more than just an acquaintance, he had been one of the commissioners representing Bess at Ashford in 1585, who had heard the pros and cons of the dispute with Shrewsbury. There would also be a marriage connection. It all added up to a friendly association which went back a few years.

Eighteen months after Shrewsbury died, Sir Francis had written tactfully to Gilbert Talbot, saying that Bess had offered him the lease of ironworks at Oakamoor and woods at Alveton,[5] both in Staffordshire, and asking permission to do business with her. Alveton or Alton woods were Talbot property which had come to Bess under the marriage settlement. What Sir Francis said was not strictly true, for the initiative had not come from Bess but from Loggin, his own ironmaster, who proposed putting up two of the new blast furnaces at Oakamoor. The idea was attractive to Sir Francis who was looking for new ways to rescue his rocky finances, but there was the drawback that he had no capital to finance the new furnaces. Loggin had approached Bess in the matter and arranged a loan of £400, secured on Willoughby lands, and that the nearby Alton woods should be used for fuel to fire the furnaces, with payment to Bess for what timber was taken. The matter had been proposed as early as May 1591 and the whole thing signed and sealed by August that same year. The arrangement suited Bess for she was able to exploit the woodland at no cost to herself, receiving an annual £172 in rent and for stock, with £40 interest on the loan. The losers were the Talbots who got Alton back at her death with the timber gone. Unfortunately Sir Francis fell out with Loggin, and Bess had to lend her own ironmaster, Sylvester Smyth, to keep the investment paying until a replacement was found.

But when Bess was at Wollaton that summer of 1592, the business of the ironworks was running smoothly and would not have occupied much of their time. Sir Francis may have broached the subject of a much bigger loan with Bess that evening: he wanted to borrow the huge sum of £3000. From her experience over the ironworks, Bess would have been aware of the state of the Willoughby finances and for such an enormous sum she required very good security. There was a lot of protracted negotiation before the money was handed over in May 1594. The arranging of the security was made difficult by the entail, settlements and mortgages on the Willoughby estates – the problem was to find land not already earmarked. In return for this loan, Bess took an annual interest of £300 on the security of five manors, the mortgage made out in Arbella's name.

These deals with Sir Francis are fairly typical of Bess and her methods of business. In the event Bess received the interest on her loan of £400 for the ironworks and an income from the sale of timber in Alton woods until her death in 1608 – a very good investment. On the loan of £3000 Bess did even better: the capital was never repaid and Arbella took over the mortgaged properties, said to be worth £15,000. For an outlay of £3000 Bess had secured a magnificent dowry for Arbella.

Bess returned to Hardwick no doubt anxious to restart the building programme held in suspense for eight months. What she found must have pleased her for both Rhodes and Balechouse, who had been left in charge, received rewards for work well done. With Bess's return the building was restarted and more labourers engaged. Bess had little to distract her now from completing her new Hardwick Hall.

'SPEAK SOFTLY MY MASTERS'
1592-1598

Within days of Bess's return the walls of the top floor of the new building were begun. To make the old Hall more habitable, the glazing was finished and fireplaces put into bedchambers; Bess was keeping the draughts out of the stairway leading to her apartments and making her own rooms snug for the winter months. Either the old Hall was too uncomfortable or she had more pressing reasons to prevent her staying, for Bess was only at Hardwick for ten weeks before she left for Chatsworth. A plot to kidnap Arbella had been discovered, but it was dealt with and Bess was back again at Hardwick by the end of the year. The reason for her return is clear. On 17 January 1593 Bess signed a contract with Edward Savage to buy the manors of Heath, Stainsby and Owlcotes for £3416 and the sum was paid in two parts on 18 January and 14 March. So was ended the fealty owed by Hardwick to the Savages in the manor of Stainsby, which had existed for centuries – they were all now under the same ownership. Bess was building up a solid holding of lands round Hardwick.[1]

By now her own apartments in the old Hall were comfortable enough to pass the winter in. No outside work was done in cold weather, this had been the pattern from the beginning; the bitter months of January and February had always seen the casual labour laid off. But by April after work had restarted, the walls of the top floor of the new house were sufficiently completed for Bess to sign a contract with a carpenter, Peter Yates, to make the roof of the new Hardwick for £50, and he received his first payment on 3 May. As a memorial to Yates this roof remains as the worst piece of work put into Hardwick. That it has stood the test of time is due to the massive timbers used and not Yates's skill.

It is obvious that the erection of a building such as Hardwick required a considerable amount of organisation. But it required far more different planning than a modern building construction job for Bess was supplying nearly all her own materials. Until the roof was complete, no internal work such as the laying of floors could be done, and until the floors were down the fireplaces and door frames could not be built. Whilst the roof was going on, trees to make the great floor beams were being felled in nearby Teversal woods, and stone for fireplaces and doorways was being worked at the same time. None of the timber was seasoned; it all went in 'green' and as it slowly dried out, sagged under its own weight, leaving many of the floors uneven to this day. Mortar had to be made on the spot and the North Orchard – the present car park – was given over to many kilns burning the locally mined limestone and puffing out their smoke away from the house in the prevailing south-west wind. Their ash, a final economy, was used to make the floors throughout the house, and laid on hay harvested in the fields that summer. The credit for all this organisation which apparently went so smoothly was due to John Balechouse or 'Painter', a favoured servant of Bess's, who was paid an annual wage of £2 as well as having a farm on Bess's land at Ault Hucknall at Hardwick's back door. (His son James, also working for Bess, was still living there in 1618.)

At the end of May 1593 Bess left Hardwick again for Chatsworth, and she did not return for just over a year. It was during this period of Bess's absence, when the first turret was being completed in April 1594 – that on the north-west corner – that Balechouse must have realised that the height of the turrets would not be sufficient to give a balanced elevation. Every two weeks Balechouse made a trip to Chatsworth, possibly taking Jenkinson's accounts for checking, and on every visit she rewarded him with a gift of 10s (50p); it says a great deal for her trust in Balechouse's ability that Bess left him to increase the height of the turrets without first seeing the effect of the low silhouette for herself.

Bess returned to Hardwick about mid-June and in general must have approved of what she saw. The interior work was well in hand and both staircases were being constructed. It is true of Hardwick as of any other great Elizabethan house that the layout of the rooms was severely controlled by the life which was to be lived in them. The plan of Hardwick was strictly based on the demands of the ceremonial which was to be carried on within its walls. From the moment that Bess would have risen in the morning until she went to bed at night, her servants performed a ritual around her which went on whether Bess was in the room or not. This ritual was based on that of the royal Court and may even have been inherited from Byzantium. It had the advantage of giving every member of a large household a definite and distinct position in the hierarchy, which was divided into gentleman servants, who were better paid and who took the greatest part in the ceremonies, and yeoman servants, who did most of the work. Everyone knew his place and his job, and seemingly nothing was allowed to interfere with the strict ceremonial which went on within the walls of these great Elizabethan houses.

It is not immediately obvious to modern eyes why the great hall at Hardwick should have separate doors from the kitchens and from the pantry, but these were two distinct catering departments, although both were under the clerk comptroller. From these doors at mealtimes would have come two separate processions, led by the usher carrying his rod and calling 'Speak softly my masters' to silence the hubbub. Respectfully, the servants would stand in the hall as the food was carried away to the upper servants and family above stairs – all this before any could dine in the hall. The kitchen, with its servery and dresser, and the pantry were essential for these Elizabethan puppets to perform their ritual: without them the service due to Bess would have come to a halt.

Because Hardwick was a matriarchal household, there were slight differences which had not been taken into account in the original plan; Bess's closest servants were women and this caused Bess to alter the lesser staircase during its construction. The hall was given over to the yeoman servants and the like visitors; the gentleman servants and similar visitors ate in the low great chamber upstairs; and Bess probably dined in her own withdrawing room in winter and the high great chamber in summer. By altering the course of the lesser stair in November 1594 she gained a small paved dining-room, which should have been a landing, and lost the privacy of the chapel which then became a landing as well as a chapel, leaving no doubt where her priorities lay. This small dining-room would supposedly let the women dine separately from the gentlemen in the low great chamber and gave them a certain superiority, which would have been the intention in this matriarchal household. It also emphasised the importance of Bess at the top of the pyramid.

The organisation of Bess's servant hierarchy was also different from that of other great households in her need for expert legal advice, necessitating extra places on what can be called her board of management. William Cavendish took a great deal of Bess's work into his own hands but only under his mother's direction. By then William had a London house managed by Henry Travice, his steward. Directly under Bess was Timothy Pusey, whose responsibility was enormous: receipts and expenditure of large sums of money went through his capable hands and he must have known almost more of Bess's business than Bess herself. Pusey had a legal training and drafted many of Bess's indentures and complaints; he wrote her letters and he kept the greater part of the accounts; he might be termed a managing director under the chairmanship of Bess. It is doubtful if he ever had time to himself for he seemed to be at everything.

In the 1590s Bess's estates were under the management of seventeen bailiffs who were responsible for the collection of rents and arrears. An obvious example is George Russell, bailiff of the western lands. Twice a year Russell collected his rents and either sent or brought them himself to Hardwick. Like the other bailiffs he gave the money to Bess's receiver William Reason, submitted his report to Bess, was rewarded by his mistress and departed with his expenses paid. Reason noted the amounts received in his books, then passed the sums over to Pusey who accounted for these in his records but with less detail than Reason.

It is impossible to get completely accurate figures from Elizabethan account books. They were never kept for that purpose but were simple imprest accounts of receipt and expenditure of monies entrusted to the keeper of the account. For instance, if a bailiff gave his rents to William Cavendish, then that sum would not show in Reason's book for he had never received it; neither was Reason concerned with the cost of collection nor the overheads of the estates. It was Pusey's job to pass the rents to Bess who would have put them in one of her many locked coffers, kept in a closet off her bed-chamber. In the 1590s Bess's gross annual receipts were an average £8300 of which an average £3000 came from her Talbot marriage settlement; by the end of the century the total had probably risen to a gross annual £10,000. But this was only her personal gross income: it does not account for the income from lands she had made over to William, to Charles and to Arbella; if these are taken into account the total is nearly doubled. It was an astonishing wealth for a woman who had started her life seventy years earlier with nothing at all.

It was also astonishing that Bess should have taken such initiatives in furthering her enterprises. After all she had more than enough for herself, and the only explanation must be that she was not doing it for herself but to ensure that her dynasty had the greatest foundation of wealth it was possible for her to provide. In November of 1593 Edward Jones, the bailiff of the Oxfordshire lands, was sent to Devon to 'talk with men touching the Alum mines'. Alum was used in tanning and dyeing and it may have been that Bess was having trouble in getting hold of the stuff, but whatever the reason 'the Alum men' were brought up from Devonshire to prospect for alum on the Shropshire estates. Finding none, they returned to their homes and the matter was forgotten.

It might be expected that Bess would have preferred to exploit the minerals in her lands for herself, but this was not the case. Lead, which is plentiful in Derbyshire, hardly concerned her at all; she had ore deposits at Winster, Aldwark and Bonsall which were left to William to develop. On one occasion, Bess had to buy lead from Henry Cavendish, indicating that she had none of her own. At Wingfield, she had blast furnaces and an iron works under her iron-master, Sylvester Smyth, and possibly a small glass works there as well, but coal, which lay just beneath the surface of nearly all her Derbyshire lands, Bess preferred to farm out for others to exploit. Her pits at Hardstoft and Tibshelf were let out, but she kept the Bolsover pits in her own hands, even sinking another shaft there in 1595. It may have been the trouble and cost of transporting the coal which deterred Bess, for from Bolsover the waggons dragged their heavy loads to Hansworth and Clown Moor to get a better price than could be obtained at Bolsover.

Timothy Pusey, although occupying the position of a steward, was never called anything other than 'Tymothy' by his mistress. She paid him £10 a year and by 1600 had given him the lease of a farm and a mill. In the autumn of 1592, Mr Levy came as official steward at double what Pusey was paid and this may have caused some resentment. Levy left after two years and the office of official steward was never revived; Pusey took over everything in his capable hands from the day Levy left. Directly under Pusey was the clerk comptroller, Rowland Harrison, a gentleman servant who kept the fortnightly accounts of household expenditure. Every item was covered: the sums paid to the clerk of the kitchen, rewards of money to visitors and tips to their servants, the amounts paid to Ellen Steward, the housekeeper at Chatsworth, and to Robert Allwood at Wingfield; the bi-annual wages totalling £140 included payments to milkmaids, laundresses, millers, gardeners, warriners and a mercer's boy. Sometimes Harrison's entries in his accounts conjure up pictures of a world which never was: 'Given to a maid that went to Chatsworth with the tame hind' might have a mark of eternal sunshine but August 1594,[2] when the maid was leading her hind through the lanes of Derbyshire, was in a particularly wet summer and she would have been lucky to get away without a drenching.

The marriages of her servants usually brought a generous response from Bess. One of her ladies-in-waiting, Anne Cooper, received a gift of £50 in April 1592 when she married Rowland Harrison and her wages increased, although she continued to be known as Mrs Cooper. Abraham Smith, one of the master masons who cut so much of the special decoration at Hardwick, was given a wedding gift of 40s (£2) when he married in September that same year. But only Henry Cook, appropriately the cook, had the honour of a special supper party on Bess, as well as £5 as a gift: Bess paid for sixteen of her staff to have supper with Henry and his new wife at Stainsby. It cost her 5s 4d (27p) and the guests cut right across the gentleman and yeoman structure for there were four of the gentlemen servants as guests, yeoman servants and kitchen staff, even the kitchen boy. That supper party in June 1594 must have been a night to remember and talk about. All these household expenses were noted and totalled in Harrison's fortnightly accounts, totalled again by Pusey and finally confirmed under Bess's distinctive hand and spelling 'E Shrouesbury'; she signed her name at the bottom of every page. The household accounts cast a brilliant and blinding light on life in a great Elizabethan household in the 1590s. Visitors come and go; horses are put up at Beightons at Chatsworth or Bradshaws, the inn at Hardwick's gate; huge sums of money are given to William to pay out for land purchase; gifts of money go to Bess's family; the mysterious comings and goings are recorded of John Hacker of East Bridgford, who acted as her occasional legal adviser and strategist for matters in Nottinghamshire; the visits are registered of her kinsman George Chaworth of Annesley, another of Bess's legal advisers, married to Mary Kniveton. All these pass through Harrison's pages – a pageant of Elizabethan life tramping through the halls of the old and the new Hardwick.

The buying of special provisions in bulk for the household posed a problem. At intervals William Jenkinson, who may have been clerk of the kitchen, was sent to Hull to buy dried fruits, hops, imported salt, salad oil, claret and, once, a topknot of figs for 6s 8d (33p); all to be laboriously hauled by water as far as Stockwith, then by waggon to Bawtry on the North Road, from there to Worksop and then on to Hardwick. Or they would go to Stourbridge Fair to buy fish, soap, cork and candlewicks. Bess's servants, sent so busily throughout the Midlands on their various tasks, wearing the distinctive blue livery cloaks and velvet caps with Bess's badge, or despatched post haste on the London road with letters to the Queen or Burghley, were hard-working and well rewarded. They were also surprisingly young. John Bamford, who offended Bess and left her service in 1595, was only twenty-nine. Elizabeth Digby's husband John, who died in 1641, would have been about Bamford's age as, no doubt, was also Timothy Pusey, who stayed on with William Cavendish after Bess died, for after he left William's service, Pusey married a daughter of John Clay of Crich, another of Bess's occasional servants. He bought Selston Manor, was a justice for Nottinghamshire for over twenty years, and Sheriff of the County in 1625, and died in the time of the Civil War; Pusey was a successful man.

By the time the new Hardwick was finished, the hall must have been filled with young servants, some of whom were later successful.

The house must often have echoed to the sound of music. On a September night in 1599 Bess was entertained by the Nottingham waits, the Earl of Rutland's musicians, and those of the Earl of Essex; a year later, the Queen's players, as likely as not, played Shakespeare in the great hall of Hardwick, with Bess watching from the gallery over the screen. Fond though Bess was of visiting musicians, in her late years she had no troupe of her own, although there were those in the household who could play instruments and did so when commanded. The household at Hardwick was a young and buoyant one. There was laughter in the hall and song in the kitchen, with Bess drawing her strength from the enthusiasms of youth, and as can be the case with the elderly surrounded by the young, living far beyond her allotted span.

But this is only one side of the picture. The years 1594, 1595, 1596 and 1597 brought heavy rains – a catastrophe, washing away the harvests and bringing famine, starvation and disease throughout England. Bess's revenues from her lands suffered a twenty-five per cent drop yet she continued her building without hesitation. Indeed the employment of so much local labour must have brought some alleviation of hardship to the area around Hardwick. In the cold of the winter of 1595–6, the poor huddled round the lime kilns for warmth in the North Orchard and were given alms. But the distant estates such as the Western Lands whose revenues were sucked into William's pocket must have suffered severely under their absentee landlord. As husbandry decayed, the government enforced meatless days in 1597 to preserve what livestock was left; Bess built fishponds at Hardwick, Wingfield and Shirland, stocked with pike, carp, tench, bream and perch, but her fish farms only came into useful production in 1600 when the crisis was over.

With famine stalking the country in the 1590s, life at Hardwick went on as if there was no distress outside. By now nearly seventy, Bess obviously considered that she had not much time left to complete her plans to leave her dynasty housed in suitable mansions. Charles Cavendish had married again, Catherine, daughter of Cuthbert, Lord Ogle, who brought with her northern lands including Ogle Castle, and gave Charles his only two sons. Charles was well equipped with houses: he had Stoke Manor in Derbyshire, and had taken a lien on Bolsover Castle in 1588 giving him the right of first offer by Gilbert Talbot after Bess's eventual death; he also rented Welbeck Abbey from Gilbert in 1597, buying it outright ten years later.

It was William and his growing family who still had no home of their own. He had apartments in the old Hardwick beneath the hill great chamber, which would have served as his reception room when he was Sheriff in 1595–6, and in the new Hardwick a chamber was set aside for him on the ground floor. But with the purchase of the Stainsby estate from Edward Savage in 1593, this situation was changed. On 8 March that year, before the final sum was paid over to Savage, five wallers working on the new Hardwick signed a contract with Bess and William to build the walls of a house at Owlcotes just three miles to the north-west of Hardwick. There was a house on the site already which was to be incorporated in the new Owlcotes manor. The new house was to be of the Hardwick type with a spine wall but only two turrets; it was not to be splendidly finished in smooth ashlar but merely scappled; and the hall, probably transverse as at Hardwick, was to be twenty feet high. This house was built to give William and his family a chance to escape from the demands of his mother; it was still standing in 1688 when it had become Pierrepont property, but gone by 1817. Owlcotes had served its purpose as William's refuge and with the passing of Bess it was no longer of use. All that is left is an early seventeenth-century building standing in a corner of the court wall – perhaps once a lodge but now a farmhouse – some stone strapwork and one delightful scalloped alcove, better than any decoration at Hardwick.

William had become Bess's shadow, seemingly with no purpose of his own other than that directed by his mother's ambitions; as Sheriff of Derbyshire he would have been able to give their joint purpose considerable help. William appeared to act as Bess's errand boy and representative in all things involving detail which Bess did not wish to be troubled with; she was bothered by rheumatism restricting her accustomed activity and William, now in his forties, was sent here and there on his mother's behalf.

Because Bess had acquired a great deal of land in recent years, she became the target of legal suits by aggrieved parties who felt that they had been the losers in bargains made over their heads. The law was a game with incredibly complicated rules; given sufficient money a suit could be spun out for decades until one side died, became bankrupt or simply wearied of the contest. There were short cuts which could be taken: the Star Chamber was a court set up to watch over the rights of the Queen's subjects and if a plaintiff could show that his rights had been interfered with, such as bribing a jury to bring a verdict unfavourable to the plaintiff, then he could make a complaint to the Star Chamber and the matter would be dealt with quickly. This exciting game of legal snakes and ladders required almost inexhaustible funds and in this respect Bess was well placed. The legal department at Hardwick was kept constantly busy and Edward Dean, her solicitor, sent regular annual bills, for example, in one term in 1594: 'Disbursed in the Easter term about the suit of Clifford's cause etc. £95.' In one whole year, 1599, William had paid out £209 for an annual item he called 'legal causes'. This was the cost of the game.

Years before in the 1570s Bess had bought lands in Edensor at Chatsworth's doorstep. She probably took them over when a loan made to Henry Clifford, Second Earl of Cumberland was not repaid.[3] These lands had belonged to Sir Ingram Clifford – a kinsman of the Earl, who had no heirs; Sir Ingram granted them to the Second Earl who then used the Edensor properties as security to raise the loan from Bess. Old Sir Ingram died about 1573, the Second Earl also died and his son George became the Third Earl of Cumberland, who with his brother Francis inherited their father's lands including those which had belonged to Sir Ingram. For reasons too labyrinthine to discover, Francis Clifford chose to challenge Bess's title to the Edensor lands. Instead of tackling the case head-on, he attacked from a flank, two of his supporters disputing with one of Bess's old tenants the legality of a lease at Edensor. On the face of it the case was a simple one and no mention was made of Cavendish or Clifford. Bess's old tenant, who had long ago left Edensor, confessed that he married the natural daughter of the man from whom he had originally taken over the lease, who in turn had leased from Sir Ingram, and there the matter might have rested, for Bess, or rather her old tenant, won the case heard in the Court of Common Pleas in London at Easter Term 1595. It all appeared to be a run-of-the-mill dispute – but it dragged on through the rest of the decade.

With the declaration of the verdict, Francis Clifford broke cover. He made a complaint to the Star Chamber that Bess and William Cavendish had corrupted and bribed the jury and others in the case. This was a nasty one for they very likely had done just that, though they denied it and produced convincing evidence to the contrary. Even if guilty, Bess would have been doing no more than others in a similar position of power were doing. The case is worth looking at, for it shows Bess's legal department working at its best.

The complaint to the Star Chamber, which came to Bess in October, was no surprise, for Clifford had visited Bess at Chatsworth in late June. He and three servants, with his legal adviser, stayed a night and no doubt discussed with her what Clifford was planning, but he found Bess unyielding and was forced to go forward with his case.

The jury for the case in Common Pleas had been empanelled by John Rhodes who preceded William Cavendish as Sheriff. Bess sent for Rhodes to come to her at Hardwick before the trial. At the time he owed her £500 which he had on loan: Bess gave him a list of twenty-four names, some of whom were tenants of hers who owed rent, and they turned up on the empanelled jury. That was the substance of Clifford's accusation and he had got his evidence from one of Bess's disaffected gentleman servants, John Bamforth. Bamforth was the nigger in Bess's woodpile: he left Bess's service in June 1595 – just about the time when Clifford visited Bess at Chatsworth. Bamforth claimed to have seen a great deal. He had held a position of trust which he now betrayed. Against the payment of his wages when he was dismissed was written 'to be allowed hereafter if he deserve yt'. Here was a man with a grievance and Clifford had secured him, but whether Bamforth's life was ever worth living after all the dust had settled cannot be said.

Bess was also accused of saying that she would spend more than the land was worth before Clifford should get it. Very likely she had said that during the Chatsworth interview; it was exactly the sort of thing Bess would have said to such a threat. But was she actually guilty? Likely enough yes, but none of the statements by Bamforth can now be proved. One of the jurors was John Calow who rented Bess's coal pits at Hardstoft. Clifford claimed that he owed £16 in rent. Calow had owed rent and would do so in the future, but at the time of the case in Common Pleas he did not. John Rhodes was to borrow money of Bess and a Mr Rhodes repaid £150 to her in October 1596, but there is no record of John Rhodes actually owing money to Bess in 1595. Rhodes was the son of Francis Rhodes who had made a fortune as judge of Common Pleas: John should not have been short of money, but in fact he was, for in 1600 he sold lands to Bess worth £2500, which shows that he had a need. Bamforth said that Rowland Harrison gave £20 to the jurors to cover their expenses, and in the Common Pleas case a witness claimed that money had been given him by 'Timothie ... to bear his charges to London, but from who he gave he knoweth not'. Who else could that have been but Timothy Pusey?

When all is said and done, it would have been very hard indeed to draw a jury from Derbyshire without involving men who were concerned with the Cavendish family in one way or another. It is quite likely that Bess had lent money to John Rhodes, for he could help her as he demonstrated, and she in turn could help Rhodes; quite likely too Bess paid the jurors' expenses for they could not have afforded their own and if she had not found the money then Clifford would have done so. For one gleaming instant the full details of Bess's methods are shown and one is left to wonder how many more of the hundreds of cases which involved her and her family were so managed. Possibly all of those she won, for that was what she paid her legal servants for, but her own head for legal matters must not be underestimated. Pusey wrote out the answer to Clifford's bill of complaint and it is a very long and involved piece of evidence; plainly he was no novice in such things, but how much of it was Bess's work? She did not pay high wages for nothing, but at the same time, being the person she was, it cannot be doubted that a lot of the drafting was her own work. Bess had said that she would spend more than the land was worth or until the plaintiff wearied – her old virtues of patience and perseverance perhaps – but unfortunately the verdicts of the Star Chamber are lost, and the results in these cases cannot be known. They went on year after year, perhaps until Clifford was wearied and Bess had spent more than the land was worth. The Under Sheriff must have echoed the sentiments of many when he said, 'I would that I was honestly shut of it' – Bess kept Edensor and the Cavendishes still hold it to this day.

Bess's wealth had given her power, but she depended on the Queen for that power. She would not have made such progress without influence in Court circles, a word here, some persuasion there, a present at the right time and a gift at New Year: this was not a lesson which her son-in-law Gilbert Talbot ever learnt.

In 1592 John Puckering was made Lord Keeper; in May Bess wrote in congratulation on the appointment.[4] This was the sort of diplomatic contact which had served Bess so well in the past. It had never been her policy to fall out with anyone in power. Not so Gilbert Talbot: he too wrote to Puckering that same year, not in congratulation but about the festering and regrettable business of the Stanhopes' weir across the Trent and near their house at Shelford in Nottinghamshire. The matter was absurd and no business of Gilbert's. It had been going on for years, and by the end all must have been heartily sick of Gilbert's disputatious nature. The episode had grown out of all proportion. Gilbert claimed that the Stanhopes had no right to build a weir on the Trent; they may or may not have had, but Gilbert, unlike his father, was not Lord Lieutenant of Nottinghamshire and this was the cause of his resentment. The honours which had been awarded to Shrewsbury had not automatically come to Gilbert who, although he had been made Lord Lieutenant of Derbyshire in 1591 and admitted to the Order of the Garter in 1592, was not involved in the Queen's confidences and State affairs like the Stanhopes – and this too Gilbert resented. He took his bad feelings towards the Stanhopes so far as to attack their weir with organised rioters. Eventually the case went to the Star Chamber and the Stanhopes were vindicated. It all led to bad blood between the two families: Bess's daughter, Mary Talbot, wrote to Sir Thomas that he was 'more wretched, vile and miserable than any creature living and for your wickedness, become more ugley in shape and the vilest toad in the world', which must have caused Sir Thomas some surprise, but it shows how far the matter had gone.

Gilbert generated disputes. In 1594 he challenged his brother Edward to a duel, trouble having arisen over a disputed lease. Edward declined to meet his brother with dagger and rapier. This episode too culminated in the Star Chamber when Edward brought a complaint against a Mr Wood. Wood had been an apothecary in Mary's household for two and a half years, compounding nostrums for her gout. This Wood spoke out of turn, a thing he must have regretted, for he was imprisoned for his slander claiming that Edward Talbot had offered him an annuity of £100 to poison Gilbert. The case brought a counter-complaint from Gilbert who revealed that the method of administering the poison had been by means of doctored gloves. The constant quarrels involving Gilbert made him unpopular with the Queen, who had found Shrewsbury difficult and now considered his son doubly so. After the affair of the poison Gilbert was banned from Court.

Gilbert's disgrace did not last long, however. An alliance between England and France was confirmed in 1596 and Essex was to head an embassy to wait on Henry IV of France. But Essex was engaged on his flamboyant expedition to Cadiz and unable to attend, therefore Gilbert was appointed in his place with an allowance of £6 per day. The purpose of the delegation, apart from the political significance, was to present the Order of the Garter to the French King and to introduce Sir Walter Mildmay as Ambassador. This mission, together with the earlier honours, went some way to restoring Gilbert's self-confidence.

Not only was Gilbert involved in these rather ridiculous disputes, but they tended to rebound on his friends. In 1592 Charles Cavendish had challenged John Stanhope to a duel early one morning at Lambeth Bridge, but after some absurd posturing the thing was called off because Stanhope had arrived wearing a padded doublet for safety. Obviously Stanhope did not forgive Charles for he made a cowardly attack in 1599 at Kirkby-in-Ashfield.

In 1597 Charles Cavendish had started to build a house for himself at Kirkby in Nottinghamshire, only a few miles from Hardwick. Bess gave him a total of £400 towards the building costs, but the house was never finished. In June 1599 Charles was staying at a house near Kirkby when

about 10 of the Clock in the morning, Sir Charles Cavendish being at his new Building at Kirkby which is some quarter of a mile from his little house where he and his lady did lie and going from thence ... being attended only by these three persons, Henry Ogle, Launce Ogle his page and one horsekeeper; he discerned to the number of about 20 horse on the side of a hill, which he thought to be Sir John Byron with company hunting; but suddenly they all galloping apace towards him, he perceived he was beset; whereupon being on a little nag, he set spurs to him, thinking to recover the new buildings, but the tit fell with him and before he could recover out of his stirrup, he was overtaken and ere he could draw sword, 2 pistols were discharged upon him, the one of them with 2 round of 2 bullets hit him in the inside of his thigh but missed the bone, and yet lyeth in his flesh near the point of his buttock.... He with his two poor men and a boy unhorsed six of them and killed two of them in the place; a third fell down in the Forest and is thought dead also.... Upon this, some of the workmen coming towards them though without any weapons, John Stanhope was now foremost in running away....

It was a nasty and untoward experience which put Charles off ever finishing his new building and the stones were later used to build Bolsover Castle which he bought off his friend Gilbert Talbot in 1608. The wound was a bad one but not dangerous: Bess gave the surgeon of Chesterfield 10s (50p) when he came from attending Charles. However, the injury was still giving trouble in January 1600 for the Queen sent her own surgeon Mr Clowes, to 'meddle with his probe'.

Now that Bess had left Court for the last time, she lost interest in the central struggles for power around the Queen. Nearly into her seventies and gloriously replete with wealth, she had no compulsion to become involved in games she had played so often in the past. In the 1590s all her energies were taken up with the profitable running of her many enterprises and the completion of her new Hardwick. By the beginning of October 1597 – in what looks like a rush job on a sudden decision of Bess's to move into her new house – the window alcoves were panelled in a bedchamber where 'Abraham's terms are'. This bedchamber can be identified as Bess's own, for Abraham Smith, a mason, carved and chiselled grotesque 'terms' – human figures terminating in a pedestal – on each side of the overmantel, and they are still there. Obviously Bess had insisted on getting this room completed for her immediate occupation. The great hall was panelled and the privies completed in the court outside.

Bess moved into the new Hardwick on Tuesday 4 October 1597

to the sound of music. Of the four amateur musicians who played her in, fate had tragedy in store for two: Starkey, the household chaplain, would commit suicide over his involvement with Arbella and her schemes; and John Good, another of Bess's favoured servants, would throw away his service by betraying Bess for the same cause, ending up locked in the Gatehouse Jail at Westminster. The remaining two musicians were Francis Parker, a gentleman servant who was witness to Bess's will made in 1601, and Richard Abrahall whose mother had been lady-in-waiting to Arbella.

Both old and new Hardwicks were not finally completed for another two years and Bess can seldom have been spared the sound of hammering and banging echoing through those yet unfinished rooms. John Balechouse or 'Painter' employed his skills in painting the frieze of the long gallery, the Hatton hangings went up in the gallery in July of 1598, and yards of Hardwick matting at 4d (2p) per yard was brought in from Shropshire and Leicestershire to lay on the gallery floor and elsewhere. John Good was sent off to Owlcotes to mat the gallery there in 1600. And although the construction of new Hardwick was more or less complete by the end of 1599, the furnishing of the interior went on until 1601. The total cost of Bess's building programme can only be estimated, for her accounts which open on 18 October 1587 do not show what the work already done had cost. Nevertheless, from 18 October 1587 until 17 January 1598, when the accounts end and the work was all but completed, the cost for the two Hardwick Halls was £3700 and the total building cost would have been about £5000 – or nearly half Bess's gross annual income.[5]

As the building of Hardwick was completed, the labour was laid off and the master craftsmen moved on to other work. It was a trade which gave occasional well-paid employment to masons, and after that was over they looked out and waited for other work – they were not known as freemasons for nothing, free of any master and free to move as they wished. As the men were laid off, the remaining lodges at Hardwick must have buzzed with rumours of other employment in the offing, of buildings already going up or planned by Smythson. Houses such as Doddington Hall in Lincolnshire, a building of the same time as Hardwick, on which at least one of Bess's masons worked (its builder, Thomas Tailor, seemingly ran out of money, for the interior was never finished in his lifetime); and Quenby Hall in Leicestershire on which two more Hardwick masons found work. But not all Bess's men drifted away. Wisely she kept her two best masons permanently on her pay roll: Abraham Smith who had first come to her at Chatsworth in 1581, and Thomas Accres who had worked for Bess as far back as 1576. These were old friends to Bess and men she could rely on. It suited her to have them permanently tied to her service and it suited them. Both had leases of farms from Bess which gave them something to fall back on when work was scarce: Smith had fifty-five acres at Ashford where the best blackstone had been found for Hardwick's over-mantels, and was still living there in 1616; Accres too had a farm on Bess's lands and died in 1607. This arrangement was convenient to all, as Bess had their skill at hand when needed, and the matter for their part, was summed up in 1670 when Sir William Coventry noted that few building craftsmen 'rely entirely on their Trade as not to have a small Farm, the Rent of which they are the more able to pay by the gains of their Trade'.[6]

Bess's patronage did not stop with Smith and Accres. Renold Plumtree, a waller who had worked at Hardwick and Owlcotes, settled at Hardstoft and died there in 1631. Robert Ashmore, another waller, had come to Bess in 1577. He too had worked at Hardwick and Owlcotes, and died at Edensor in 1617. Both Ashmore and Plumtree were very likely tenants of Bess – did these old men meet in Derbyshire inns and talk of the old days when Hardwick was building, of the ingenious engine built by Accres to cut blackstone at the Chatsworth quarry; did they embellish their own mantels with decorated stone?

With the completion of Hardwick, Bess had not finished her building. Chatsworth, Hardwick and Owlcotes were evidence of her material splendour, but to ensure the future of her soul in afterlife Bess sought redemption in this world by building and endowing almshouses in Derby for twelve almsfolk of the town. The building was started some time in the spring of 1598 and by March 1600 the first twelve old people had moved in, one of whom had been a servant of Bess's, Isabell Heyward. Twice a year each received their bounty of 33s 4d (£1.67) and a livery when they first arrived. With her spiritual and material business settled, Bess was clearly putting her house in order against her inevitable death, but fate had not finished with the ageing Countess; there were still to be a few more years left to her and some of that time was not to be passed in the tranquillity which Bess may have felt she had earned.

'WEARIED OF MY LIFE'
1598-1603

Arbella was twenty-two when with her grandmother she moved into the new Hardwick, and she was still unmarried. Bess was about seventy years old. Age and youth do not make easy companions and it was an epoch when years were valued for their wisdom and experience – youth took second place and Arbella had to conform to her grandmother's wishes in most things. It was not easy for the two women: there were disagreements and Bess with her sharp tongue could lacerate deeply. Also the fact that she was not married was becoming something of a disaster to Arbella: at the same age Bess had already been married twice.

In almost every way grandmother and grand-daughter were opposite in character. Where Arbella was extrovert, Bess had learnt to keep her feelings to herself; Arbella was inclined to let her heart rule her head, a thing Bess would never entertain; where Arbella was impatient, Bess looked on patience and forbearance as virtues. Arbella had been taught all the necessary skills for a lady of the Court; Bess had to acquire these for herself – she never learnt French and it is doubtful if she understood Latin, whereas Arbella was reported to have studied Greek and Hebrew, as well as speaking French, Italian and Spanish and reading Latin and, being fond of music, she played the viol. Only in determination did Arbella share her grandmother's character.

In appearance Arbella should not have been called beautiful, although the Venetian Ambassador flatteringly reported her to be of great beauty. She was an amusing and lively girl, and in life and movement her appearance, which by her portraits is only pleasant and attractive, may well have become beautiful in the eye of the beholder.

In the new Hardwick, Arbella probably occupied the comfortable bedchamber in the south-east turret, on the same floor as Bess's own. Nearby was an unheated chamber for her lady-in-waiting, Bridget Shirland, which is now two bathrooms. Arbella called her chamber her 'quondom study' and although in 1601 it had a bed in it, Arbella's bedstead, with its gilt knobs and canopy in blue and white, was in her grandmother's bedchamber – where Bess could keep a closer eye on her charge, a restriction which must have added to Arbella's resentements.[1]

For the moment, however, there was the novelty of the new house to distract them both. Bess's drawing-room, where she and Arbella spent so much time, still has the same six tapestries 'with personages' above the panelling, but Bess's chair 'of black leather gilded' and its footstool and footcarpet have long since gone. Likewise what may have been Arbella's chair 'of wrought cloth of gold with gold and red silk fringe' has vanished. Two chairs 'for Children' were for Bess's grandchildren, William's children, in the schoolroom below: Gilbert, the oldest, who died young and William aged seven in 1597; but 'little James' and the daughter Frances would have had to sit on one of the many stools. The room was a hotch-potch of clutter and colour. As well as the red and gold trimmings of the chair there were cushions of gold and damask, of crimson velvet, and a screen to set against the draughts in a 'violet coloured cloth'. Bess's bedchamber, a smaller room, was even more crowded: in addition to the two bedsteads, were a great iron chest, three great trunks, two little trunks, three desks, no less than six coffers, a cupboard, two chairs and stools. It must have been a difficult room to walk about in without tripping against some of the jumbled contents. But this was the room Bess probably used in winter more than her withdrawing-room; here was a folding table to eat from, here were desks for her writing and coffers for her money; against the cold draughts from the two huge windows were red curtains with three coverlets to hang before them, as well as another coverlet to hang in front of one of the three draughty and ill-fitting doors, whilst her bed, the final defence against those bitter Derbyshire blasts, was a cocoon of coverings. With the five bed curtains drawn around her, Bess lay on a featherbed with a mattress beneath and with two quilts and eight Spanish blankets on top of her. Before the roaring fire Bess could sit in her 'chair of russet satin, striped with silver and a russet silk fringe', whilst a lady-in-waiting read aloud from Calvin on Job, Solomon's proverbs, or a book of meditations – all good, safe reading.

As Bess walked through the rooms of her new Hardwick, leaning on her stick, the splendour she had created could only have given her satisfaction. The superb high great chamber still has the same Ulysses tapestries, but the wainscoting painted with heads which Byng noted in 1798 has gone and there are only the remnants in the two sides of the window bay.[2] In the adjoining state withdrawing-room with the hangings of the virtues; and the 'drawing table carved and gilt, standing upon sea dogs inlaid with marble, stones and wood' – a French table made in Du Cerceau's design – was likely enough a present from Mary, the Scots Queen. All this magnificence Bess had created from nothing and it was her gift to future genera-tions of Cavendishes who, she was certain, would be a credit to their founder.

There were still some inconveniences, however. Arbella gives a pungent comment on the discomforts of a smoking chimney in the low great chamber. In her coming crisis she wrote: 'My cousin [Mary Talbot] and I had spent a little breath in evaporating certain court smoke ... which made some eyes besides ours run awater, we walked in the great chamber for fear of wearing the mats in the gallery (reserved for ... courtiers) and then went down to dinner on the floor below.'

But the troublesomeness of smoking chimneys was a small price to pay for the splendour and the story Bess was telling. Here is the foundation of the Cavendish dynasty, she tells us. By the enormous heraldic overmantels, the story proclaims her lordship, and her authority is not to be doubted. Her presence was established throughout the house and still is after four hundred years for those prepared to read the heraldry of the plasterwork. As one climbs the shallow treads of the stair, the story changes in the state apartments high on the third floor: here Bess acknowledges the authority of the Queen as being greater than her own. In the high great chamber, the first of the succession of these apartments, the arms of the over-mantel are the royal arms of Elizabeth, the Tudor Queen. The great plaster frieze which runs continuously round the room shows Diana, the goddess, queen and huntress, with her court of nymphs in a forest setting: it is the first thing to be seen on entering the chamber, it dominates all and is a compliment to Elizabeth. Diana symbolises Elizabeth in all her virtues, whilst in the surrounding forest, the wild animals, the lions, the elephants, the placid deer and the camels are at peace with each other and the Cavendish stags run through the trees with the unicorn – a symbol of the Queen's purity. This is the story of the fourth eclogue, when the goddess Diana/Astrea returned to bring peace to a blood-soaked and wicked world; there is no more war; the crops grow without travail and the animals are at peace. To Elizabethans this is what life under their Queen meant: she came to the throne after the blood-bath of Mary's reign, she brought peace and unprecedented prosperity to England, and two years before the building of Hardwick was started, Philip's Armada was vanquished. To Bess and her contemporaries, Elizabeth was Diana, Astrea and Ceres, the goddess of plenty, who appears on the overmantel of the little dining-chamber. The Queen's attributes of justice and mercy are symbolised in the statues of the overmantels of the long gallery; her charity is shown in that of the state bed-chamber; and if the originals had survived in the second state bed-chamber and the state withdrawing-room there would have been two more of Elizabeth's conferring attributes, probably Clementia and Temperantia. It is a completely classical story told in a strangely gothic fancy, utterly in the spirit of the English renaissance. The same tale is related in those hangings of applied work, showing the virtues and their attributes, made with Mary's help twenty-five years before – these Bess used as the best hangings in the state bedchamber.

For all its apparent size, Hardwick Hall was not a large house. It only had fourteen principal bedchambers and the accommodation for the yeoman servants was negligible. Before the invention of the bell-pull servants were obviously expected to be at hand when called, for the landings and passage-ways of Hardwick were filled with their truckle beds and beds which folded back into chests. The halls and stairways at night would have been occupied with snoring figures sleeping on temporary pallets, at hand if needed, but the luckier servants would have been in rooms across at the old house, where the rule, in line with other great houses, would have been

two in a bed, yeoman with yeoman and gentleman with gentleman.
Mrs Digby's husband had a room to himself in the old house, as
did William Reason, but in no sense were they comfortable, having
only the barest of furniture. Pusey had no room of his own at all
and was likely enough sleeping near Bess's chamber in some
draughty corridor uncomfortably on hand when called for.

In April 1601, Bess made her will[3] and at the same time had the
great inventory made, listing the contents of both old and new Hardwicks. The contents of both houses were left to William. The
trouble between her and Gilbert Talbot had still not been settled
and it rankled: 'whereas there hath been unkindness offered me by
my son-in-law, the Earl of Shrewsbury, and my daughter his wife
... I do notwithstanding ... pray God to bless them'. Bess left
£1000 to her servants, and money to buy mourning rings to her
immediate family. To Arbella went £1000 and a crystal glass cup
set with lapis lazuli and precious stones, her sable and her pearls.
To her eldest daughter, Frances Pierrepont, she left that book which
Sir William Cavendish had made for her over fifty years before,
set with stones 'with her father's picture and mine drawn in it'. And
to Henry Cavendish she left the contents of Chatsworth. None of
her family was forgotten, her grandchildren were all left something,
and finally the Queen was asked to accept 'this poor widow's mite'
of £200 to buy a gold cup – with this bribe was a request asking
the Queen to accept Arbella back again at Court. The request had
followed letters to Elizabeth in which Bess asked that a husband
be found for Arbella and had culminated in a conversation between
the Queen and the seventy-four-year-old Lady Stafford when she
had presented Bess's New Year gift of twenty gold pieces. The
Queen had expressed a preference for Arbella's offering and had
promised to be 'carefull of her'. Bess was using her will to help
Arbella.

Bess ordered that she be buried at All Hallows Church, Derby,
'in the place appointed' beneath her tomb which was then 'finished
and wants nothing but setting up'. The tomb had been designed
by Robert Smythson and was to stand over vaults which Bess was
still having finished in October that year. So Bess, with her houses
finished, the almshouses built, the will made and her tomb and
vaults ready, had set the seal to her long life and composed herself

to wait for her death, future tranquillity and eventual salvation. But immediate tranquillity was something which Bess would be denied, for Arbella was about to cause her grandmother acute distress and weariness.

Arbella had been the centre of many rumours of marriage, chiefly caused by Catholic plottings to marry her to a Catholic and use her claim to the throne as a means to restore the 'true faith' to the benighted and heathen England, but these proposals had been without the consent of the Queen, Bess or Arbella. The Queen would have preferred the Prince of Condé, nephew to the French King Henry IV – this was her view in that spring of 1601 when Bess was making her will. Elizabeth was visibly ageing but reported to be still 'frolicky', and although Cecil had committed himself to the obvious choice of his Queen's successor in James of Scotland, Elizabeth, prevaricating as ever, had not herself made any such undertaking. Her choice of Condé was then quietly dropped, having served its purpose to keep France happy in temporary courtship with England whilst the Tyrone rebellion in Ireland was put down.

The Queen was content to use Arbella as a piece on a chess board to be kept locked away at Hardwick and to be played with when it suited her and then put back again. As time passed and Arbella grew older, she realised the disability of her royal blood and grew exasperated with the Queen, her grandmother and her lot.

Arbella's frustration was expressed to James Starkey in March of 1602.[4] Starkey, one of the witnesses to Bess's will, who was household chaplain and tutor to William's children, was like Arbella dissatisfied with his fate and so they had a common bond, she against her grandmother and he against William, who had kept Starkey on with the promise of giving him a living which in eight years had not been awarded. Starkey had noticed that Arbella 'oftentimes being at her books would break forth into tears'. She had already told him that 'she would use all the means she could to get from thence by reason she was hardly used ... in dispiteful words, being bobbed and her nose played withal which she could not endure'. Plainly Arbella was finding Bess an elderly tyrant, and Bess was finding the keeping of her grand-daughter a trial which had become a tribulation for both sides.

Starkey left Hardwick and William's service during that summer

and went to London. He had promised to carry letters for Arbella
and spend some £75 on her behalf. About the same time Arbella
sent her jewels and her money up to Yorkshire out of Bess's reach
because she had threatened to take them from her. Arbella was
deliberately planning to escape from Hardwick and from Bess.

Hearing nothing further from Starkey by the beginning of
December, Arbella asked one of Bess's old and trusted servants,
John Dodderidge, 'if he would go a little way for her'. Not long after
that she asked him if he would go a hundred miles, but Dodderidge
took fright for fear of losing his job and said as much to Arbella.
What she asked him to do when he had gone a hundred miles
frightened him even more, for she wanted him to go to a solicitor
by the name of Kirton, whose son had married a daughter of Sir
William Cavendish (not by Bess), and ask him to reopen the matter
of a suggested marriage between herself and Hertford's grandson
Edward Seymour, a proposal which had been floated before and
which had come to nothing. Dodderidge hesitated and to get over
his fears, Arbella promised her protection.

By involving himself behind Bess's back, Dodderidge was being
very foolish indeed – Arbella's persuasion must have been powerful.
Dodderidge was one of the few old men in Bess's household. He
was one of her trusted servants, even witness to her will, and Bess
was paying for the education of his son at school. She had also given
him the lease of a farm – Dodderidge had a great deal to lose. This
trusted servant had an alias, John Good, whom we have already met
matting the gallery at Owlcotes and playing Bess into Hardwick.
That he had two names was not due to any attempt at deviousness
on his part, for it was not uncommon for Elizabethan servants to
have two names. John Good or Dodderidge had much to lose by
falling in with Arbella's plans.

In order to carry out Arbella's request, Dodderidge asked one
of Bess's gentlewomen, possibly Mrs Digby, if he might have leave
to visit a relative. He asked five or six times but his request was
not granted. Meanwhile, perhaps because of the delay with Dodderidge, Arbella was in touch with Starkey again. She promised a
reward for his help and there was the inexplicable involvement of
a silver fire shovel for Arbella, which Dodderidge in a later confession oddly remembered was valued at 5s 8d (28½p) the ounce.

Notes passed between Arbella and Starkey and he ungallantly backed down on his former offer of help, so that side of Arbella's plotting came to nothing. Arbella, therefore, was forced to go back to Dodderidge as her messenger. This time Dodderidge was to go straight to the Earl of Hertford himself with her proposal.

Accordingly Dodderidge set out from Hardwick after dinner on Christmas Day 1602 with Arbella's message memorised. Henry Cavendish provided the horse. He was always happy to annoy Bess and did not earn his mother's title of 'my bad son Henry' without reason.

Edward Seymour, Earl of Hertford, was by nature a timid man; he had spent some years of Elizabeth's reign in the Tower because of his marriage to Catherine Grey. But notwithstanding heavy fines, he had somehow managed to repair his fortune. Fate's wheel had turned a full circle: Bess, for her innocent involvement in the earlier marriage, was now to be involved again innocently, but this time over their grandchildren. Timid though Seymour was, he was not to be diverted in one direction: to prove the legitimacy of his two sons by Catherine – their marriage by the enquiry of 1561 having been declared illegal and void. His two sons, although accepted everywhere as Lord Beauchamp and Lord Thomas Seymour, were therefore on the face of it illegitimate. It was to Edward Seymour, the eldest son of Lord Beauchamp, that Arbella was proposing herself.

Edward Seymour was a boy of sixteen in 1602, when Arbella was an ageing Princess of twenty-seven. It is a measure of Arbella's desperation to escape from Hardwick that she should have picked the one family in England which the Queen would have had most reason to resent her marrying into, and to have chosen a boy eleven years her junior whom she had never seen. Not that the difference in their ages would have raised many eyebrows, but since the point of most marriages in that society was to unite estates to build up wealthy dynasties, then Arbella's reasons for thinking that the Seymours might accept her proposal were unsound: all she had was her royal pension of £200 a year, the income of £300 from the mortgaged Willoughby lands in Nottinghamshire and an unknown income from Skegby lands in Lincolnshire which were bought in 1599 with Bess's money. Her total income was not much above £700, so that all she had to offer tangibly was her royal blood, which to the Seymours would have been a liability. For an intelligent woman the proposal was a foolish one but Arbella was driven to extremity.

Dodderidge arrived at the Earl's house in Tottenham on the afternoon of 30 December. Hertford was immediately suspicious and made the old man repeat his memorised message in front of two witnesses. He abused the poor Dodderidge, by now a thoroughly frightened man, denied that he wanted any such marriage and said ominously, 'Thou art prepared for punishment.' Prepared or not, Dodderidge had no option. He was taken away, locked in a room overnight and interviewed by the Earl again next morning in his dining-room. Hertford could not bring himself to believe what Arbella's messenger proposed: the suggestion that his grandson should ride up to Derbyshire, to Hardwick, with some old man, taking with them proof of identity which Arbella would recognise, such as a picture or letter of Jane Grey whose handwriting she knew – Jane Grey had been dead nearly fifty years! All this to get admittance to Hardwick under pretence of having land for sale, seemed as far-fetched as the marriage proposal to Hertford. He suspected something deeper and ways were used to frighten the truth out of Dodderidge. But these means were nothing by comparison with the stronger measures later used on the old man – by ten o'clock he was escorted, a prisoner, to Sir Robert Cecil.

Cecil was the second son of Lord Burghley. Although he was the Queen's most trusted councillor, he never gained the same confidence from the Queen as his father had done; they were not of the same generation. Short, with a slight curvature of the spine giving him a hunchbacked appearance, he was unkindly called 'her pigmy' by the Queen. He made up for his appearance by his brilliance and was a very good servant to Elizabeth, painstaking and industrious. Cecil had his network of spies and he may have been surprised that he had picked up no hint of Arbella's proposal to Hertford; if he had he may have dismissed it as just another rumour amongst many concerning Arbella. However, once Dodderidge and his evidence were safe with Cecil, he took the matter very seriously indeed. Painstakingly and with astonishing speed and thoroughness, he went about getting to the bottom of what had the first appearance of being a dangerous business.

Dodderidge made a confession to the Privy Council on 2 January 1603. In his efforts to leave nothing out he repeated himself and with this overlong unbosoming he produced a short note written to Arbella in worried haste when he had been with the Earl of Hertford, warning her that his 'entertainment here is contrary to all expectation'. His entertainment was indeed contrary to expectation; he was still shut in the gatehouse jail at Westminster fourteen days later, his good position with Bess lost for ever – Arbella would have been powerless to help him even had she known.

Nothing of Dodderidge's 'entertainment' was known at Hardwick. Arbella looked out hopefully for the arrival of the disguised young Seymour with the old man, but the visitor who came was someone she did not expect. Cecil had inherited his father's gift for choosing the right man for the right job – he was a good judge of character. Sir Henry Bronker, a Queen's commissioner, was the type of courtier who always seems available when needed. By Monday 3 January, briefed by the Queen personally, he was on his way to Hardwick. Sir Henry was intensely loyal to his Queen and no personal suffering was allowed to interfere with his duty. Only eight months earlier, when he believed himself to be dying 'with the stone', he had written to his patron Cecil, committing his wife and family to Cecil's care. Yet in mid-winter, at a moment's notice, Bronker made what must have been a painful journey of 145 miles in three and a half days.

The sudden eruption of Bronker, a Queen's commissioner, unannounced at Hardwick on 7 January, can only have caused consternation. His report only put his arrival baldly, 'I came to Hardwick and found the house without strange company, My Lady of Shrewsbury after she had my name, sent for me in her gallery where she was walking with the La:Arbella and her son William Cavendish.' For Bess, with her shrewdness and understanding of Arbella, this arrival of Sir Henry Bronker must have made her guess that her grand-daughter had been up to something and that whatever it was had been discovered. But Bess was completely unaware of the nature of Arbella's deceit. For Arbella, on the other hand, who was waiting for a message from Hertford, the visit of Sir Henry can only have given her an awful sense of foreboding. As Sir Henry walked down the matting of that very long gallery towards the three, both women and William must have had their minds filled with speculation.

With tact, Sir Henry opened his difficult mission by giving Bess friendly greetings from the Queen. Sir Henry noted, 'The old lady took such comfort at this message as I could hardly keep her from kneeling.' Bess, perhaps suspecting that Arbella might have offended the Queen in some unforgivable fashion, no doubt had the lesson of her past visit to the Tower in mind: the message from the Queen would have been a comfort. Then Sir Henry, drawing Bess on with compliments towards the far end of the gallery and so getting her apart from Arbella, gave the Queen's letter to Bess. Perhaps it was not as reassuring as she would have liked, for it told her nothing of the reason for Bronker's visit, but again he reassured her of the Queen's good opinion and favour. Sir Henry deserves some admiration for his tactics: he had arrived at Hardwick after a tiring journey, knowing nothing of the lay-out of the house, but he succeeded with tact in separating Bess and Arbella to opposite ends of the gallery and was able to interview both of them in the same room without either overhearing. This at least would have spared Bess the further anguish of having to leave Arbella alone with Sir Henry. Bess, left at the far end of the gallery with William while Sir Henry spoke to her grand-daughter, must have had her mind set in a turmoil Her eyes were giving her trouble and she would have had difficulty in peering at the two figures talking together at the far end of the long chamber.

Sir Henry began by softening Arbella with flattery. Without actually saying what it was, he hinted that he knew what had been going on; in fact Sir Henry had Dodderidge's confession in his pocket. Arbella, knowing that something had gone very wrong with her plans, improvised as she went. And Sir Henry, watching her closely, noted 'it seemed by the comings and goings of her colour that she was a little troubled'. Arbella denied that she had anything to confess and that if Sir Henry would only tell her what he accused her of, then she could justify herself. He then came into the open and told her that he knew that she had been in touch with the Earl of Hertford, whereupon Arbella, resolved on the moment to lie, denied that she had. Even when Sir Henry showed her Dodderidge's confession she continued doggedly to deny any involvement. Arbella was terrified out of her mind.

Bess, at the far end of the gallery, can only have been consumed with anxiety and impatience. On that no doubt cold January day the fires crackled in the two enormous grates, the flames reflecting warmly on the great copper handirons; the pictures of the Queen and of her Tudor ancestors, of Bess's last three husbands and of Arbella herself gazed down at the drama below. Bess and William waited.

Eventually, after Sir Henry had kept up his tactful pressure, Arbella said that she would tell him everything, but what she said was such a jumble of hysterical nonsense that Sir Henry could make nothing of it. Finally, on a promise from Sir Henry that he would tell Bess nothing, Arbella said that she would write down all the facts, and eventually all left the chamber. Bess would still have been ignorant as to what the business concerned and would have been more worried as a consequence; Arbella, now thoroughly frightened, was incapable of coherent thought. Sir Henry wrote, 'For that night I left her to herself and the next morning expected her letter.'

If Arbella had been left to herself she might have been able to think constructively, but with her bed in the same room as her grandmother, privacy was something she was denied and Bess would have done her very best to wring out of her reluctant grand-daughter what the grave trouble was. This was hardly the time to write out any sort of confession. That night must have seemed a long one to Bess and even longer to Arbella. Indeed the next morn-ing, when Sir Henry read her letter, 'he perceived it to be confused, obscure and in truth ridiculous'; hardly surprising after Arbella had passed a night with Bess in one of her most penetrating moods. Arbella made another attempt which was no better, and in com-promise Sir Henry wrote the confession himself and Arbella signed it. His comment on her state of mind was to the point: 'her wits were somewhat distracted either through fear of her own grand-mother or conceit of her own folly', but perhaps that was an under-statement. Arbella, in desperation, had discussed her problem with William, and Sir Henry, knowing that Bess would hear everything from her son, felt 'in duty and discretion to disclose all unto the old lady'. He noted that 'she was wonderfully afflicted with the matter and much discomforted ... that she took it so ill as with much ado she refrained her hands'. Again this must be an understatement, for Bess was never one to mince words and without doubt she would have subjected Arbella to some strong verbal violence which would not have been Sir Henry's part to repeat to the Queen.

Before Sir Henry left Hardwick on the Sunday, Bess wrote a letter for him to take to the Queen. It was concise; she denied any previous knowledge of Arbella's plottings and furthermore she would be glad to be rid of the girl. Would the Queen please take her off her hands, to Court, in marriage, anything to be rid of the responsibility of keeping the deceitful Arbella? In effect Bess was denying her granddaughter and supporting the Queen.

Sir Henry, by his tact and persuasion, had reached the bottom of the matter. He had felt some sympathy for Arbella and more for Bess, who he could see was innocent of any implication; his treatment of both had been beyond reproach. In a difficult two days both women had come to feel that Sir Henry was their friend – Cecil would not have found a better man for the mission. Nothing more remained but for him to return to London with all speed. As he left Hardwick on the Sunday, Bess offered him a purse full of gold 'in honour of your Majesty', which, Sir Henry told the Queen, he refused for her Majesty's honour. This offer was in no sense a bribe, it was simply the custom, and that Bess wanted him to know that she felt he was worth the gift, and she would have felt no distress at his refusal.

As the hoofbeats of Sir Henry's horse died away, Arbella's position would have been unenviable. Bess would have lashed her granddaughter mercilessly with her tongue, reminding her that her duty lay to the Queen and not in any way whatsoever in her own desires and wishes, and Arbella, who had learnt that it was pointless to oppose her grandmother, would have meekly answered with a simple 'yes' or 'no', possibly infuriating Bess more than ever. Sympathy and understanding on Bess's part would have saved the relationship, but Bess was beyond caring. She felt the Queen and herself had been betrayed by Arbella and only wished to be rid of her ungrateful grandchild. For her part, Arbella wished to be rid of her ungrateful grandmother and to escape from Hardwick: at least they were sharing a common ambition, but one which could only be achieved with the Queen's permission. With impatience, both women waited for Bronker's letters.

Bronker did not reach London until 13 January. He was delayed by a severe fall from his horse and was still in considerable pain when he made his report to Cecil and the Queen. Meanwhile at Hardwick, Arbella was closely confined. On 15 January she wrote to John Hacker, who was occasionally employed and rewarded by Bess, asking him to persuade her aunt Mary Talbot to come to Hardwick. With this went another letter from Arbella's lady-in-waiting, Bridget Shirland, who made a similar appeal. As Hacker responded to neither letter it is doubtful if he ever received them, and certainly Arbella's aunt Mary made no move to visit Hardwick. Moreover, Arbella made mysterious comments to Bess hinting that she might leave Hardwick, causing Bess to believe that her grand-daughter had more tricks up her lively sleeve. All these letters and the comments and conceits of Arbella were passed on to the Queen by Bess. And both women still waited for Elizabeth's reply. Nearly three weeks after Bronker had left Hardwick the reply was delivered, but it was a letter which gave no hope to either Bess or her grand-daughter; it merely stated that Arbella was to remain at Hardwick and to be closely watched.

The Queen's answer only served to increase the struggle between the spirited young Arbella and the equally spirited but ageing Bess. Their relationship had become so bad that Arbella was able to communicate with her grandmother only by letter. In a long, illogical, rambling account to Bess, Arbella hinted that she had a 'dearest' but did not reveal who the man was. Bess forwarded all the 'scribbled follies' to Cecil and Sir John Stanhope. Stanhope had been made vice-chamberlain of the royal household and, ironically, a Privy Councillor on the same day as Gilbert Talbot. Arbella could expect no help from Stanhope, who had murderously attacked her uncle Charles only three years earlier. This did not prevent her from writing to him and Cecil jointly, asking to see Bronker again when she would explain to him what was in her mind.

John Starkey, Arbella's erstwhile helper, had been very closely questioned by Cecil's men on his part in her scheming, and he found the trust she had given him and the responsibility of his very minor part altogether too much to sustain. About 1 February he hanged himself, leaving a confession asking for Arbella's forgiveness – the matter gave the appearance of getting out of hand.

Cooped up at Hardwick, Bess showed no sign of losing her head; this was one of her great attributes and no doubt the Queen was relying on it when she refused the request to release Arbella from her charge. Bess was displaying her many remarkable gifts in this crisis, all the more astounding in view of her seventy-five years. The redoubtable old Countess had no certain idea of what her grand-daughter was planning and the girl's hysterical outbursts, her dark hints and long obscure letters to the Queen, to Cecil and Stanhope and to Bronker, must have worried her. But Arbella did not know herself what she would do; she was playing her lines as the situation and her feelings directed – a proceeding almost beyond Bess's understanding. Her only aim was to escape from Hardwick and this Bess was loyally determined to prevent.

Attempting to find help where she could, Arbella then wrote to Edward Talbot asking him to come and see her. Just why she should have written to him was something that she possibly could not have explained, for there was no chance of his becoming embroiled in what had the aspect of a serious matter. Arbella, in fact, was appealing to those who were least likely to help her; apparently, for the moment at least, she avoided the more obvious ally, Henry Cavendish. Her next move was to go on hunger strike, refusing to eat until she was free of Hardwick and her grandmother. Bess wrote to Cecil telling of this latest development on 21 February, not because she was worried by Arbella's not eating but because the girl was obviously ill with an acute pain in her side, and to ask that Bronker be sent up with all speed. But Bronker was already on his way to Hardwick.

Cecil, after he had digested Bronker's report and the statements from Dodderidge, Starkey and others, had concluded that his one fear, that Arbella was a secret Catholic, was unfounded. The pro-posal to Hertford was seen in its proper light and the whole matter was no more than a foolishness on the part of Arbella. Cecil would have let the matter drop there, leaving the two women to stew it out in wildest Derbyshire. Either he had underestimated the state of hostility existing between Bess and Arbella or he did not see that Bess's determination had been inherited by her grand-daughter.

To give herself some respite, Bess had Arbella sent to Owlcotes in William's care. As she commented to Cecil, 'I am wearied of my life and therefore humbly beseech her Majesty to have compassion on me' – the responsibility of her wilful grand-daughter was taking its toll.

By the time Bronker arrived on 2 March, Arbella had been brought back to Hardwick. At this second encounter with Sir Henry, Arbella was as exasperating as she had been with Bess. He was quite unable to get out of her who her secret lover was, which, since there was none, is understandable. Bronker returned to London carrying a letter from Bess to Cecil asking for Arbella's removal, and a verbal request from her grand-daughter to the same end, which he had been unable to grant on his own authority. After Sir Henry had left, Arbella wrote an unfinished letter to him on 4 March, in which she described the tension at Hardwick:

After dinner I went in reverent sort to crave my grandmother's blessing ... after I had with the armour of patience, borne of a volley of most bitter and injurous words, at last, wounded to the heart with false epithets and an unlooked for word only defending myself with a negative (which was all the words I said, but not that I could have said in my defence), I made a retreat to my chamber, which I hoped ... should have been my sanctuary....

She found no peace there, where she was pursued by Bess, her waiting women and William who asked for a 'parley'. This broken note to Bronker was followed by another on 6 March and yet another on 7 March and the longest of all written on Ash Wednesday, 9 March, the anniversary of the execution of Essex, as she reminded Bronker. The last letter, which was as rambling as her others and to as little point, shows a surprising knowledge of Essex and lends strength to a suggestion that she had been banned from the Court in 1597 for becoming too fond of the Queen's favourite.

Neither Bess nor Arbella were able to move the Queen or Cecil to granting their wish. The only reply they received was on 14 March when they suggested that William should take some of the burden off his mother's shoulders. The volatile situation had been bubbling in a constant state of suspended tension for over nine weeks, but Bess had great reserves of strength and no matter how 'wearied' she was of the whole business, she was still going to be able to dominate and subdue members of her troublesome family.

The sinister absence of Henry Cavendish from his mother's irritations was now explained. Somehow he had been in touch with Arbella and, behind Bess's back, they concocted a plan of escape for her with the help of a Catholic, Henry Stapleton. The first attempt on 10 March, which was badly planned, proved abortive. Henry and Stapleton with a party of eight men had gone to Ault Hucknall to watch from the church tower for when Arbella took her exercise before Hardwick Hall – but they had been unable to get the key of the church from the vicar, and in any event Arbella was prevented from passing through the porter's lodge at Hardwick. Bess explained the whole episode in a letter to Bronker which she wrote in the guttering light of the best candles late that same night. At two o'clock, after the plan had failed, Henry and Stapleton presented themselves at the porter's lodge, but Bess would only let Henry in: 'For that Arbella was desirous to speak with my bad son Henry, I was content to suffer him to come into my house and speak with her, rather than she to go to him.' Bess gave Henry a time limit of two hours and remarked that she disliked Stapleton and for that reason kept him outside the gates.

Henry had got himself inside Hardwick and was with Arbella; it now remained for him to get her through the guarded gates of the high walled courtyard and outside, where he had thirty to forty men waiting hidden around Hucknall village. He and Arbella walked down the stairs through the hall and out into the walled forecourts with Bess, no doubt, watching from her windows, for she reported exactly what followed. She must also have had absolute confidence in the loyalty of her servants. Across the court went the two to the gates and Arbella tried to pass through to Stapleton outside, but the porter prevented this and sent to Bess for instructions, saying that Arbella wished to talk to Stapleton. There must have been a deal of to-ing and fro-ing between the party at the gates and Bess in her withdrawing-room, for Bess refused Arbella's request to speak to Stapleton and Arbella replied by asking if she was a prisoner. However, after a few pleasantries spoken through the closed gates, Stapleton and Henry were forced to withdraw, leaving Arbella behind, completely beaten by the old Countess who from start to finish had dominated the whole scene. Bess concluded her stark account of the day's dramas with 'And so, being very late this Thursday night the 10 March, I cease, wishing you all happiness.' She did not add that she was even more wearied than before.

Bess had been wise to stick to the bare facts in her account to Cecil. In trying to kidnap Arbella with a force of forty men and associating with such a Catholic as Stapleton, Henry was very close to treason, but whatever Bess may have felt about her 'bad son Henry', she would not have wished to see him put on trial as a result of her evidence. The episode was taken seriously in London when Bess's fast messenger arrived with her letters, taking only two days on the journey. On 15 March Bronker set out again on what had become a familiar route to Hardwick, and all the justices of Derbyshire were instructed by warrant to assist him as necessary.

Bronker made a very fast journey, arriving on 17 March, having taken two and a half days only on the way. He sent at once for Henry Cavendish 'by friendly letter' rather than by warrant, as his instructions had ordered. He interviewed Arbella, her servants, the vicar of Hucknall and the villagers, in fact everyone remotely connected with the matter, except Stapleton who had fled to London. Bronker reached the only conclusion possible, that Arbella should be removed from Bess's care, 'so settled is her mislike of the old lady', and then he added that Bess 'groweth exceeding weary of her charge, beginneth to be weak and sickly by breaking her sleep and cannot endure long this vexation'.

Bess was not only tired of her charge, she was also exceedingly angry with both Arbella and Henry. On 20 March she signed a codicil cutting them both out of her will and by the end of that month, Arbella had been removed to the care of Henry Grey, Earl of Kent, at Wrest Park in Bedfordshire, who was by way of being a relative, for his nephew had recently married the second daughter of Gilbert Talbot. Henry Cavendish avoided any punishment and the whole matter was discreetly forgotten, for another drama was being played out at Richmond Palace, and another chapter in Bess's life was ending. Queen Elizabeth was dying.

'NOT OVERSUMPTUOUS'
1603-1608

Gloriana, who brought stability and prosperity to England, had lived too long. The Queen who had been worshipped for the brilliance and luck of her earlier successes, for which she was only partly responsible, was now denigrated for the distress of the nineties, a failure which was no fault of hers; it had been beyond the power of the primitive government system to alleviate the suffering. The younger generation saw only an ageing woman, often ridiculous, whose policies were worn out. Her contemporaries such as Bess, who was about five years her senior, remembered her earlier magic and still saw her as the Astrea they had always thought her to be. They would have forgiven her mistakes and the vagueness of age, when younger generations would have treated them with impatience born of frustration.

A Jesuit priest, Father Rivers, writing to Father Parsons in March twelve months before, had noted the change in the Queen: 'the ache in the Queen's arm is fallen into her side, but she is still, thanks to God, frolicky and merry, only her face showeth some decay'. And now the end was not far away. The Queen, unable to sleep, was also eating nothing, but never one to admit to a sickness or infirmity, even in these last days she refused to submit. From 1 March to the 12th, her malady began to get the better of her willpower; on 12 March she revived a little but this was followed by a more serious relapse and she gave way so far as to allow herself to be put to bed when previously she had lain on cushions on the floor. The Privy Council had received no direction from Elizabeth as to her successor. Cecil knew that James of Scotland was the only true candidate and so did the Queen, but refusing to acknowledge that she was dying she refused to name her heir. Only at the last minute did she name 'our cousin of Scotland', and died at two in the morning of 24 March.

As Arbella rode south to Wrest Park, the news of the Queen's death was speeding up the road north to Hardwick. And the news, although not unexpected, would have upset Bess; she had known Elizabeth well through all the forty-five years of her reign, had been her most loyal and well-beloved subject, and the Queen in return had supported her through all those dreadful years with Shrewsbury. The relationship between the two women was the closest friendship which Elizabeth allowed herself to have with another woman, and it was founded on the basic understanding between a subject who acknowledged her sovereign's authority and a sovereign who knew that her old friend would never turn against her, a mutual understanding which was of benefit to both. As recently as 1599 the Queen had sold a valuable assortment of vicarages and parsonages to Bess for a cheap £12,750:[1] sold to a loyal friend as a gesture of appreciation and paid for by a loyal subject to a Queen who needed the money. There was too much of a common past of shared hopes and fears for Bess to have been unmoved by the sad news of Elizabeth's death, and it would have reminded her of her own mortality.

James, the new King, entered his realm by the Scottish border and made his triumphal way down England, staying with Gilbert Talbot at Worksop on 20 April. Here he was diverted by 'excellent soul-ravishing music' and so much of fowl, fish, meat and wine 'that it was left open for any man that would, to come and take'. Did James ever stop to think of his mother Mary, who had been at Worksop for two visits twenty years before? Perhaps he was too diverted by Gilbert's extravagant hospitality. And Gilbert, who should have been diverted by mounting debts, was casting money he did not have before a monarch who would give him no reward. The opportunity of the interlude at Worksop was not missed by Mary Talbot who pressed James to release Arbella from her confinement at Wrest Park.

Bess did not stir from Hardwick, neither did she see James. The episode of the past months had wearied her; nor had she any wish to make the long, uncomfortable trip to London for the Queen's funeral on 28 April. Arbella was invited to the funeral but refused in a haughty manner, saying that as she had been unacceptable in the Queen's lifetime, then she would not attend at her death. One of James's first minutes was directed to the Earl of Kent and concerned Arbella, 'for as much as we are desirous to free our cousin the Lady Arbella Stuart from that unpleasant life which she hath lead in the house of her grandmother with whose severity and age she, being a young lady could hardly agree'. Bess was acquiring a reputation as an ogre, but it is difficult to see how else she could have acted, with Arbella behaving as she did, for it had been the Queen's command that Bess should keep her confined. James had nothing to fear from Arbella personally and soon released his cousin, making her free to attend Court.

No sooner was James on the throne than the counter-reformation began plots to remove him. It was Arbella's fate that she was the only alternative to James and so was the pivot to any plot to depose the King. Arbella had no wish to be a Queen and was innocent of any personal involvement. To have successfully avoided being incriminated in any of the plots involving her name and to have survived at Court was an achievement which can only have been due to her transparent lack of any ambition to take the Crown or to be other than what she was.

In July the Main Plot and its off-shoot, the Bye Plot, came near to Bess, for the instigators of the secondary Bye Plot were her old acquaintances, Henry Brooke the Eleventh Lord Cobham, his brother George (a godson to Bess) and Sir Griffin Markham, a near neighbour of Bess. Raleigh too was involved but extricated himself by a brilliant defence at the trial. The Brookes and Markham, however, were condemned to be beheaded. Markham and Henry Brooke were reprieved at the last moment in a grisly manner on the scaffold, but there was no such redemption for George Brooke. There were hints of the involvement of Henry Cavendish and Gilbert Talbot, and certainly Bess's daughter Mary Talbot, Gilbert's wife, was known to be a Catholic. It was a strange twist of beliefs that Bess, who was a Protestant through and through and who had over the mantel of her low great chamber at Hardwick the Protestant device 'The conclusion of all things is to fear God and obey his commandments', should have produced a daughter who became an avowed Catholic in defiance of her husband Gilbert;

and another daughter Frances married to Henry Pierrepont, who was often suspected of Catholic tendencies, though these were never proved.

These were struggles at the centre of power which only affected Bess through her old friendships; she had seen it all before so many times. She remained serenely glad to be out of everything, safe at Hardwick where the hours seemingly meant little to the old lady, for Hardwick, unlike Chatsworth, had no clock-tower pointing to the passing time. The one clock in the house was inconveniently placed on the top landing of the north turret, and in her bedchamber there was only an hour glass to show the passing minutes. Bess may have had a watch, but her letters in this period show a vagueness of time: 'about two of the clock', 'at dinner time' or 'written late at night'. Bess had disposed of her wealth and taken care of her spiritual future. Apart from the irritating law suits with Gilbert Talbot which still rumbled through the Courts as late as July 1606, Bess had little to do but wait for her inevitable end and pass the time in sponsoring marriages for her grandchildren.

The recent disputes with Francis Clifford were forgotten when George Clifford, Third Earl of Cumberland, proposed a marriage between his daughter and one of Bess's Cavendish grandsons. But it was a proposal which came to nothing. In 1604 her grand-daughter Mary Talbot married William Herbert. Third Earl of Pembroke who, with his brother, made up Shakespeare's 'incomparable pair of bretheren'. The Earl of Arundel made enquiries about Alathea Talbot, resulting in their marriage in 1606. Not long afterwards Alathea wrote a dutiful letter to Bess on pretty paper, painted and decorated with coloured flowers and once tied with white silk: a non-committal letter to a legendary grandmother, apologising for not writing before and for Arundel's not calling, but she assured Bess, as did all her grandchildren, 'you have no child that can more sincerely and affectionately strive to serve you'.[2] When their first son and Bess's great-grandson was christened at Court in July 1607, Arbella was proxy godmother for Bess, the other godmother being Queen Anne.

Henry Cavendish, meanwhile, continued to give trouble. Timothy Pusey thought it well to tell William Cavendish in April 1604 that 'My La: this night is informed by a gentlewoman here, that a gentleman of good credit now here sayeth there is no good agreement between Mr H Cavendish and ye La: Grace and that he hath lately charged her to be a harlot to some of his men and names men to her.' Bess may have reflected that this was too much coming from Henry who had scattered his own bastards throughout Staffordshire and Derbyshire, but whatever Henry and Grace got up to had little meaning for Bess: he had no heirs and was cut out of her inheritance, as was his illegitimate heir, Henry Junior, although Bess had welcomed the latter to Hardwick in 1596. It might have moved her to know, however, that from this oldest illegitimate son of Henry came the Lords Waterpark, founded on Cavendish wealth and living at Doveridge on Cavendish lands. Had she also known that William was to buy Chatsworth from his brother Henry in 1609 for £8000 she would certainly have been contented, for in 1603 she had gone as far as possible in disinheriting Henry: she had denied him the furnishings of Chatsworth by leaving them to William, but she could in no way interfere directly with the entail of the property itself on Henry made by Sir William Cavendish in 1553. Chatsworth without its contents was of no use to Henry – he could not afford to furnish it – and he was forced to sell to William; but perhaps Bess, in her astute way, had foreseen that outcome.

Although Bess had retreated to the seclusion of Hardwick for her last years she was not cut off entirely from the mainstream of events. Her family, mainly through William, kept her informed of what went on at Court, though William wrote particularly dull letters – the Cavendish family lacked any ability to write amusing or lively communications, Arbella being the only exception. In these late years Bess, like many old ladies, reposed a lot of her confidence in a clergyman. She developed a friendship by letter with Dr James Montague,[3] Dean of the Royal Chapel and later Bishop of Bath and Wells, leaving him £20 in her will. Practical in all things, this exchange of correspondence had its uses: Montague, through his job, was close to the King and in fact he saw and spoke with him many times every day. He was thus able to keep Bess informed on what went on in the immediate royal circle and conversely could pass on to the King whatever Bess wanted him to know.

In the spring of 1605 Bess was reported unwell and in a forgiving spirit Arbella asked if she might make a visit to her old grandmother at Hardwick. James provided a letter of recommendation, an unusual step, which in effect made the visit a royal command. Bess, suspicious in most things concerning forgiveness, particularly when defaulting members of her family might be after her money bags, wrote to Montague that she thought it strange of Arbella to wish to come to Hardwick again when she had previously been so anxious to leave. Suspecting that Arbella was coming to ask for money she told the Dean – for the King's ears of course – that her granddaughter had been provided with land bringing in £700 and that she had received gifts which would have brought in another £100. But money was not the purpose of Arbella's visit and it had rather less to do with forgiveness than Bess imagined. James had given Arbella a patent for a peerage with a blank for the name to be filled in as she wished and she wanted to insert her uncle William's name. For once Arbella could indulge in some horse-trading with her powerful grandmother and when she left Hardwick by the first week in April, she took back with her a gift of £300 and a gold cup worth £100. William was awarded his peerage in May – it cost him £2000 – and Arbella was forgiven for past misbehaviour. Bess would have found the money of course; she knew the value of a title for her dynasty and the privilege it brought.

With William now a peer, Bess may have felt she had achieved all she set out to do and had at last earned some repose. Seemingly fate thought otherwise, for the struggles at the centre of power threw out shock waves which washed up even on the shores of Bess's retirement. If the Main and Bye Plots had been worrying to authority, they were child's play compared with the Gunpowder Plot of November 1605, and again Bess was affected by its association with her family. Gilbert Talbot was caught up in the accusations; for Father Garnet, executed for his passive involvement, was well known to Mary Talbot, Gilbert's wife and Bess's daughter. Gilbert's cousin, John Talbot, was asked for asylum by Richard Winter, one of the conspirators on the run. It is curious that the Privy Council, very alarmed by the discovery of the plot to blow James and parliament sky-high, should have sent instructions to the Derbyshire justices to watch over the safety of Bess:

In consequence of the horrible treason intended by Thomas Percy and his adherants, we require you to be very vigilant in suppressing any disorder in your country. And as Lady Shrewsbury, Dowager, dwelling at Hardwick is a widow and solitary, we request you to have a care of her safety and quietness, and if Lord Cavendish shall have occasion to ask your assistance in her behalf that you will aid and assist him for securing her safety.[4]

It is difficult to understand why anyone might have had violent designs on Bess. Perhaps the Council was showing a kindly care for the old widow, though more likely this covered a desire to watch for the involvement of Henry, Mary or Gilbert in the comings and goings at Hardwick.

Bess continued on at Hardwick, still resolute but with fluctuating health, and as her health fluctuated so did the interest of some of her family. By 1607, when Bess had just reached her eighties, Gilbert Talbot was deep in debt and desperately needed the income from the Talbot lands settled on her. Henry Cavendish, also in debt, would not be able to sell the Cavendish lands entailed on him until Bess's death released them. Rumours circulated. In February 1605 it had been reported that Bess was confined to her room, that John Bentley, a chaplain and her bailiff at Duffield, was having to act on her behalf, and that Henry Cavendish was hopeful that the contents of Chatsworth would revert to him. Poor John Bentley had been one of eight witnesses to Bess's first codicil made in March 1603 when Henry and Arbella had been cut out of the will and he claimed that he had had to go to London on that account. Within days of Bess's death he was complaining that he had been left nothing so much as to cover his expenses: 'Yesterday's experience breeds this day's wisdom' was his comment.[5]

In July 1606 Gilbert Talbot was told that his mother-in-law was walking with a stick and was well but 'impatient and mindful of the Earl's suit against her'. And a year later Mary Talbot, who had fallen out of favour through Gilbert's intransigence over the settlement and his suits, wrote from London to Bess saying that she was glad the pain in her hip had declined. In December that same year of 1607 Gilbert and Mary with Charles Cavendish made a ceremonial visit to Hardwick to be reconciled, for Charles too had been marked with disfavour through his association with Gilbert and now that the tiresome suits were settled there was no more to quarrel about. They found 'a lady of great years, of great wealth, of great wit, which yet still remains'. She received Gilbert with all respect and affection.

They stayed with Bess the whole of one day and there was not so much as one word of any former unkindness – but that was according to Gilbert in a letter to Cecil now Lord Salisbury. He was more truthful writing to Henry Cavendish about the same visit: both would gain by Bess's death.

When I was at Hardwick she did eat very little and not able to walk the length of the chamber betwixt two, but grew so ill at it as you might descern it. On New Year's eve, when my wife sent her New Year's gift, the messenger told us she look pretty well and spoke heartily; but my lady wrote that she was worse than when we last saw her, and Mrs Digby sent a secret message that she was so ill that she could not be from her day or night. I heard that direction is given to some at Wortley to be in readiness to drive away all sheep and cattle at Ewden instantly upon her ladyship's death.

That was on 4 January 1608 and the mention of driving the cattle south from Yorkshire riled Gilbert; plainly Bess still distrusted him. Uden Park was Talbot settlement land and Bess knew that as soon as Gilbert heard of her death he would claim back all his inheritance without delay and all that grazed on it as well.

It was by now plain to all, including Bess, that the end was not far away. William spent his nights and most of his days at Hardwick from the first warnings of Bess's deterioration in January. The two ladies-in-waiting, Elizabeth Digby and Mary Cartwright, were in attendance all the time, taking turns nursing their sick mistress night and day. One morning about the middle of January, after one particularly bad night of extreme sickness when Bess had nearly sent for William, believing that she was dying,[6] Bess was sitting weakly in her chair of 'russet satin striped with silver' before a blazing fire in her bedchamber when William came to her and she told him then that she felt she had not long to live. But like her old friend the late Queen, she had an amazing and tough constitution and the struggle was not to be over so quickly. During those long nights when Bess lay awake, her main concern was not for the past but the future and her favourite son William, of the pitfalls she could foresee and he could not, of which she had to warn him.

One morning, towards the end of that over-long January, Bess told William that she had thoughts 'of matters that might concern him much, and which perhaps he had never thought of', then telling Elizabeth Digby and Mary Cartwright to leave them together, they 'saw her continual care and love towards him'; Bess wanted only William to be with her. In those eternal and agonising nights when death would not come, Bess's thoughts were on William: it was through him that she would achieve some sort of eternity, he was to carry on the dynasty she had founded. Bess was concerned too by what Gilbert Talbot and Henry Cavendish might do to deprive William of some of his inheritance. 'She showed herself very offended with some, for that the well was poisoned' was one way of putting her feelings about Gilbert and Henry. Once when Elizabeth Digby was holding her mistress's stomach, and William was with her, Bess told him to let the Chancellor of Lichfield know that she had made her will and none were to interfere with it. But William did not send to Lichfield and was reminded again a day or so later by Bess, who was offended that he had done nothing.

On the last day of January Bess again thought she was dying and forgave Mary Talbot her past unkindnesses. This was a touching deathbed forgiveness, for she specified that Mary was to have the pearl bed, with its coverlet of black velvet embroidered all over with silver and pearls, though not the hangings 'which she would not give her.' That pearl bed had ties of sentiment, for Bess and Sir William Cavendish had shared it at Chatsworth as far back as 1553.

Dr Hunton from Sheffield, who had been Bess's physician for the previous ten years, moved into Hardwick on 2 February to nurse his greatest patient. Perhaps his remedies brought some relief to Bess in her struggle to die. He prescribed a plaster for her back or for her spleen, and when he left for a brief time on 9 February a messenger found him and brought him back to dose Bess with Venice treacle and London treacle, perhaps remedies for a troublesome cough.

Bess lay night after long night on her bed, cocooned in Spanish blankets and coverlets, pained in her back and in her stomach, her thoughts turning on William and wishing to warn him of future dangers which she saw so clearly and to which he was so blind. The fire crackled in the grate and the two weird terms of the overmantel, carved by Abraham only ten years before, watched impassively; one of Bess's ladies-in-waiting dozed in a chair. Bess heard the Derbyshire wind whispering in the thousand leaded panes like voices from the past, the silence of the great house lay about her broken only by the quiet stirrings of the servants sleeping on the truckle beds by her chamber doors. In the distant winter countryside a dog barked, an owl hooted and still Bess was suffered to live through another night. As she lay there too slowly dying in her great bed, she could see the bed posts covered with scarlet overlaid with silver lace, the matching curtains and yet more curtains of purple baize drawn around her. She regretted nothing of the past and in the way of her times she had nothing to regret. She had led a long life and a successful one. She had obeyed God's laws and those of her sovereign; she thought only of the future. The making of money had been no sin and she had brought up her family to fear God and serve Him, and they were to carry on her dynasty. She meant to die in charity with all men – all men, that is, except Gilbert and Henry whom she never forgave for going against her.

Wishing to die in those long and painful nights, Bess found she was unable to. The household was hushed about her, the servants went through their rituals just as if she were up and about. Pusey and William were kept busy answering the messages of well-wishers bringing their last respects to the great lady. From the moment that Dr Hunton arrived Bess battled on for eleven long days and even longer nights, until too tired and weary to continue living, she died.

On 13 February 1608 Elizabeth Talbot, Dowager Countess of Shrewsbury, died. Her exact age none knew, perhaps she had not known herself; she was most likely eighty, an enormous age to live in those days. 'Given to Dr Hunton at my Lady Shrewsbury's departure: £13 6s 8d (£13.33).' – exactly forty marks – was entered in William's accounts. Bess's body was drained of blood, disembowelled and embalmed by an apothecary, for she was to lie in state at Hardwick whilst her funeral was arranged by Garter King of Arms. The tomb and vault were made ready.

Bess lay in state for three months, which was a long time even for the period, and William, Lord Cavendish's eldest son, was married during those months. William was eighteen and was knighted on 7 March, within weeks of his grandmother's death, and on 10 April he was married in London to Christian Bruce, sister to Lord Kinloss. His bride was only twelve – another arranged marriage. For the ceremony to take place at this time was an unusual complication and it can only have been allowed because Bess expressly wished that nothing should delay so important a matter. It would have been typical of Bess to request that her funeral be postponed for the marriage to go on as already planned. In delaying, anything might have happened – Christian Bruce might have died, which would have lost for the Cavendishes the Bruce estates she was bringing with her. Practical in living, Bess was practical in dying; the future of her dynasty came before her own funeral.

There is no eye-witness account of Bess's lying-in-state, nor of her funeral. Her remains after embalming would have been sealed in wax and put into a lead coffin. The coffin would have been laid in the great chamber at Hardwick and the whole room draped in yards of black cloth, possibly the stairs too would have been swathed in black and the hall become one enormous black tent. Arbella made a visit to Hardwick and these sombre decorations in March to pay her last respects to her grandmother and returned to London with a drawing of Chatsworth for Lord Salisbury, to remind him of Bess. Arbella herself, for the help she had given in getting William's peerage, had been forgiven by Bess for past vexations and was left £1000. Charles Cavendish had been partly forgiven: there was nothing for him but Bess left 4000 marks between his two sons to buy them land. Gilbert Talbot and Henry Cavendish were left nothing at all, not even a small sum to buy mourning-rings.

When Bess made her will in 1601, she had £5102 counted out into bags and put into one of her money coffers. This was to pay the various cash legacies and the funeral expenses. Elizabeth Digby was left £100, likewise the Lord Chancellor and the Archbishop of Canterbury had £100 each in gold. King James got the £200 for the gold cup intended originally for Queen Elizabeth; and £1000 went to servants, whilst £2000 was to cover the expense of the funeral. In mentioning the latter, Bess requested that it 'be not over sumptuous or performed with too much vain and idle charges', nevertheless she would have been unable to avoid the full treatment accorded to the rank of countess – Garter King of Arms would have seen to that.

The ceremony took place at All-Hallows, Derby (now All Saints Cathedral) about 4 May. A macabre procession entered the church headed by a mourning knight carrying a great banner painted with Bess's arms, followed by heralds and officials of the College of Arms, then came the coffin carried by six gentlemen. The coffin was covered by a black velvet pall, the corners of which were held by four knights. After this centre-piece came two hooded gentlemen ushers carrying white rods and then the lady chief mourner, Mary, Countess of Shrewsbury, supported by two hooded barons, her train carried by one of her waiting-women. Behind followed Bess's family, her servants, the twelve poor folk from her almshouses and mourning women hired for the gloomy occasion.[7]

In 1572 the procession of the Earl of Derby had stretched for two miles behind the coffin; it is likely that Bess considered this 'over sumptuous' and William, who was accounting for all, would have seen that the ceremony was smaller but impressive for all that. As well as Bess's waiting-women, Elizabeth Digby and Mary Cartwright, there were the waiting-women of the high-ranking mourners – two baronesses at the service had seven women between them. Apart from Henry Cavendish and Gilbert Talbot, who seemingly did not attend, all Bess's family were there. Inside the church, draped in black and garnished with escutcheons of arms, stood a vast hearse built like a four-poster bed and covered in many yards of black velvet: on this the coffin under its black velvet pall was laid. The Archbishop of York, Toby Matthew, preached a funeral sermon based on Solomon's description of a virtuous woman, and Bess was laid to rest in the vault beneath the sumptuous monument made by her architect Robert Smythson.

By 1848 more than forty Cavendish descendants had joined their ancestor, their coffins piled haphazardly on top of each other until the weight crushed those beneath. When the vault was recently cleaned, there was not even Bess's coffin-plate remaining – looted perhaps by earlier souvenir hunters.

The epitaph on Bess's tomb is not contemporary. As can be judged from the detailed description of the awards given to the Duke of Newcastle which takes up more room than those of Bess, it was put up about sixty-nine years later when her exact age had been forgotten. But Bess herself was not forgotten or unmourned. Gilbert Talbot was surprised at Mary Talbot's distress over her mother's death and manlike 'hoped to set workmen on soon to take her mind off it'. Nearly thirty years later a dramatist, William Sampson, born in the Midlands, gave Bess first place in a book of poems called *Virtus Post Funera Vivit*, dedicated to those lately dead. Her greatest memorial today is Hardwick Hall, but that is not how Bess would have seen it; her ambition was to found a great dynasty and it was for that she would have wished to be known.

There is no question but that Bess succeeded in her ambition; to prove it her descendants are with us today. From William Cavendish, her favourite son, the present Duke of Devonshire is directly descended and still lives at Chatsworth. From Charles Cavendish who bought Welbeck from Gilbert Talbot came the Dukes of Newcastle and from them, indirectly, the present Duke of Portland who lives at Welbeck. From her daughter Frances, who married Henry Pierrepont, came the Dukes of Kingston, and from them the Earls Manvers. A descendant still lives at Holme Pierrepont Hall, the same house in which Frances dwelt. Mary Talbot became mother-in-law to the Earls of Pembroke, Kent and Arundel, and from the last is descended the present Duke of Norfolk. And the bad son Henry fathered illegitimately the Lords Waterpark. By the end of the last century, almost every noble family including the royal family had Bess's blood diluted in their veins. This is the size of the achievement of Bess's ambition and she would not have been surprised. But if Arbella had been a boy, then the course of history would have been different; only in that was Bess denied her full ambition.

As far as wealth was concerned, Bess only regarded this as a means to an end. She would have been surprised to be called the wealthiest woman in England, for that was not what she set out to be; she gave away to her family as much as she kept for herself. In 1600 Bess's gross income revenue was a third of Cecil's, and it would not have troubled her had she known. Immediately after their mother died, William and Charles Cavendish commissioned a survey of their estates: they started in 1608 and by the time it was finished in 1627 both families had 100,000 acres each. This was the means Bess provided; the end was the positions of power which her descendants were able to achieve through her means.

Bess has always been judged unjustly according to morals later than her time – morals which she could not have understood – and she has been cruelly misrepresented. To judge Bess fairly she must be seen in the light in which her contemporaries saw her. In the opinion of her times she obeyed the laws of God and her Queen; to acquire wealth for her family was a pastime of the epoch; she married four times and on certain evidence made three of her husbands very happy, two completely so – and even the failure of her marriage to Shrewsbury was not through want of effort on her part for Shrewsbury's misery was of his own confusion. None of these was a black deed, although at various times they have been painted thus.

Bess has been accused of trampling down others in the pursuit of her ambition and indeed she did. But in any battle someone has to win, and it was an entirely Elizabethan occupation and no one saw wrong in defeating a weaker opponent. Today, ambitious men still trample down the less able. Bess in fact often helped others and charitably gave where the need was greatest. We may think less of her for her habit of using 'the language of the bank' and for the cruel words she could employ when roused; we may find her unlovable, yet three husbands loved Bess, and Mary Talbot was very distressed when her old mother died; Bess's lovability eludes us or I suspect cannot be translated from its Elizabethan meaning. Her children and her contemporaries admired her for what she had achieved and we can do the same; her success we must applaud. She ended her life with no regrets and that is how we must judge her.

APPENDIX I

The Hardwick accounts for the period 1592 to 1601 are the most complete run of Bess's accounts to survive. It is beyond the scope of this biography to attempt the hideous complexity of converting Elizabethan accounts into modern profit-and-loss accounts. However, some figures can be drawn which will be useful to students of the period. The expenditure for these years covers the building of Hardwick Hall, loans made and land purchases – in one case only has the exceptional cost of land purchase been noted in the tables. The receipts cover the period of the bad harvests of 1594–7 which caused very severe famine; these events are reflected in the drop in Bess's gross receipts of twenty-five per cent, and she only regained her former gross income in 1600–1.

It must be emphasised that the Hardwick account books are simply records kept by servants who were accounting to Bess for money passing through their hands. William Reason, as Bess's receiver, took all the rents from the bailiffs of seventeen collections, or estates; he was not concerned with the cost of running the estates nor with the expenses of the bailiffs; he was only accounting for money he received and from whom it came, then he passed it over to Timothy Pusey who accounted for the receipt again in his account book. The gross receipts given below are compounded from Reason's figures when they exist and, failing these, from Pusey's less detailed accounts. MSS 9a and 10 are Reason's own accounts covering the years 1592–4. But MS 9 is a collection of Reason's and Pusey's accounts bound together as one, probably in the last century. I have distinguished one from another by a series numeration. There is no complete record for expenditure for the years 1597–8.

YEAR	REF.	GROSS RECEIPTS FROM TALBOT LANDS	TOTAL OF ALL GROSS RECEIPTS	EXPENDITURE
1 Oct 1592– 29 Sept 1593	MS 9a	£3500	£9500	£8400
30 Sept 1593– 29 Sept 1594	MS 10	£3400	£7900	£7500 (MS 9:5th Series ff30–31)
4 Oct 1596– 29 Sept 1597	MS 9 ff1–18 (2nd Series)	£2850	£7690	£4364 (MS 9:5th Series ff34–34v)
11th Nov 1597– 29 Sept 1598[1]	MS 9 ff0–15v (3rd Series)	£2540	£7100	No figures for the whole year
30 Sept 1598– 29 Sept 1599	MS 9 ff1–2v (4th Series)	£2800	£8200	£5300 (MS 7:ff34v–67)
30 Sept 1599– 29 Sept 1600	MS 9 ff4–5v (4th Series)	£3000	£9700[2]	£16,900 (MS 7:ff72–104) Includes purchase of parsonages for £12,750.
30 Sept 1600– 29 Sept 1601	MS 9 ff6–8 (4th Series)	£3250	£9500	£5900 (MS 7:ff105–150)

[1] The first and last pages are missing and therefore the figures are not complete.
[2] Includes receipts by Henry Travice in London (Drawer 143/42).

APPENDIX II

It is often asked 'How much did it cost to build Hardwick?'

Those who are familiar with Elizabethan accounts will know that they are often ambiguous and it is possible to make what you want of them; therefore the response to the question is likely to raise contention, the computation of it is hazardous and the provision of it perhaps foolish. However, I have attempted this foolishness; the distillation of the final figure has been hideously complicated and an explanation is necessary.

The building accounts for Hardwick Halls both old and new (MS 6) cover a period from 18 October 1587 to 17 January 1598. These are supplemented by the household accounts (MS 7) which carry the fortnightly payments 'for the buildings' from 14 October 1592 until 18 January 1598, when apart from wainscoting and the like the building was to all intents finished. MS 6 is not just one account book but eighteen, which were bound up as one in the nineteenth century totalling over six hundred pages. In 1590 there were four accounts books running concurrently, which makes any computation difficult; there are pages missing which, although not a great many, will make any result inaccurate – I give my figures in round totals. MS 7 does not present so many hazards; it totals four hundred pages; the fortnightly payments are uncomplicated but some building wages are included in the half-yearly payments to servants. I have ignored Bess's rewards for good workmanship.

From the start of MS 6 in 1587 to 27 March 1591, when the building administration changed due to Bess's departure to Wingfield and eventually London, David Fludd acts as clerk of works but only responsible for payment of 'bargains in great' (contract work); Bess pays the day-labourers; the two figures for the period total £1340. With Bess in London, Fludd vanishes from the accounts and Henry Jenkinson, the family priest, takes over as clerk of works, but he has nothing to do until Bess returns; the work in progress is accounted for by John Roods from 11 December 1591 to 23 December 1592, and John Balechouse from 10 December 1591 to 7 April 1593 – which totals £190 (these periods overlap Bess's return in August 1592 but this is accounted for by the fact that work in hand was not completed).

With Bess's return, the computation becomes more simple, for Jenkinson the clerk of works is paid from MS 7 in fortnightly sums which are accounted for in MS 6. These payments total £2200.

From the three totals covering the period 18 October 1592 to 18 January 1598 comes a grand total of £3700 over eleven years, making an average annual expenditure of £340. When MS 6 opens in 1587,

Bess has already been building for some time; one wing is completed and is being added to. Exactly when this work began cannot be said, but she could have started in 1584 when she was chased out of Chatsworth and retired to Hardwick, and if the annual average is used for those three years, a round figure of £1000 can be added to the figure arrived at for the later years, making an estimated total of £4700. But to allow for the missing pages it would be fair to inflate this figure to £5000 for all the buildings of both Hardwick Halls including the stable yard, from 1584 to January 1598.

This final figure may strike some as ludicrously low and I can only claim that I have drawn the figure from the accounts which are the only evidence available. But it may be compared with the figure for the building of Wollaton Hall, £5200, which was computed by P. E. Rossall in a thesis presented to the University of Sheffield in 1957 – Rossall explains his computation and provides a transcription of the accounts and it is not a figure I would dispute. Again in *The Making of the English Country House 1500–1640*, Malcolm Airs provides computations for other Elizabethan buildings which tend to confirm the Hardwick figure. Furthermore it must be pointed out that Bess was providing practically all her own materials and her costs were for labour only – a very cheap commodity in the 1590s.

At the other end of the scale, in *Family and Fortune*, Lawrence Stone gives a figure for the building of Hatfield House from 1607–1612, (which includes some very costly gardening and extravagant imports from abroad) totalling £38,848, but he fails to say how this figure is arrived at.

NOTES

A list of abbreviations used in the notes appears on pages 246–7

CHAPTER I : YOUNG BESS OF HARDWICK

1 The quotations given from this notebook are taken from *Historical Collections* of *Noble Families*, by A. Collins. Also an article in the *Derbyshire Archaeological Society Journal* for 1907. Both quote entries from this notebook belonging to Sir William Cavendish. Unfortunately the notebook has vanished. In *A Catalogue of Letters and Historical Documents existing in the Library at Welbeck Abbey*, 1903, the notebook is given as reference 111 C4. The present Duke of Portland does not know of the notebook and it is not with any of the deposited manuscripts.

2 Lodge, Edmund, *Illustrations of British History*.

3 Chatsworth, *Schedule of manuscripts in the muniment at Hardwick Hall*, 1812, p. 246.

4 All the details of the date of John Hardwick's death, his will, the Hardwick lands and his widow's problems with the Court of Wards are found under the following references: P.R.O. (I.P.M.) C/143/50 102; P.R.O. (I.P.M.) C/42/47/25; P.R.O. Wards Books 149 and 150; P.R.O. Star Chamber, Hen. VIII, vol. VII, ff15–16.

5 P.R.O. Wards 9/129. Survey 1527/8.

6 P.R.O. (P.C.) vol. VIII, file 1022/28.

7 The details on the Barley wills, estates and marriages are from: P.R.O. Wards 9/152; P.R.O. (P.C.) C1/1101/17; *Barlow Family Records*, by Sir Montague Barlow, 1932.

8 Manuscript is at Chatsworth.

9 Chatsworth, Drawer 367.

10 N.R.O.(Port.) DDP 42/27.

CHAPTER 2: 'UTTERLY UNDONE' 1547–1557

1   S.P.(Dom.) 26. Hen. VIII, nos. 1250 and 481.
2   Details of William Cavendish's life and family are taken from: *Life of Cardinal Wolsey*, by George Cavendish; *The Cavendish Family*, by Frances Buckley; S.P.(Dom.) 37. Hen. VIII, Grants, February. Details of the dates of his marriages and the births and sponsors of his children are from the missing notebook mentioned in note 1, chapter 1.
3   Details of living in London and at Northaw are taken from the two earliest surviving of Bess's household account books: Folger Xd 486; Hardwick MS 1.
4   P.R.O. (Star) Edwd. VI, Bundle 1, no. 49.
5   Folger Xd 486, f15.
6   Details of the Northaw/Chatsworth land exchanges are from: P.R.O. (Chan. Misc.) Bundle 54, file 1, Derby no. 20, 14 Eliz. 1; Folger Xd 486 f26; B.M. Add. MSS 5861 (I.P.M. Sir W. Cavendish); Cal. Pat. Rolls: 6 Edw. VI, 23 June 1552.
7   Folger Xd 486 f27.
8   *Ibid.*, f23v.
9   Hardwick MS 1, Pt. 1
10 *Ibid.*, Pt. 2.
11 Details of land purchases are found in: B.M. Add. MSS 5861, ff198v–200; Folger Xd 428 f20v.
12 P.R.O. E101/424/10.
13 Chatsworth. An envelope marked '143'.
14 Hardwick MS 3, ff1–1v.
15 Details of the charge against William Cavendish and his reply are taken from: P.R.O.(P.C.) VI, 182; P.R.O. E101/424/10.

CHAPTER 3: LADY ST LOE 1557–1565

1   These details and those of Bess's movements during the accession of Queen Elizabeth are taken from: Hardwick MS 3. The Parl. Bill: Longleat MSS Thynne corrs., vol. 13 no. 3 A+B tt 9–11.
2   The figures of Bess's income and expenditure are computed from: Hardwick MS 3.
3   This outline of Sir William St Loe's life is composed from the following sources: his marriage; Longleat MSS Thynne corrs., vol. 3 no. 5 t29 hre 15 August 1559. Cal. Pat. Rolls, 2 Eliz. 1, Pt. V, m5, and Pt. VIII, m25; *The Retrospective Review*, vol. 2, 1828, 'Memoires of Sir Wm St Loe'; 1821 Schedule, *op. cit.*, p. 147, no. 6; Acts of

the Privy Council 1553-4. The value of the St Loe lands is given in Lansdowne 40/42.

4   Folger Xd 428 (75) 4 Sept 1560; *ibid.*, (76) 12 October 1560; *ibid.*, (77) 24 October 1562 (?).

5   Eton Manuscript 272 (Phillipps 14788) is a short account book kept by a manservant when Henry and William Cavendish attended Eton College in 1560-1. The details fit in neatly with the St Loe account book at Chatsworth (Phillipps 15081) which has been used in the chapter to chart St Loe's travels and purchases.

6   The astonishing facts for this story of the quarrel between the St Loe brothers are taken from: *Archaeologia*, vol. XII, pp. 98-9; *The Tower of London*, by John Bayley, p. 448 and Appendix; Chatsworth Drawer 143(3); Sir William St Loe's replication, 1561; *The Retrospective Review*, op. cit.

7   Chatsworth Drawer 143(3).

8   Calendar of Patent Rolls, 2 Eliz. 1, Pt. VII, m10.

9   All the details of this sad affair are taken from B.M. Harl. 6286: the interrogations and answers of all those involved except Bess herself.

10   H.M.C.(Sal.), vol. 1, 153/87.

11   H.M.C. (Long) vol. IV, pp. xiv–xv.

12   Univ. Nottm. (Manvers) Probate Inventory, 7 April 1564.

13   The details of the marriage negotiations are briefly covered in letters: Folger Xd 428 (69) and (70).

14   *The Retrospective Review, op. cit.*

15   The figures and details which follow are taken from: Hardwick MS 2. The two letters of instructions from Bess: Folger Xd 428 (84) and (85). The detail of the 'Great Gate': Chatsworth, St Loe Accounts, p. 64. William St Loe's comment: Folger Xd 428 (78).

16   Cal. Pat. Rolls, 5 Eliz. 1, Pt. 2.

17   These latter events affecting St Loe are taken from: *A Survey of London*, by John Stowe, 1908, vol. 1, p. 172; Folger Xd 428 (78); S.P. (Sup.) 46/13, f298.

CHAPTER 4: MY LADY SHREWSBURY 1565-1570

1   Cromp's letter referring to the Cavendish boys and to Jackson: Folger Xd 428(18). The troubles of the unfortunate Jackson are covered by two letters dated 29 September 1567 addressed to the Archbishop of Canterbury, one from the Queen and the other from the Privy Council: S.P.(Dom.) Eliz. 1, Addenda 1567, vol. XIII. Earlier troubles are reported in *Visitation of Merton College 1562* published

by Canterbury and York Society, vol. 11, pp. 688–99. Rumours of marriage H.M.C. (Sal.) vol. 1, p. 325. Court pension in Nicholls' *Progress of Elizabeth*, vol. 1, p. 269.

2 Chatsworth Drawer 143(6): fragment of an inventory for Chatsworth 1564(?).
3 The inventory of jewellery was bought by Sheffield Public Libraries at Sotheby's in June 1974, ex collection of John Wilson of Broomhead Hall, MS 15074. And the Wingfield letter: Folger Xd 428(129).
4 Chatsworth Drawer 278, Item 1.
5 This letter and the following letter, both written in the autumn of 1568 from London: Folger Xd 428(86) and (87).
6 H.M.C.(Pepys) p. 144.
7 Strickland, *Letters of Mary Queen of Scots*, vol. 11, p. 161.
8 The details of the preparations at Tutbury and the furnishings are taken from: H.M.C.(Pepys), p. 147, Cal. of Scots Papers, vol. 11, nos. 961, 962 and 969. White's letter: H.M.C.(Sal.), vol. 1, no. 1279. Shrewsbury's letter of 13 March: Cal. of Scots Papers, vol. 11, no. 1022.
9 The embroidery details are taken from: *The Needlework of Mary Queen of Scots*, by Margaret Swain; *English Domestic Embroidery Patterns of the 16th and 17th Centuries*, by John Nevinson (Walpole Society, vol. 28); 'Stitched for Bess of Hardwick', by John Nevinson (*Country Life*, 29 November 1973); 'Embroidered by Queen and Countess', by John Nevinson (*Country Life*, 22 January 1976); 'An Elizabethan Herbarium' by John Nevinson (*National Trust Year Book 1975/6*).
10 Passport for Ange Marie: S.P.(Sup.) 46/14, f187. The 'Rich Bed', etc., Labanoff, vol. IV, p. 403.
11 Letters concerning the illness of Mary and that of the Earl are found in: Cal. of Scots Papers, vol. 11, nos. 1050–89.
12 S.P.(Dom.) Eliz. 1, vol CCVII, no. 59: this is part of the evidence of the quarrel between the Shrewsburys.

CHAPTER 5: THE SCOTS QUEEN 1570–1575

1 The comment about the state of the wells at Tutbury is given in Cal. of Scots Papers, vol. 3, p. 129, and the later reference to the cost of keeping Mary, in the same vol. p. 118.
2 H.M.C.(Sal.) vol. 1, p. 499.
3 Strickland vol. 1, pp. 246–9.
4 Indenture dated 22 April 1572. Chatsworth. Cupboard no. 1, Shelf 3.

5 The travels of Gilbert Talbot and Henry Cavendish are covered by letters: Lambeth MS 697, f83, 23 June 1570; *ibid.*, f71, 1 November 1571; Col. of Arms, vol. P, f571, 4 November 1570.

6 *Ibid.*, vol. F; f33.

7 The Hall at Buxton was built by Shrewsbury as a guest house for his visitors taking the waters. They were visitors who covered the glass of his windows with scratched verses, mottoes and Latin tags. Mary's farewell to Buxton which was scratched on one window of the Hall is printed in Strickland's *Mary Queen of Scots*, vol. 11, p. 376: though the date of its destruction given in the footnote must be incorrect (mid-eighteenth-century) – the Hall was burnt down in 1670. Other examples of visitors' memorials on the windows of the Hall are given in H.M.C.(Bath) vol. 11, pp. 20–2. Dr John Jones's expression of the merits of Buxton was published in 1572. *The Benefits of the Ancient Bathes of Buckstones.*

8 Folger Xd 428 (9).

9 *Ibid.*, (30).

10 S.P.(Dom.) Eliz. 1, 1547–80, vol. XCIX, no. 13.

11 The main details of this account are taken from *Correspondance Diplomatique de la Mothe Fénélon*, vol 6, (edited by J. Teulet) pp. 249, 245, 261, 293, 298, 319, 328 and 357. The Acts of the Privy Council for 1574. The two letters written by Margaret Lennox on 3 December, one to Burghley and the other to Leicester are found in S.P.(Dom.) Eliz. 1, 1547–80, vol. XCIX, no. 12, and one letter on 10 December to Leicester is in the same volume, no. 13.

12 The letters which Shrewsbury wrote to the Queen are in: Strickland, *Mary Queen of Scots*, pp. 346 and 347, dated 5 November. (Strickland quotes Cotton Caligula CIII and gives no folio number. I have been unable to find this letter.) Cotton Caligula CV f243, 2 December. Col. of Arms, vol. E, f103, 2 December. Cotton Caligula CIV, f308, 4 December.

13 Charles Lennox's secretary, Thomas Fowler, was examined in the matter. The Interrogatories are given in Cal. of Scots Papers vol. 5, nos. 21 and 22. These have been dated July 1574 which is incorrect; it must have been December 1574. Fowler's answers have not survived.

14 S.P.(Dom.) Eliz. 1, 1547–80, vol. XCIX, no. 15.

15 Lodge vol. 2, p. 126.

16 Cal. of Scots Papers vol. V, nos. 93, 94, 126–41 and 211.

17 Shrewsbury's two letters: Col. of Arms vol. P, f719, dated 10 February 1575; Lodge vol. 11, p. 128, dated 3 March 1575. And

a general description of the violent tremor is given in *Chronicles of England* by John Stowe (1587).

CHAPTER 6: 'MY JEWEL ARBELLA' 1575–1578

1   Letter to Mary Queen of Scots from Margaret Lennox, Cal. of Scots Papers vol. V, no. 202.

2   Col. of Arms vol. F, f93. The reference to Anthony Wingfield is found in *Documents relating to the Office of Revels in the Reign of Queen Elizabeth* by Albert Feullerat (1908), p. 47.

3   The references to the New Year gifts are numerous but have mainly been quoted from: Folger Xd 428 (127) and (130); Hardwick MS 5, ff2, 19 and 26; an article by John Nevinson in *Costume*, 1975, vol. 9, p. 28. The references to Jones as the Queen's dressmaker are taken from Folger Vb 308, fiv; Hardwick MS 7, f16; and Wardrobe Warrants 1589 P.R.O. L.C. 5/36.

4   A letter bought by Sheffield Libraries at Sotheby's, July 1974, ex Phillipps MS 20556.

5   The will is printed in Labanoff vol. IV, 360.

6   The loan is mentioned in S.P.(Sup.) 46/30, f333, and the dowry in Lansdowne 40/41.

7   Hardwick MS 4.

8   The Queen's letter which she thought better of sending, Cal. of Scots Papers vol. V, no. 253; and the letter which she sent and Shrewsbury received, Col. of Arms vol. P, f819.

9   Gilbert's letter to Bess July 1575, bought by Sheffield Libraries at Sotheby's July 1974 ex Phillipps MS 20556; and the letter of October 1575 was included in the same purchase. The reference to Shrewsbury's writing is from Batho's introduction to his *Calendar of Shrewsbury Papers in the College of Arms*, p. xii.

10 The letter of the Scots Queen is found in S.P.(Dom.) vol. CCXXXI, p. 99; the references to Bessie Pierrepont are from Cal. of Scots Papers vol. VII, nos. 366, 551 and 624. Bessie had a very strong affection for Jacques Nau, usually known as Claude Nau (see H.M.C. Bath vol. 2, p. vii), and their marriage was seriously considered by her father and the Scots Queen; Bessie eventually married Richard Stapleton, heir of Brian his father.

11 Letter from Gilbert to Bess dated 1 August 1577, Folger Xd 428 (112); and the long letter dated only 1577 but which was in fact about the same time, is printed in Hallamshire, p. 87. The original of the letter has vanished.

12 The references to the sad death of little George are taken from Folger Xd 428 (112); Cal. of Scots Papers vol. V, nos. 264 and 267.

13 Shrewsbury's letter anticipating the death of Margaret Lennox, dated 4 March 1578, is in Col. of Arms vol. F, f233; and the follow-up letter from Bess thanking the Queen for awarding the wardship to Elizabeth Lennox is H.M.C.(Sal.) vol. 2, p. 174.

14 The references to the allowance are found in S.P.(Dom.) vol. CLII, pp. 42, 43 and 53, also Cal. of Scots Papers vol. VI, nos. 95 and 96.

15 Bess's London visit in the autumn of 1578 is covered by: H.M.C.(Sal.) vol. 2, pp. 205, 223 and 226; Lambeth vol. 697, ff161 and 181.

CHAPTER 7: 'THE OLD SONG' 1578–1580

1   This is a curious reference for although the Manor of Keighley was a rich estate there is no reference to it in any rentals or estate papers until William Cavendish married Anne. The only reference at all is a grant dated 7 July, 32 Henry VIII (1540) giving Sir William Cavendish Lord of the Manor of Keighley, rights to hold fairs and markets in Keighley. The reference is Hardwick Drawer 337.

2   Elizabeth Lennox addressed a letter to Bess at Hardwick carrying no date but written before her marriage in 1574, Folger Xd 428(50). The reference to timber at Hardwick, Col. of Arms vol. O, f66; and the purchase of Hardwick for £9500 on 2 June 1583, Landsdowne 40/41. The references to James Hardwick being in the Fleet are in H.M.C.(Rut.) vol. 1, pp. 118 and 131. James's letters are in Folger Xd 428 (34) and (35); the letter to Bess from her mother, Folger Xd 428(50). James Hardwick's survey of his estates in 1570 survives in Hardwick MS 12; and the reference to Shrewsbury not paying for Hardwick is in Lansdowne 40/41.

James Hardwick's career towards bankruptcy is a classic example of foolish speculation in buying Church lands on borrowed money, the return on the purchase being monstrously overshadowed by the interest he paid on the loans.

3   The references to the ship *The Talbot* are from Col. of Arms vol. G, ff92, 202 and 255. The Voyages and Colonising Enterprises of Sir Humphrey Gilbert by A. B. Quinn, vol. 1, pp. 78–9.

4   The wartime experiences of Henry Cavendish are covered by S.P.(Span.) 1578, nos. 488, 491, 573 and 578; S.P.(Dom.) Eliz. 1, Addenda vol. xxv, nos. 85 and 86; whilst his borrowings are found in S.P.(Dom.) 1584–6 (5) and Statutes Staple C152/55, pt. 4.

5   The reference to the 'Platte' being sent to Giles Greves is in a letter

from Shrewsbury dated 5 August 1577, Col of Arms vol. P, f837. Greves was working at Worksop in 1585, Lambeth vol. 698, f87. The request to send Accres is scrawled across Folger Xd 428(140) dated 10 October 1580. Mary's first visit to Worksop was in June 1583 and is mentioned in the Cal. of Scots Papers but particularly in Col. of Arms vol. G, f225, a letter dated 3 November 1583. Mary visited Worksop again in September 1584.

6 The problems with the tenants are covered by Hallamshire, p. 85; Folger Xd 428(39); and Col. of Arms vol. F, f331 and vol. P, f973.

7 Shrewsbury's complaints about his finances at this time are found in H.M.C.(Sal.) vol. 2, no. 1079 and Cal. of Scots Papers vol. VI, no. 80.

8 The will of Elizabeth Lennox dated 16 January 1581/2 is in Chatsworth Drawer 279(4), and the detail of the payment to Arbella of £3360 is given in Hardwick MS 7, f83v.

9 The letters are found in S.P.(Dom.) vol. CLII, pp. 42 and 43; vol. CLXXXIII, no. 56.

10 The details of Bess's land purchases are very involved and are found when taken as evidence during their great quarrel. S.P.(Dom.) 1581–90, vol. CCVII, covers evidence from Bess and from Shrewsbury, neither agreeing on any point. H.M.C.(Sal.) vol. III, presents similar evidence with the same problem. The most reliable details are those which Burghley used himself and are under Lansdowne 40/47. The Earl's pathetic comment is from Col. of Arms vol. G, f311.

11 From *A Survey of Staffordshire* by Sampson Erdswick (1717). And Harl. 1093 shows Henry Cavendish as leaving eight illegitimate children.

12 William Cavendish's financial benefits are taken from Lansdowne 40/47.

13 Purchase of Stoke Manor, Derbyshire: N.R.O.(Port.) DDP 114/20. Shrewsbury's refusal to make a settlement: Lansdowne 40/41. The reference to George Wilbye, the madrigalist, is taken from *Robert Smythson and the Elizabethan Architects* by Mark Girouard, p. 212.

CHAPTER 8: 'NO GOOD AGREEMENT' 1580–1584

1 Gilbert's letter to his father, 15 May 1579: Col. of Arms vol. F, f331. Shrewsbury's letter to Bess, 21 June 1580: Folger Xd 428 (102). Marmyon's letter to Willoughby, 28 October (1582): H.M.C.(Mid.) vol. 1, p. 153. Frances Battell's letter to Lady Paulet, 23 March 1584: Cal. of Scots Papers vol. VII, no. 46.

2   The two letters are printed in S.P.(Dom.) vol. CLVIII, nos. 57 and
     58. The account of Shrewsbury's farewell to Bess is given in Lans-
     downe 40/57.
3   Col. of Arms, vol. G, ff116, 124 and 300.
4   Col. of Arms vol. G, f256, is Shrewsbury's warrant. The attack on
     Charles Cavendish is described in S.P.(Dom.) CCVII, no. 14, and
     William's defiance from the battlements of Chatsworth in the same
     volume, no. 32, with the subsequent results under no. 34 and Bacon/
     Franks 2/64. Booth's earlier incitements are in Col. of Arms
     vol. G, f957.
5   Hardwick Building accounts MS7.
6   Letter from Shrewsbury to his bailiff Avery Copley, 7 June 1584:
     Folger Xd 428 (105). The account following is based on Miss Lloyd's
     MSS at Althorp, principally from pp. 6–20. The quotation on
     Shrewsbury's health comes from Folger Xd 428 (113).
7   The mention of Mary's overtures in Bordeaux is from Cal. of Scots
     Papers vol. VII, no. 82. The rumour of the Shrewsbury/Mary affair
     is quoted in Lambeth vol. 698, f39v; whilst Copley's court action
     is taken from Queen Elizabeth and her Times, vol. 11, p. 241. The
     important statement by Mary on the rumours is in Harl. 1582, f311.
8   Bess's letter to Walsingham, 6 April 1584: S.P.(Dom.) vol. CLXX,
     no. 6. Shrewsbury's letter to Leicester, 8 August 1584: Col. of Arms,
     vol. G, f257, repeated in Lloyd/Althorp, p. 20. Shrewsbury's veno-
     mous comments on Bess come from S.P.(Dom.) vol. CCVII, nos.
     15 and 20; Col. of Arms vol. G, f277. Whilst Bess's opinion is given
     in a letter to Shrewsbury from Leicester shortly after his visit to
     Chatsworth, it is dated 26 June 1584, from Lloyd/Althorp,
     p. 14.
         William Overton's letter to Shrewsbury, dated 12 October 1590:
     Col. of Arms vol. I, f92; and his borrowings from Bess appear in
     Hardwick MS 7, f133 and Drawer 143, f19.
9   The proposed marriage between Arbella and Leicester's son Robert
     is mentioned in S.P.(Dom.) vol. CLIX, no. 8; and Labanoff vol. V,
     p. 436.
10   The correspondence between Leicester and Shrewsbury over the
     death of Leicester's son is given in Lloyd/Althorp, p. 21 and Col.
     of Arms vol. G, f257.
11   Mary's letter to Mauvissière is printed in Leader's Mary Queen of
     Scots in Captivity, p. 549, giving the reference Colbert MSS no. 470,
     f 27. Chenelle's duplicity was divined by Labanoff and is explained
     by Conyers Read in a footnote to p. 380 of vol. II of Sir Francis

Walsingham. Mary's 'scandal' letter is printed in full in Labanoff vol. VI, p. 51.

12 This verse is quoted in Strickland's *Mary Queen of Scots in Captivity* in a footnote to p. 376. However, the verse is not given in H.M.C.(Bath) vol. II, pp. 20–2, and Strickland's account in the footnote of the glass being broken in the mid-eighteenth century, when the then dowager Countess of Burlington attempted to have it removed, is not reconciled by the fact that the Hall was burnt down in 1670, H.M.C.(Bath) vol. II, p. viii.

13 Topcliffe's connection with the rumour is given in Cal. of Scots Papers vol. VII, no. 72; S.P.(Dom.) vol. CLXXII, no. 8. And in Folger Xd 428 (113), Bentall is shown as being Bess's enemy.

14 William's detention in the Fleet is mentioned in Cal. of Scots Papers vol. VII, no. 268. Bess's short note to Shrewsbury, dated only 1584, is in the Longleat MSS, Talbot Letters, vol. II, f267, but this same letter is quoted in Lloyd/Althorp with the date 25 August 1584. Shrewsbury's letter to Manners of 24 September 1584 is in H.M.C.(Rut.) vol. I, p. 170.

15 This account is taken from Strickland, vol. II, p. 382–3. Sadler's letter is from *The Life Letters and Papers of Sir Ralph Sadler*, p. 422, and he also gives the key to the code. Baldwin's imprisonment is mentioned in S.P.(Dom.) vol. CCVII, no. 1; Gilbert's claim for £100 from Baldwin, Col. of Arms vol. H, f855. Shrewsbury's decayed health is demonstrated in Cal. of Scots Papers vol. VII, no. 417.

CHAPTER 9: THE FALL OF THE LEAF 1584–1590

1 Leicester's warning to Shrewsbury is taken from his letter of 26 June 1584 Lloyd/Althorp, p. 17. Walsingham writing to Bromley, the Lord Chancellor, on 22 December 1584, stated that both sides had been advised of the date of the commission: Lansdowne 40/55. Shrewsbury's undated letter to the Queen is in Lloyd/Althorp, p. 25; and his visit to Oatlands is covered by S.P.(Dom.) vol. CCVII, no. 8 (1). Shrewsbury's chastened mood is caught in a letter to Leicester, 30 April 1585: Col. of Arms, vol. G, f272. Leicester's belated letter to Bess giving the expected result of the enquiry, 12 July 1585: S.P.(Dom.) vol. CXXX, no. 22.

2 Lloyd/Althorp, pp. 45–51.

3 Letter to Shrewsbury dated 1 March 1585: Bacon/Franks 2/73. The account of the misfortunes of Henry Beresford is taken from S.P.(Dom.) vol. CCVII, nos. 4 and 5. Justice Clenche's report is

is the same volume, no. 16. The stay of execution is in Folger Xd 428 (24) and S.P.(Dom.) vol. CCVII, no. 8 (1).

4 The references to this commission are taken from S.P.(Dom.) vol. CLXXXV, nos. 10 and 11; H.M.C.(Rut.) vol. 1, p. 187. Charles Cavendish's report on the Earl's disobedience: S.P.(Dom.) vol. CCVII, no. 6.

5 The details of the Earl's partial good behaviour are from S.P.(Dom.) vol. CCVII, no. 14. Bess's letter to Shrewsbury of 9 June 1586; Col. of Arms, vol. G, f.331. Shrewsbury's accusation of Walsingham, 15 June 1586: S.P.(Dom.) Vol. CCVII, no. 15; and Lloyd/Althorp. Roger Manner's letter to Rutland, 8 July 1586: H.M.C.(Rut.) vol. 1, p. 199. Shrewsbury's complaints of his treatment at Richmond: H.M.C. 6th Report Appendix Bacon/Franks vol. 19.

6 Shrewsbury's bond for £40,000 is quoted in S.P.(Dom.) vol. CCVII, no. 60. Roger Manner's letter to his brother, dated 20 July 1586: H.M.C.(Rut.) vol. 1, p. 200. Shrewsbury's complaint to Walsingham, H.M.C.(Sal.) vol. III, no. 321.

7 Gilbert Talbot to his uncle (Rutland?) 6 April 1587: H.M.C.(Rut.) vol. 1, pp. 212–3. Bess's letter to Burghley reporting Shrewsbury's neglect, 6 October 1587: S.P.(Dom.) vol. CCVII, no. 31. Kinnersley's letters to Bess are in Folger XD428(44) and (45).

8 The details of Shrewsbury's purchase of Barley are in N.R.O.(Port.) DDP51/19 and 42/27.

9 The Queen's last letter to Shrewsbury, dated December 1589: S.P.(Dom.) vol. CCXXIX, no. 50. The obsequious letter to Shrewsbury from an unnamed correspondent, reporting rumours of Bess's visit to London: Col. of Arms vol. I, f37. The description of Shrewsbury's funeral is from Hallamshire, p. 73.

CHAPTER 10: 'ARBELLA WAS MERRY' 1590–1591

1 Shrewsbury's will is printed in *Surtees Society*, 1912, 1, 'North Country Wills 11', pp. 148–50. Bess's letter to Burghley 11 April 1591: S.P.(Dom.) vol. CCXXXVIII, no. 116. The foolhardy challenge to a duel by Gilbert Talbot is mentioned in Col. of Arms, vol. 1, f188.

2 Fox's original manuscript of this journey is at Chatsworth but it was printed in full in *Camden Miscellany*, vol. XVII.

3 The account of the progress of the building of both old and new Hardwick Halls in this chapter is distilled from Hardwick building accounts MS 6.

4 *Robert Smythson and the Elizabethan Architects* by Mark Girouard.

5 See Appendix II.

6 S.P.(Dom.) vol. CCXXXIII, no. 73.

7 Charles Cavendish's letter to Bess undated (but, from internal evidence, July–August of 1587): Chatsworth Drawer 143, no. 10. The inventory of plate dated 21 August 1587: Chatsworth Drawer 143, no. 8. Arbella's first surviving letter to Bess dated 8 February 1587: H.M.C. 3rd Report, p. 420. Goodman's comment on James and Ann is taken from *The Court of King James by Goodman*, edited by J. S. Brewer, 1839. James's proxy marriage 20 August 1589. Reget Scots P.C., vol. IV, p. 411 n.

8 S.P. (Ven) IX, 541.

9 The cost for John Rood's house is given in MS 7, f235.

CHAPTER 11: 'SOMEONE VERY DESIROUS' 1591–1593

1 The details for the visit Bess made to London are taken from two sources, both account books: Hardwick MS 7, ff1–33v, which covers the period from her departure in November 1591 until her return on 5 August 1592; and an account book kept by her London steward, Edward Whaley, mainly showing legal expenses from 9 September 1589 to 12 July 1592. Bess's gift to Cordell at New Year 1591 is from Drawer 143, no. 8.

2 The references in this paragraph are from S.P.(Dom.) vol. CCXL, no. 53 and vol. CCXXXIX, no. 164; H.M.C.(Sal.) vol. IV, p. 144.

3 The entry for these payments (MS 7, f30) is confused by a correction. I give the entry as it was intended, ignoring the correction. Erna Auerbach, in *Nicholas Hilliard*, gives the full entry on p. 254.

4 MS 8, f29v.

5 The details of Bess's collaboration with Sir Francis are taken from Col. of Arms, vol. H, f353; Univ. Nottm. (Midd.) 6/171/46; and an article 'Sir Francis Willoughby's Ironworks, 1570–1610' by R.S. Smith in *Renaissance and Modern Studies*. vol. XI, pp. 90–140.

CHAPTER 12: 'SPEAK SOFTLY MY MASTERS' 1593–1598

1 The contract for the purchase of Heath, etc., is mentioned in the 1821 Schedule of Manuscripts, p. 21. This schedule is at Chatsworth and is valuable as some of the manuscripts have vanished since it was made. The details of the payments for Heath are in MS 7, ff50–4. Peter Yates's first payment for the roof of Hardwick: MS 6, f239. The alum reference is MS 7, ff77v and 81v.

2 The reference to the maid with the hind is in MS 7, f98. And the half-year's payments for wages occur regularly in MS 7. The Earl of Rut-

land's musicians play in MS 8, f61, and the Queen's Players are in the same volume, f104.

3 The Clifford case is taken from the Star Chamber records: P.R.O. Star C5 C62/38 and C32/6. The references made by Bess are in MS 8, f24; MS 7, f124v and Drawer 143 (10). The loan to Rhodes is given in MS 7, f133.

4 Bess's letter to Puckering 28 May 1592: Harl. art 67, f71. Mary Talbot's letter to Stanhope: *Lives of the Earls of Shrewsbury*, a manuscript by Nathaniel Johnson at Chatsworth, vol. VI, p. 217. Edward Talbot's trouble with the alchemist Wood from: *Les reportes del cases in Camera Stellata 1593–1609* by W.P. Baildon, pp. 13–16. Charles Cavendish's duel is in Sloane 4161, no. 6, and his wounding at Kirkby in *Historical Collections of the Noble Family of Cavendish* by Arthur Collins, p. 21; MS 8, ff55v and 80. Abraham Smith's 'Terms': MS 6, f253.

5 See Appendix II.

6 I am indebted to Malcolm Airs for this reference, Sloane 3828: 208. The earlier reference to Abraham Smith at Ashford is from the great survey of William Cavendish's estates, 'Senior Survey', at Chatsworth, p. 148. Accres's death is recorded in William Cavendish's account book for MS 29 March 1607: 'Given by my Lord's command at Thomas Akers burial, 5s'. No will or inventory for either Accres or Smith has been found at Lichfield, York or Canterbury.

CHAPTER 13: 'WEARIED OF MY LIFE' 1598–1603

1 The details of the furnishings are taken from the 1601 inventories of Hardwick Hall.

2 The reference to Bess using a stick is from: Col. of Arms vol. M, f349. Byng's comment comes from *Torrington Diaries* vol. III, p. 31. Arbella's comment on the interior of Hardwick: *Life of Arbella Stuart* by Bradley, vol. II, p. 139. The Queen's reference to Arbella: Folger Xd 428(120).

3 Bess's will is printed in part in *Historical Collections of Noble Families* by A. Collins, pp. 15–19. The copy in the P.R.O. is under Prob 11/ 111/C1123 and there is another copy at Chatsworth.

4 The details of Arbella's adventure over her proposal to Seymour and the subsequent repercussions are from H.M.C.(Sal.) vol. XII, pp. 681–96; also *Life of Arbella Stuart* by Bradley, vol. II; and the story is told again in *Arbella Stuart* by P.M. Handover.

CHAPTER 14: 'NOT OVERSUMPTUOUS' 1603–1608

1   Details of the payments are found in MS 8, f69v. The account of James I's visit to Worksop: *The Progresses, Processions and Magnificent Festivities of King James the First* by John Nicholson. And James's minute for Arbella's release: H.M.C.(Sal.) vol. XV, p. 65.

2   The letter was sold at Sotheby's on 26 June 1974 and is illustrated in their catalogue, Lot 2840. Pusey's letter to William Cavendish, dated 22 April 1604, is under Drawer 143 (14). The visit of Henry Cavendish Junior to Hardwick is shown in MS 7, f150v, when Bess gave him £10.

3   Montague's letters to Bess: Col. of Arms vol. L, f7; Folger Xd 428 (59) and (60). The payment by William Cavendish for his peerage is quoted in *Crisis of the Aristocracy 1558–1641* by Laurence Stone (abridged paperback edition, Oxford University Press, 1967, p. 50).

4   H.M.C.(Rut.) vol. 1, p. 399.

5   Bentley's complaint: Col. of Arms, vol. L, f143. The comment to Gilbert is made by Sir John Harpur in a letter 31 July 1606: Col. of Arms vol. M, f349. Gilbert to Salisbury, 14 December 1607: H.M.C.(Sal.) vol. IXX, p. 379, and Gilbert's letter to Henry Cavendish describing the same visit is printed in *Bess of Hardwick and her Circle* by Maud Rawson, p. 346: the original has not been traced.

6   The account given of Bess's last days is an amalgam of details taken from the following: Pusey's 'Memorandum of Declarations made by the Countess of Shrewsbury subsequent to her will', Drawer 143(17); Mrs Digby's evidence of a nuncupative codicil to the will of the Countess of Shrewsbury, Lambeth vol. 710, f61; and the payments made out of William Cavendish's account book MS 29, covering the period of Bess's illness and death.

7   The description of Bess's funeral is drawn from the payments given in MS 29 and the background is filled in from details given in: Col. of Arms, Vincents Precedents 151 (1610) (a manuscript of instructions to heralds on charges and procedures), the section headed 'Funeral of a Countess'.

LIST OF ABBREVIATIONS

The following abbreviations have been used in the note references: Manuscript Collections calendared by the Historical Manuscript Commission:

H.M.C.(Long): Longleat MSS at Longleat House.

H.M.C.(Pepys): Pepys Library, Magdalene College, Cambridge.

H.M.C.(Rut.): Rutland MSS at Belvoir Castle.

H.M.C.(Sal.): Salisbury MSS at Hatfield House.

Col. of Arms: A calendar jointly published by the H.M.C. and the Derbyshire Archaeological Society, edited by G.R. Batho, covers the Shrewsbury collection of MSS in the College of Arms.

Lambeth: Another joint calendar published by the H.M.C. and Derbyshire Archaeological Society, edited by E.G.W. Bill, covers the Shrewsbury collection of MSS in the Lambeth Palace Library.

Calendars of State Papers published by the Public Record Office:

P.R.O.(C.R.): Close Rolls.

P.R.O.(Pat.): Patent Rolls.

P.R.O.(P.C.): Proceedings of the Privy Council.

S.P.(Dom.): State Papers: Domestic.

S.P.(For.): State Papers: Foreign.

S.P.(Span.): State Papers: Spanish.

S.P.(Ven.): State Papers: Venetian.

Reference to the Calendar of Scots Papers covers the volumes under that name which have collected all references to Scottish State Papers from wherever they have been found.

British Museum:

Harl: The Harleian MSS.

Cotton: the Cottonian MSS.

Chatsworth: the collection of manuscripts at Chatsworth House, Derbyshire which was augmented by manuscripts brought from Hardwick Hall in 1959, the latter being distinguished by the abbreviation: Hardwick.

Folger: Folger Shakespeare Library, Washington, Mass, USA.

Althorp, Lloyd: Rachael Lloyd's manuscript at Althorp House, Northants.

Sheffield Libs: The manuscripts in the Local History Department of the Sheffield City Library.

Arundel: Catalogue of Arundel Castle MSS in the Sheffield City Library.

B/F: The unindexed addendum to the Arundel Castle Catalogue, listing the Bacon Franks collection of manuscripts in the Sheffield City Library.

The fact that two collections calandared by the H.M.C. have since been deposited with the University of Nottingham: the Middleton and Manvers MSS; and the Portland MSS with both the University of Nottingham and the Nottinghamshire Record Office, can give rise to confusion. I have therefore ignored the H.M.C. references and give the new references:

N.R.O.(Port.): the Portland MSS in the Notts. Record Office.
Univ. Nottm.(Port.): the Portland MSS in the University of Nottingham.
Univ. Nottm.(Manvers): the Manvers MSS in the University of Nottingham.
Univ. Nottm.(Midd.): the Middleton MSS in the University of Nottingham.

MANUSCRIPT SOURCES

(in chronological order)

Hardwick MS 1. 5 November 1551–23 June 1553.

Hardwick MS 3. 20 August 1557–1 March 1559.

Hardwick MS 2. 8 October 1559–6 October 1560.

St Loe Accounts August 1560–December 1560 (bought by the Trustees in 1974)

Hardwick MS 12. James Hardwick's survey of Hardwick lands. 1570.

Hardwick MS 4. 7 January 1577–30 September 1577.

Hardwick MS 5. September 1579–July 1584.

Hardwick MS 6. 29 July 1587–20 January 1599 (Hardwick building accounts)

Hardwick MS 7. 23 November 1591–8 January 1598.

Hardwick MS 9a. 13 October 1592–29 October 1593.

Hardwick MS 10. 30 September 1593–29 September 1594.

Hardwick MS 9. 30 September 1593–16 April 1598.

Hardwick MS 8. 15 April 1598–August 1601.

Hardwick MS 24. Book of Remembrances.

Hardwick MS 29. William Cavendish's accounts, 1608–28.

Manuscript 'Lives of the Earls of Shrewsbury', by Nathaniel Johnson.

Basil Stallybrass, in an article on the building of Hardwick in *Archaeologia*, vol. lxiv, quotes from an account book which he called Hardwick MS 4 and the earliest date he gives is July 1577 and the last is 24 December 1580. This manuscript book has vanished.

Hardwick drawers 143, 144, 145 and 367 also Box 6. Also Hardwick Charters.

Xd 486 The earliest accounts of Bess to survive covering 1548–50.

Vb 308   Richard Whaley's London account book. 9 September 1589–12 July 1592.
La 843–4   Bagot Letters.
Xd 428   Cavendish/Talbot letters.

ALTHORP HOUSE, NORTHANTS

Manuscript by Rachael Lloyd 'Memoires of Elizabeth Hardwick Countess of Shrewsbury and her descendants'. (Miss Lloyd was housekeeper at Kensington Palace and a friend of Gorgiana, Countess Spencer. Together they visited many country houses and Miss Lloyd occupied her time copying letters from the muniment rooms. There is a part of Hardwick garden called 'Spencer's Walk'. Many of the letters quoted by Miss Lloyd cannot be traced to the originals and I would like to think that Miss Lloyd saw letters at Hardwick reported by Torrington Byng as being in the old hall 'and which would bear a hearty rummage'. That was in 1789; Miss Lloyd died in 1803.)

BRITISH MUSEUM

Additional Manuscript no. 21,404. Account of sums paid to the Earl of Shrewsbury for the maintenance of Mary Queen of Scots.
Additional Manuscript no. 27,532. Bailiff's accounts for the Earl of Shrewsbury covering the 1580s.
Additional Manuscript no. 5,861. St Loe Kniveton's notes on the Cavendish family.
Additional Manuscript no. 22,563. Arbella's life at Court from the Weymouth Collection.
Harleian vol. 6286. Contemporary transcription of the examinations in the Hertford-Grey marriage.

UNIVERSITY OF NOTTINGHAM

Middleton Manuscripts.
Manvers Manuscripts.
Portland Manuscripts.

NOTTINGHAMSHIRE RECORD OFFICE

Portland Manuscripts.

CALENDARS

Public Record Office
State Papers Domestic.
State Papers Foreign.

State Papers Scottish.
State Papers Venetian.
State Papers Spanish.
Acts of the Privy Council.
Close Rolls.
Patent Rolls.
A Calendar of Shrewsbury Papers in the Lambeth Palace Library, ed. E.G.W. Bill.
A Calendar of Shrewsbury and Talbot Papers at the College of Arms, ed. G. Batho.
Catalogue of the Arundel Castle Manuscripts in the Sheffield City Library and Talbot Correspondence (part of the Bacon Franks MSS), ed. R. Meredith.
Historical Manuscripts Reports.
Salisbury (Cecil), 24 volumes.
Rutland 4 Volumes.
Bath IV, 1 Volume.
Middleton, 1 Volume.
Pepys, 1 Volume.

A Catalogue of Letters and other historical documents exhibited at Welbeck Abbey, 1903 (compiled by A. Strong).

SOURCES
FROM
ARTICLES

Batho, Gordon, 'Gilbert Talbot 7th Earl of Shrewsbury' (*Derbyshire Archaelogical Society Journal*, 1973, vol. xciii).

Braisford, W., 'Bess of Hardwick' (*The Antiquary*, 1887, vol. xv).

Brodhurst, Revd. Francis, 'Elizabeth Hardwick Countess of Shrewsbury' (*Derbyshire Archaeological Society Journal*, vol. xxx).

Brodhurst, Revd. Francis, 'Hardwick Old Hall' (*Thoroton Society*, 1904, vol. VIII).

Brodhurst, Revd. Francis, 'Sir William Cavendish' (*Derbyshire Archaeological Society Journal*, vol. xxix).

Brodhurst, Revd. Francis, 'Was Mary Queen of Scots ever at Hardwick Hall?' (*Thoroton Society*, 1901, vol. V).

Cornforth, John, 'Chatsworth, Derbyshire' (*Country Life*, 18, 25 July, I, 29 August, 5 September 1968, vol. clxiv).

Currey, H. E., 'Almshouses of Elizabeth Countess of Shrewsbury' (*Derbyshire Archaeological Society Journal*, 1894, vol. xvj).

De Serre, J., 'Furnishings at Hardwick Hall' (*Country Life*, 23 April 1927).

Drury, Charles, and Hall, Walter, 'The Parish Register of Sheffield' (*Hunter Archaeological Society*, 1917).

Durant, David H., 'A London Visit' (*History Today*, July 1974).

Gilchrist, I., 'The Countess of Shrewsbury' (*The Antiquary*, 1885, vol. xii).

Gilchrist, I., 'Elizabeth Hardwick Countess of Shrewsbury' (*The Antiquary*, 1908, vol. xiv).

Girouard, Mark, 'Elizabethan Chatsworth' (*Country Life*, 22 November 1973).

Girouard, Mark, 'The Development of Longleat House' (*Royal Archaeological Institute*, vol. cxvi).

Hawkesbury, Lord, 'Catalogue of Pictures at Hardwick Hall' (*Derbyshire Archaeological Society Journal*, 1903, vol. xxviij).

Hunter, Revd. Joseph, 'Memoirs of Sir William Saint Loe' (*Retrospective Review*, 2nd series, vol. ii, 1928).

Hunter, Revd. Joseph, 'The expenses of Two Brothers at Eton College in 1560' (*Retrospective Review*, 2nd series, vol. ii).

Hussey, Christopher, 'Hardwick Hall' (*Country Life*, December 8, 15 and 22, 1928, vol. lxiv).

Jourdain, Margaret, 'Needlework at Hardwick Hall' (*Country Life*, 26 February 1927, vol. xxx).

Jourdain, Margaret, 'Some Tapestries at Hardwick Hall' (*Country Life*, 26 March 1927, vol. xxx).

Kirke, Henry, 'An aristocratic Squabble' (*Derbyshire Archaeological Society Journal*, 1911, vol. xxxiii).

Lees-Milne, James, 'Chatsworth, Derbyshire' (*Country Life*, 11, 18 and 25 April, 2 May 1968, vol. clxiv).

Nevinson, John, L., 'English Domestic Embroidery Patterns of the 16th and 17th Centuries' (*Walpole Society*, vol. xxviij).

Nevinson, John, L., 'New Years Gifts to Queen Elizabeth 1584' (*Costume*, vol. 9, 1975).

Nevinson, John, L., 'An Elizabethan Herbarium: Embroideries by Bess after the Woodcuts of Mattioli' (*National Trust Year Book*, 1976).

Nevinson, John, L., 'Stitched for Bess of Hardwick' (*Country Life*, 29 November 1973).

Nevinson, John L., 'Embroidered by Queen and Countess' (*Country Life*, 22 January 1976).

Stallybrass, Basil, 'Bess of Hardwick's Buildings and Building Accounts' (*Archaeologia*, 1913, vol. lxiv).

BIBLIOGRAPHY

This is not an exhaustive list of sources used in the preparation of this book but a list of references used and which would be of interest to readers who wish to deal with the subject matter more fully.

Auerbach, E.,   *Nicholas Hilliard* (1961).
Baildon, W.P., (ed.),   *Les Reportes del cases in Camera Stellata 1593–1609* (1894).
Bayle, M.R.,   *Lives of Most Eminent Persons* (1748).
Bayley, J.,   *The History and Antiquities of the Tower of London* (1821).
Birch, T.,   *Memoirs of the Reign of Queen Elizabeth* (1754).
Black, J.B.,   *The Reign of Elizabeth 1558–1603* (1969).
Buckley, F.,   *The Cavendish Family* (1911).
Boynton, L., and Thornton, P.,   *The Hardwick Hall Inventories* (1971).
Bradley, E.T.,   *Arbella Stuart* (1889).
Burke's Peerage   (1963 edition).
Burnett, J.,   *A History of the Cost of Living* (1969).
Camden, W.,   *Britannia*, ed. R. Gough (1789).
Camden, W.,   *The History of Annals of England* (1615).
Cheney, C.R.,   *Handbook of Dates* (1961).
Clifford, A., (ed.),   *The State Papers and Letters of Sir Ralph Sadler* (1809).
Collins, A.,   *Historical Collections of the Noble Families of Cavendish, etc* (1752).
Cooper, C.D.,   *The Life and Letters of Lady Arbella Stuart* (1866).
Cooper, C.P., (ed.),   *Correspondance de La Mothe Fénélon* (1838).
Copnall, H.H.,   *Nottingham County Records of the 17th Century* (1916).
Cust, L.,   *Authentic Portraits of Mary Queen of Scots* (1903).
Devonshire, W. Duke of,   *Handbook to Chatsworth and Hardwick* (1845).
De Vries, J.V.,   *Architectura* (1563).

Du Maurier, D.,   *Golden Lads* (1975).

Foley, H.,   *Records of the Provincial Society of Jesus* (1877).

Fraser, A.,   *Mary Queen of Scots* (1970).

Feuillerat, A.,   *Documents relating to the office of Revels of Queen Elizabeth* (1908).

G.E.C.,   *The Complete Peerage of England, etc* (1910–40).

Gesner, C.,   *Historia Animalium* (1551–8).

Girouard, M.,   *The Smythson Collection, Architectural History* vol. 5 (1962).

Girouard, M.,   *Robert Smythson and the Architecture of the Elizabethan Era* (1966).

Gotch, J.A.,   *Early Renaissance Architecture in England* (1901).

Handover, P.M.,   *Arbella Stuart* (1951).

Hardy, B.C.,   *Arbella Stuart* (1913).

Hunter, J.   *History of Hallamshire* (1869).

Hurstfield, J.,   *The Queen's Wards* (1965).

Jarvis, S.,   *Printed Furniture Design before 1650* (1974).

Labanoff, A.I.,   *Recueil de Lettres de Marie Stuart* (1844).

Lacey, R.,   *The Fallen Icarus* (1971).

Laver, J.,   *A Concise History of Costume* (1969).

Leader, J.D.,   *Mary Queen of Scots in Captivity* (1880).

Levy, M.,   *High Renaissance* (1975).

Lodge, E.,   *Illustrations of British History* (1791 and 1833).

Lyte, M.,   *A History of Eton College, 1440–1910* (1911).

Mattioli, P.A.,   *Herbal* (1572).

Meaby, K.T.,   *Nottingham County Records of the 18th Century* (1948).

Mercer, E.,   *Furniture 700–1700* (1969).

Newcastle, M. Duchess of,   *The Life of William Duke of Newcastle* (1906).

Newcastle, W. Duke of,   *General System of Horsemanship* (1743).

Nichols, J.,   *The Progresses and Public Processions of Queen Elizabeth* (1823).

Nichols, J.,   *The Progresses, Progressions and Magnificent Festivities of King James I* (1788–1821).

Pevsner, N.,   *The Buildings of England* (by counties).

Picinello, A.,   *Mundus Symbolicus* (1681).

Plucknett, T.F.T.,   *Taswell Longman's Constitutional History* (1960) (11th edition).

Rawson, M.,   *Bess of Hardwick and her Circle* (1910).

Read, C.,   *Mr Secretary Walsingham and the Policy of Queen Elizabeth* (1925).

Read, C., *Mr Secretary Cecil and Queen Elizabeth* (1955).
Read, C., *Lord Burghley and Queen Elizabeth* (1960).
Ridley, J., *Mary Tudor* (1973).
Ripa, C., *Iconolgia* (1593).
Rogers, T., *Six Centuries of Work and Wages* (1919).
Rowse, A. L., *The England of Elizabeth* (1950).
Rowse, A.L., *The Expansion of Elizabethan England* (1955).
Seebohm, M.E., *Evolution of the English Farm* (1927).
Sitwell, S., *British Architects and Craftsmen* (1945).
Statham, E.P., *A Jacobean Letter-Writer: The Life and Times of John Chamberlain* (1920).
Stone, L., *Family and Fortune* (1927).
Stone, L., *Crisis of Aristocracy* (1965).
Stowe, J., *A Survey of London* (1908).
Stowe, J., *The Chronicles of England* (1587).
Strickland, A., *Mary Queen of Scots* (1888).
Strong, R., *Portraits of Queen Elizabeth* (1961).
Strong, R., *The English Icon* (1969).
Strype, J., *Ecclesiastical Memorials* (1820).
Swain, M., *Historical Needlework* (1970).
Swain, M., *The Needlework of Mary Queen of Scots* (1973).
Summerson, J., *The Book of Architecture of John Thorpe*, Walpole Society, vol. XL (1966).
Summerson, J., *Architecture in Britain, 1580–1830* (1953).
Thompson, F., *A History of Chatsworth* (1951).
Tuberville, , A.S., *A History of Welbeck Abbey and its Owners* (1938).
Valeriano, P., *Hieroglyphica* (1556).
Wilenska, R.H., *Flemish Painters* (1960).
Williams, E.C., *Bess of Hardwick* (1959).
Williams, N., *Henry VIII and his Court* (1971).
Williams, N., *All the Queen's Men* (1972).
Winwood, R., *Memorials of the Affairs of State in the Reigns of Queen Elizabeth and King James I* (1725).
Yates, F., *Astraea* (1975).
Yeatman, P., *Feudal History of Derbyshire* (1903).

GENEALOGICAL TABLES

HARDWICK

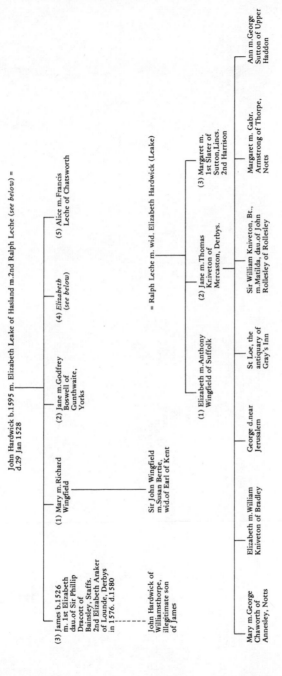

John Hardwick b.1595 m. Elizabeth Leake of Hasland m.2nd Ralph Leche (*see below*) =
d.29 Jan 1528

(1) Mary m.Richard Wingfield

(2) Jane m.Godfrey Boswell of Gunthwaite, Yorks

(3) James b.1526 m. 1st Elizabeth dau.of Sir Phillip Dracot of Bainsley, Staffs. 2nd Elizabeth Araker of Lounde, Derbys in 1576. d.1580

(4) *Elizabeth* (*see below*)

(5) Alice m.Francis Leche of Chatsworth

Sir John Wingfield m.Susan Bertie, wid.of Earl of Kent

John Hardwick of Williamsthorpe, illegitimate son of James

= Ralph Leche m. wid. Elizabeth Hardwick (Leake)

(1) Elizabeth m.Anthony Wingfield of Suffolk

(2) Jane m.Thomas Kniveton of Mercaston, Derbys.

(3) Margaret m. 1st Slater of Sutton,Lincs. 2nd Harrison

George d.near Jerusalem

St.Loe, the antiquary of Gray's Inn

Sir William Kniveton, Bt., m.Matilda, dau.of John Rollesley of Rollesley

Margaret m. Gabr. Armstrong of Thorpe, Notts

Ann m.George Sutton of Upper Haddon

Mary m.George Chaworth of Annesley, Notts

Elizabeth m. William Kniveton of Bradley

Elizabeth Hardwick b.about 1527,d.13 February 1608,m.

1st Robert Barley in 1543(?) d.24 December 1544.

2nd Sir William Cavendish in 1547, d.25 October 1557. (*see Cavendish*)

3rd Sir William St Loe by 1560, d.1565

4th George Talbot 6th Earl of Shrewsbury by Autumn 1567, d.18 November 1590

TALBOT

George Talbot 6th Earl of Shrewsbury m.1539 Gertrude dau. of
Thomas Manners, 1st Earl
of Rutland d. 1566

m. 2nd Elizabeth St Loe, wid,
dau. of John Hardwick

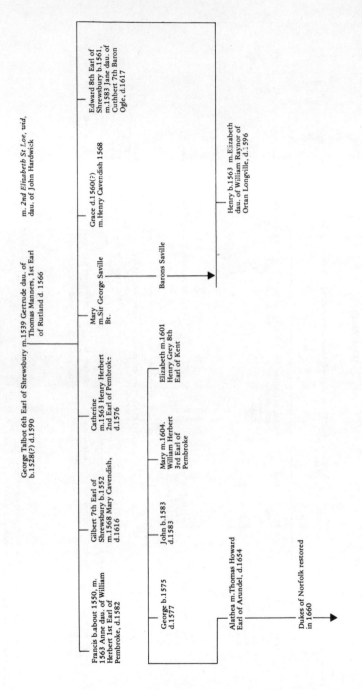

Francis b.about 1550, m.
1563 Anne dau. of William
Herbert 1st Earl of
Pembroke, d.1582

Gilbert 7th Earl of
Shrewsbury b.1552
m.1568 Mary Cavendish,
d.1616

Catherine
m.1563 Henry Herbert
2nd Earl of Pembroke
d.1576

Mary
m.Sir George Saville
Bt.

Grace d.1560(?)
m.Henry Cavendish 1568

Edward 8th Earl of
Shrewsbury b.1561,
m.1583 Jane dau. of
Cuthbert 7th Baron
Ogle, d.1617

George b.1575
d.1577

John b.1583
d.1583

Mary m.1604.
William Herbert
3rd Earl of
Pembroke

Elizabeth m.1601
Henry Grey 8th
Earl of Kent

Barons Saville

Henry b.1563 m.Elizabeth
dau. of William Raynor of
Ortan Longville, d.1596

Alathea m.Thomas Howard
Earl of Arundel, d.1654

Dukes of Norfolk restored
in 1660

CAVENDISH

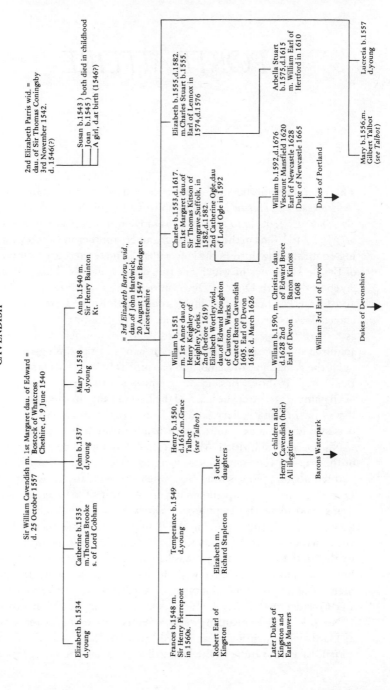

PORTRAITURE

The reference numbers quoted are those used in *Biographical notes on the Portraits at Hardwick Hall*, published by the National Trust.

Bess: nos. 9, 73, 92 and 120 In the 1601 inventory there are three portraits of 'My Ladie'. One in the low great chamber, another in Bess's withdrawing-room and the third in the long gallery. Today there are four portraits of Bess at Hardwick of which one (no. 92) is spurious. This portrait was given to the Sixth Duke of Devonshire by the Fourth Duke of Portland and formerly hung in the dining-room at Bolsover Castle. It shows a crazed-looking woman wearing a hat, and is dated by Sir Oliver Millar as *c.* 1618 (ten years after Bess had died); somewhere in its history it acquired its misleading title. Today it hangs in the dining-room.

Of the remaining three no. 120 has probably hung at Hardwick since Bess's day. It shows Bess in her countess's attire and is likely to have been painted just after she married the Earl in 1567; in the 1792 inventory it was in the long gallery, and by Lord Hawkesbury's 1903 inventory it is still in the same room; it now hangs in the hall.

No. 73, although titled 'Maria Regina', has a good claim to being one of the original 1601 portraits. It is in the style of Hans Eworth and was painted about 1560 showing Bess when she was lady-in-waiting to the Queen. In the 1792 inventory it was 'Portrait of a Lady, no name or Arms, said to be the Countess of Shrewsbury when Young, $\frac{3}{4}$ length, 40 ins × 33 ins', and it hung in the dining-room. Since then it has been cut down in size and had its royal title painted on it, possibly all done by the Sixth Duke. By 1903 it was hanging on the west side of the gallery but now hangs on the east wall. It has a claim to being the portrait mentioned in the 1566 fragment of a Chatsworth inventory Drawer 143(6) when one of 'My Ladie' was on a table in Bess's chamber.

No. 9 is a copy, probably early seventeenth-century after a portrait at Hardwick which has disappeared (Strong, *Tudor and Jacobean Portraits*). In 1792 it hung in the long gallery and had the same dimensions

PORTRAITURE 261

as now, 40 ins × 31 ins; in 1903 it was still in the gallery where it hangs today. An almost identical portrait was acquired by the National Portrait Gallery in 1859 and now hangs on permanent exhibition in the long gallery of Montacute House. There is yet another copy at Welbeck Abbey. These are the only known portraits of Bess: those at Ingestre Hall are not of 'My Ladie'.

George Talbot, Sixth Earl of Shrewsbury: no. 5 In 1601 there was one portrait of George Talbot and that hung in the long gallery; there is today one portrait of him at Hardwick and that hangs in the same room, likely enough the same portrait. Certainly it was today's portrait in the long gallery in the 1792 inventory for its size, 27 ins × 20 ins, is identical, and it was there in the 1903 inventory by Hawkesbury. But if the tentative attribution to Rowland Lockey is correct then the present portrait must be a posthumous copy, although a copy which could have been made by Lockey before 1601. There is an almost identical portrait at Welbeck Abbey and Edmund Lodge in *Illustrations of British History* (1791) used an engraving based on a similar painting but with the date 1580. Strong, in his *Tudor and Jacobean Portraits*, mentions a watercolour on white paper from the same source, which is in the National Portrait Gallery. There is another likeness of George Talbot shown as a Knight of the Garter in procession 1575, from the etching by Gheeraerts of Queen Elizabeth (Plate IV in 'Calendar of Talbot and Shrewsbury Papers in the College of Arms' by Batho). There is also a full-length portrait of George Talbot in the Tate Gallery, formerly at Rufford Abbey. At Drayton House, Northamptonshire, is a portrait labelled 'John Talbot', which is claimed by the owner, Mr Stopford-Sackville, to be of George Talbot the Sixth Earl, and said to have been painted in 1590, the year he died. Certainly there was a connection, for the Earl of Wiltshire who lived at Drayton was a cousin of George Talbot.

Arbella Stewart: nos. 1 and 83 There were two portraits of Arbella in 1601, one in the long gallery and the other called 'The Ladie Arbella her Grandchilde' in the withdrawing-room – this most likely is no. 83 showing Arbella aged twenty-three months. Today 83 hangs in the withdrawing-room and the other, no. 1, a full-length, in the long gallery; both are possibly back where they were in 1601. This was not always so for the full-length portrait of Arbella has wandered. In 1793 it was hanging in the long gallery but 'much defaced' and although back in the gallery by 1903, Hawkesbury says of the portrait, 'This picture was given by the Sixth Duke to Mr Cribb the picture cleaner, from whom it was bought by the present Seventh Duke.' He goes on to say that it was lent in 1888 for the Scottish Exhibition and finally reframed and restored in

1900 by Mr Haines. Hawkesbury also reports that the smaller portrait of Arbella was moved into the drawing-room from the gallery. In the Shrewsbury papers at Lambeth Palace is a tantalising letter from a person called Neville in London to Mary, Countess of Shrewsbury, dated 26 November 1608: 'Will send picture of the Countess with the Lady Arbella's pictures.' One wonders what became of them. For a brief informative portraiture of Arbella see Handover's *Arbella Stuart*, p. 8.

Lady Jane Grey This illusive portrait has vanished from Hardwick. Bess had one at Chatsworth in the 1566 inventory but none is mentioned in 1601 at Hardwick. When Byng made his visit and reported this in the *Torrington Diaries* (1789) he found a portrait of Lady Jane Grey, yet none is given in the 1792 inventory. However, Lyson's *Derbyshire* (1817) lists amongst the portraits at Hardwick one of 'Lady Jane Grey'.

Mary Queen of Scots: nos. 11 and 86 There was no portrait of Mary given in the 1601 inventory; today there are two ascribed at Hardwick to the Scots Queen. No. 86 is unlikely to be of Mary as it is not like any other known portrait of her. No. 11, a full-length dated 1578, is another matter, for this is undoubtedly she and there are many versions of this same painting. Stylistically – by the carpet, the draped curtain, the table carpet and the full length – this can be dated *c*. 1600–10, and it is likely to be a portrait commissioned by William Cavendish based on the 1578 miniature – the so-called 'Sheffield Portrait'. There is the puzzling matter of the words on the edge of the table carpet 'P Oudry Pinxit'. Oudry was one of Mary's embroiderers in Scotland, but there is no record that he ever came to England after Mary became a prisoner; embroiderers had to be able to draw and it is very possible that Oudry could have painted as well. However by the time this portrait was made, Oudry would have been a forgotten name, if indeed he was ever known outside Mary's little Court circle. How then did his name come to be on the portrait? I suggest that Oudry's name only came to light when Labanoff published his collected letters of Mary in 1844, just at the time when the Sixth Duke was restoring pictures and furniture at Hardwick. It appears to me likely that when Mr Cribb restored this painting the Sixth Duke had Oudry's name 'restored' as well. In his guide to Hardwick and Chatsworth printed in 1845, the Sixth Duke mentions the other supposed portrait (no. 86) but does not mention this large painting – perhaps even then it was with Mr Cribb. And certainly the portrait has had some attention since the 1792 inventory, for although the same height, it has grown wider by $3\frac{1}{2}$ ins. This picture has suffered from being heavily overpainted and has been badly 'restored'. Until it receives expert attention the Oudry question will remain in abeyance.

No. 126 is a painting of Mary and Darnley, impossible to see in its present position at Hardwick. This was in the withdrawing-room in 1601 and is a composite painting based on the Uffizi portrait of Mary reversed and that of Darnley on the Mauritshuis portrait; Strong (*Tudor and Jacobean Portraits*) dates it after 1565.

Sources: 1601 Hardwick Inventories; 1792 Inventory at Hardwick (Chatsworth); 'Catalogue of Pictures at Hardwick Hall' by Lord Hawkesbury in *Derbyshire Archaeological Society Journal* for 1903; *Handbook and Guide to Chatsworth and Hardwick* written by the Sixth Duke of Devonshire in 1844 and printed privately a year later; *The English Icon* and *Tudor and Jacobean Portraits*, both by R. Strong; *Nicholas Hilliard* by Erna Auerbach; the 1972 survey of paintings at Hardwick Hall commissioned by the Courtauld Institute; *Biographical notes on the portraits at Hardwick* by The National Trust.

INDEX